SIMONE WEIL AND THE POLITICS OF SELF-DENIAL

SIMONE WEIL

AND THE POLITICS OF SELF-DENIAL

ATHANASIOS MOULAKIS

Translated from the German by Ruth Hein

University of Missouri Press
Columbia and London

Copyright © 1998 by
The Curators of the University of Missouri
University of Missouri Press, Columbia, Missouri 65201
Printed and bound in the United States of America
All rights reserved
5   4   3   2   1   02   01   00   99   98

Library of Congress Cataloging-in-Publication Data

Moulakis, Athanasios, 1945–
    [Simone Weil, die Politik der Askese. English]
    Simone Weil and the politics of self-denial / Athanasios Moulakis ;
translated from the German by Ruth Hein.
        p.   cm.
    Includes bibliographical references and index.
    ISBN 0-8262-1162-3 (alk. paper)
    1. Weil, Simone, 1909–1943—Contributions in political science.
I. Title.
JC261.W45M6813   1998
320.53'1'092—dc21   97-38830
                                                              CIP

∞™ This paper meets the requirements of the
American National Standard for Permanence of Paper
for Printed Library Materials, Z39.48, 1984.

Designer: Stephanie Foley
Typesetter: BOOKCOMP
Printer and binder: Thomson-Shore, Inc.
Typefaces: Bembo and Carlton

CONTENTS

ACKNOWLEDGMENTS

The appearance of an American edition of this book gives me the welcome opportunity to thank the staff of the European University Institute and in particular Ursula Noccentini, publications officer Brigitte Schwab, and all the personnel of the library who helped in different ways to prepare and present the original German version. The institute itself kindly released the rights of translation. I am also grateful for the encouragement and constructive criticism of early reviewers, Heinz Abosch in the *Neue Zürcher Zeitung,* H.-M. Lohmann in the *Frankfurter Allgemeine,* and Rolf Kühn in *ARSP.*

It is not easy to transform the dense syntax of German into English. It is perhaps even more difficult to escape the structure of sentences one has formulated oneself. I am therefore doubly indebted to the translator. My editor at the University of Missouri Press, Jane Lago, was confronted with an unusually difficult manuscript. She did, yet again, an exemplary job.

ABBREVIATIONS

AD	Simone Weil, *Attente de Dieu*
C	Simone Weil, *Cahiers* (1st ed.)
CO	Simone Weil, *La condition ouvrière*
COp	Simone Weil, *La condition ouvrière,* paperback edition
CS	Simone Weil, *La connaissance surnaturelle*
E	Simone Weil, *L'enracinement*
EHP	Simone Weil, *Ecrits historiques et politiques*
EL	Simone Weil, *Ecrits de Londres et dernières lettres*
Ep	Simple Weil, *L'enracinement,* paperback edition
FLN	Simone Weil, *First and Last Notebooks,* translated by Richard Rees
FW	Simone Weil, *Formative Writings, 1929–1941,* edited and translated by Dorothy Tuck McFarland and Wilhelmina van Ness
IC	Simone Weil, *Intimations of Christianity,* collected and translated by Elisabeth Chase Geissbuhler
Leçons	Simone Weil, *Leçons de philosophie de Simone Weil,* presented by Anne Reynaud
Lessons	Simone Weil, *Lectures on Philosophy,* translated by Hugh Price
N	Simone Weil, *The Notebooks of Simone Weil,* translated by Arthur Wills
NR	Simone Weil, *The Need for Roots,* translated by Arthur Wills
OL	Simone Weil, *Oppression et liberté*
OLE	Simone Weil, *Oppression and Liberty,* translated by Arthur Wills and John Petrie
P	Simone Pétrement, *La vie de Simone Weil*
PE	Simone Pétrement, *Simone Weil: A Life,* translated by Raymond Rosenthal

PSO	Simone Weil, *Pensées sans ordre concernant l'amour de Dieu*
SG	Simone Weil, *La source grecque*
SL	Simone Weil, *Seventy Letters,* translated and arranged by Richard Rees
SWA	*Simone Weil: An Anthology,* edited with an introduction by Siân Miles
SWR	*The Simone Weil Reader,* edited by George A. Panichas
WG	Simone Weil, *Waiting for God,* translated by Emma Craufurd

SIMONE WEIL AND THE POLITICS OF SELF-DENIAL

Introduction to the American Edition

Interest in Simone Weil has increased since the German version of this book was published. It is no longer necessary to insist, with the vigor that was needed then, that her message, her religious testimony, her political and historical analysis, her exemplary existential honesty are undeservedly neglected. Her writings are being read and commented on from different points of view, and several accounts of her life and intellectual trajectory have been published. There are active Simone Weil societies in France, Italy, Japan, and the United States. This has resulted in a great deal of useful work and not a little controversy. Yet I believe that no other work does quite what the present study attempts: to concentrate on Weil's political thought and, while seeking to situate it within the context of the events and the intellectual climate of her time on the one hand, to connect it to her epistemology, cosmology, and the unfolding of her personal experience on the other. This approach has as its goal a philosophical understanding of politics, and hence of political science, that reaches beyond current affairs and ideological advocacy.

I have learned much since the original publication of this book, but in looking it over I find that there is little of substance that I need to change in the light of what has been written since then.[1] If

---

1. I am grateful to Rolf Kühn for pointing out a genuine error of interpretation in Chapter 14, which I have sought to rectify (*Deuten als Entwerden: Eine Synthese des Werkes Simone Weils in hermeneutisch-religionsphilosophischer Sicht,* 175). His is unquestionably one of the most important and comprehensive studies of Simone Weil to date. Daunting in its complexity but also in its mastery of the sources and of the issues they raise, it is the result of *lungo studio e grande amore.*

1

I were to write a different book, I would probably want to pay greater attention to Weil's reception of Kant, so ably worked out by Miklos Vetö. The vexed question of Weil's relation to Jews, Jewishness, and Judaism deserves fuller treatment than it receives within the context of this book, but not, I believe, for the purposes of the argument presented here.[2] Similarly, one could explore more fully certain aspects of Weil and her work by looking more closely at the manner in which she experienced her womanhood.

The updated bibliography should help to situate the present study within the growing body of Weil literature. In this introduction I will limit myself to elements of the reception of Weil in America. Naturally British and American responses to Weil overlap, but they do not coincide. The former are treated here mainly insofar as they affect the latter.

Weil's writings were first introduced to American readers shortly after her death, even before the end of the Second World War, in Dwight Macdonald's radical magazine, *Politics*.[3] The magazine was seeking a

2. Vetö, "Thèmes kantiens dans la pensée de Simone Weil." On Weil's reading of the Old Testament, see David Raper, "Simone Weil's Critique of the Old Testament"; *Cahiers Simone Weil* 3:2 (June 1980), devoted to "Simone Weil et l'Ancien Testament"; and Emmanuel Levinas, "Simone Weil contre la Bible." For the Veterotestamental temperament of Weil, see Leslie Fiedler, "Simone Weil: Prophet out of Israel, Saint of the Absurd." For affinities with the Cabala, see Wladimir Rabi, "La conception weilienne de la Création: Rencontre avec la kabbale juive." Martin Buber discusses Weil alongside another Jewish philosopher attracted to Christian mysticism in "The Silent Question: On Henri Bergson and Simone Weil." The most virulent attack on Weil as a "renegade," in terms borrowed from Theodor Lessing's *Der jüdische Selbsthass*, is Paul Giniewski, *Simone Weil ou la haine de soi*. Thomas R. Nevin, *Simone Weil: Portrait of a Self-Exiled Jew*, indicates a key of interpretation in its subtitle. The most judicious and balanced discussion of the question and the literature is Robert Chevanier, "Simone Weil: 'La haine juive de soi'?"

3. For the journal's political "line" see "Why Politics?" *Politics*, February 1944, 6–8. See also Staughton Lynd, "Marxism-Leninism and the Language of *Politics* Magazine: The First New Left and the Third." Weil's articles were:

(1) "Reflections on War," February 1945, 51–56, installment 4 of the journal's series "War as an Institution." This was revised from *International Review* 1:1 (1938)—strictly speaking, the first publication of Weil in English—translated from Boris Souvarine's *La Critique Sociale*, November 1933. It presents the pacifist rationale according to which preparation for war and the hierarchies imposed by the war economy are as bad or worse than the tyranny imposed by a foreign invader—a position by then long repudiated by Weil.

(2) "The Iliad or the Poem of Force," November 1945, 21–331, from *Cahiers du*

way to "democratic socialism" through nonorthodox Marxism, was concerned with popular culture and the repressive effects of the "war economy," and, in the particular historical situation, sought to expose what it took to be the intended collusion or structurally determined analogues between Stalin and Western imperialism. Its tone is reminiscent of the small groups of "left-opposition" that Weil was close to in the 1930s. A brief, admiring, yet balanced biographical note in the February 1945 issue outlines Weil's life and looks forward to the full publication of her works. It does not fail to notice her turn to Christian spirituality, but the articles are, of course, reproduced as contributing to the journal's cause.[4] They were, by the same token, destined to remain unnoticed except by a very narrow circle of readers.

Simone Weil the radical was easily overshadowed by the idiosyncratic mystic personality, concerned with the spiritual rootedness of individual and political existence, presented in T. S. Eliot's preface to Arthur Wills's translation of *The Need for Roots* in 1952. Susan Sontag has made much of this: speaking in the late 1970s she maintained that because of the "enormous influence" of the "royalist, Anglican-conservative Eliot . . . in that dim, distant era . . . the tendency was to interpret everything

---

Sud 19 (December 1940): 561–74 and 20 (January 1941): 21–34. This idiosyncratic interpretation of the *Iliad* as a parable of the inexorable workings of power is perhaps Weil's most widely read piece in English, certainly the best known of her "nonreligious" texts. Excerpts were reprinted in *Time* 46 (December 17, 1945): 65–66.

(3) "Words and War" ("War as Institution," installment 7), March 1946, 69–73, a shortened translation of "Ne recommençons pas la Guerre de Troie," which had appeared in *Nouveaux Cahiers,* April 1 and 15, 1937, and develops the theme that the most violent conflicts result from unreal, imaginary goals.

(4) "Factory Work," on the front page of the December 1946 issue, 369–75. The editor's postscript (376–77) expresses his disappointment at her meliorism and her assertion of the incapacity of effective action by the workers given their dispirited condition, despite his praise for her analysis of social evils, which he misreads in a more orthodox Marxist sense.

(5) "What Is a Jew?" winter 1949, 40, is a translation of the well-known letter to the minister of education of the Vichy government, taken from Robert Louzon's *Etudes materialistes* 17 (December 1947) and presented simply as evidence of Vichy racism.

4. The note is signed "Candide." The author quite properly notes her concern for the effect of modern technology and mechanization on workers' psychology while pointing out that "her transcendental concept of Christianity had nothing in common with the various business enterprises which go under that name" and that "she entered the Gaullist organization [in London], about which she had no illusions" ([February 1945]: 55–56).

[of Weil's] from a religious perspective."[5] Certainly much of the work on Weil in America, and some of the best, is primarily concerned with the religious dimension of her thought and its implications for community.[6] Part of the reception of Weil, in America as elsewhere, is downright hagiographic.[7] But given the nature of Weil's work and her extraordinary life, it is difficult to avoid a religious perspective, if by "religious" one means something other than dogmatic irrationalism and church apologetics. It is only if one assumes that there is a radical break between her "early" social thought and her "late" religious reflections that the supposed suppression of one aspect in favor of the other—under the influence, perhaps, of a conservative poet or the concerns of the New Left, respectively—becomes a possibility and hence a problem.

It could be argued that a bipolarity between a "Catholic" and a "radical militant" reading of Weil was encouraged by the way in which her work appeared. As Gabriella Fiori has shown very nicely, the early publications came from two sources. One "current" stemmed from the Catholic friends whom Weil entrusted with her late papers before leaving France; their compilations and editions were the first to affect the broader reading public. The other current, editorially more meticulous, stemmed from the cooperation of the Weil family and Albert Camus. The latter also involves the careful reception and transmission to the English-speaking world of Weil's writings by Sir Richard Rees.[8] If the second current is in some sense the more faithful and disinterested, it also bears out the fundamental continuity of Weil's temperament and of her search for truth. It is in fact not the case that Eliot promoted one side of her rather than the other. Indeed, he

5. See Dwight Macdonald's review of *The Need for Roots* in *New York Times Book Review,* July 6, 1952, 6. Sontag's remarks at a symposium at Princeton University in 1978 are quoted in George Abbot White, ed. *Simone Weil: Interpretations of a Life,* 182–83.

6. See for instance Eric O. Springsted's *Christus Mediator; Platonic Mediation in the Thought of Simone Weil* and *Simone Weil and the Suffering of Love.* Springsted has been the president of the American Weil Society. See also Diogenes Allen, *Three Outsiders: Pascal, Kierkegaard, Simone Weil,* and the book edited by Allen and Springsted, *Spirit, Nature and Community: Issues in the Thought of Simone Weil.*

7. A recent work in that vein is Anthony Welton, "Simone Weil."

8. Fiori, *Simone Weil: An Intellectual Biography,* bibliographical note; Rees, *Simone Weil, Selected Essays 1934–1943* (London: Oxford University Press, 1962); Weil, *Seventy Letters;* Rees corresponded and worked closely with Simone's brother, André Weil. Besides editing and translating, he produced thoughtful critical studies: *Brave Men: A Study of D. H. Lawrence and Simone Weil* and *Simone Weil: A Sketch for a Portrait.*

wrote his preface for the translation of a book edited by Albert Camus, whom no one can consider a Tory. Rather, he resisted classifying the contradictory and fragmentary materials too hastily and found the equilibrium of Weil's articulation of her experience in the very paradoxes it engenders:

> On the one hand she was a passionate champion of the common people and especially of the oppressed—those oppressed by the wickedness and selfishness of men and those oppressed by the anonymous forces of modern society. . . . On the other hand, she was by nature a solitary and an individualist, with a profound horror of what she called the *collectivity*—the monster created by modern totalitarianism. What she cared about was human souls. Her study of human rights and human obligations exposes the falsity of some of the verbiage still current which was used during the war to serve as a moral stimulant.[9]

If American readers and commentators came to emphasize the religious over the political in Weil, it is not because they read T. S. Eliot's preface, but because they did not read it carefully enough.

Sontag, of course, objects not simply to a particular interpretation of Weil, but to interpretation itself. Objecting to a tendency to treat all appearances as epiphenomena, all images and texts as standing for something other than what meets the eye, she argues for an art of energy and of immediate, sensuous experience: an "erotics of art" to replace hermeneutics.[10]

Now Eros takes many forms, including Weil's insatiable thirst for truth. But for Weil that truth is never revealed to unmediated desire or to artful formalization, both of which are to her modes of illusion and madness; rather it is revealed only by means of the methodical mediation of work as the systematic contact with a reality that impresses its necessity on the subject, by means of science understood as a mode of work, and, finally, by means of expectant, patient receptivity to divine love, which is the opposite of energetic, willful action. In this respect Sontag is at the antipodes of Weil, not only as presented or misrepresented by Eliot, but with regard to Weil's innermost convictions. In this vein

9. Preface to *The Need for Roots*, xi–xii.
10. Sontag, "Against Interpretationn," in *Against Interpretation and Other Essays*, 3–14.

Sontag necessarily departs also from Macdonald, whose position on Weil she praises because it is "on the left." For Marxist analysis, be it unorthodox and qualified in its determinism, postulates structures that *underlie* social phenomena. It is precisely because Weil seems to promise rigorous *interpretation* of social reality, while upholding the dignity of individual humanity, that her work can serve as a starting point for renewals of leftist theory.[11] Mary McCarthy's translation of *The Iliad or the Poem of Force,* a powerful and highly idiosyncratic interpretation of the Homeric poem as a parable on the "physics" of power and violence, became a crucial text for Weil's reputation with the American left. That Weil's treatment of nonviolence as well as her spirituality would appeal to Thomas Merton is hardly surprising.[12]

It is in the context of a teleology that identifies a vitalistic, artistic avant-garde with political progress that interpretation, any interpretation, can be dismissed, in Sontag's words, as "reactionary, impertinent, cowardly, stifling." Sontag grants that there may be historical circumstances, though not ours, in which interpretation can be liberating, for "it is a means of revising, of transvaluing, of escaping the dead past."[13] Weil would be horrified, perhaps to a fault, at such an idea of freedom. She would want to know what it is we are liberated from. She would ask whether wishing one's past dead were not in fact a deadly uprooting. She would resist the euphoria of "transvaluing" unless she knew the transition would be for the better. Simone Weil is a radical, but an ontologically and epistemologically foundationalist radical.

What interests Sontag is not Weil's reasoning, but her vehemence, her capacity to shock us out of a complacent "bourgeois" conformism: "The culture-heroes of our liberal bourgeois civilization are anti-liberal

11. See Lawrence A. Blum and Victor J. Seidler, *A Truer Liberty: Simone Weil and Marxism.* Among many interesting things, the authors reflect on the pertinence of Weil to movements such as Poland's Solidarity and Liberation Theology. The first case is particularly intriguing, given the combination of syndicalist underpinnings and Catholic inspiration. In the case of the latter, though Weil undoubtedly would have identified with the downtrodden, she would also have had grave misgivings about the immanentism and historicism of the movement.

12. *The Iliad or the Poem of Force,* trans. Mary McCarthy, Pendle Hill pamphlet No. 91 (Wallingford, Pa., 1956). (For the earlier publication in *Politics* see above, n. 4; this also happens to be the one text, as far as I know, to have been translated even into Greek, by Maria Woulker-Kamarinea.) Merton, "Pacifism and Resistance in Simone Weil."

13. Sontag, "Against Interpretation," in *Against Interpretation,* 7.

and anti-bourgeois; they are writers who are repetitive, obsessive, and impolite, who impress by force—not simply by their tone of personal authority and by their intellectual ardor, but by the sense of acute personal and intellectual extremity." What Sontag values in Weil is the intensity that comes across as morbid, hysterical, fanatical. The very placidity of our civilization generates a taste for the extreme in art and thought, a desire not for truth, which is, as it were, given, but for "a deepening of the sense of reality" that cuts across our hypocrisy. Sontag admires the authenticity of Weil, her willingness to sacrifice herself, to be a martyr for her views. But such martyrdom does not make her message more persuasive:

> I . . . do not doubt that the sane view of the world [as opposed to Weil's "unhealthy" one] is the true one . . . I cannot believe that more than a handful of the tens of thousands of readers she has won since the posthumous publication of her books and essays really share her ideas. . . . As the corrupt Alcibiades followed Socrates, unable and unwilling to change his own life, but moved, enriched, and full of love, so the sensitive modern reader pays his respect to a level of spiritual reality which is not, could not, be his own.[14]

This is no doubt a plausible view of the social psychology and the sociology of knowledge that conditions the reading of texts in our time. But it does reduce the seriousness of the testimony before the "sensitive reader" to a life-enhancing (Sontag's Nietzschean word) performance. It is a moving, indeed an erotic, stimulant that enhances a life without changing it. We are enriched by the experience, but we continue to operate within the confines of a sanity that leads a loving Alcibiades to disastrous megalomania and high treason.

Weil was very much opposed to philistinism as the conformity to received ideas and sought to anchor truth in reality, beyond the distortions of social opinion. She never hesitated to *épater les bourgeois* when occasion arose. But she would have found the idea of a truth that could be divorced from reality profoundly repellent.

In one important respect, Sontag's Weil is much like the one presented by T. S. Eliot: both commentators emphasize the personality, the exemplary life, and the authentic testimony rather than the doctrine.

14. Sontag, "Simone Weil," in *Against Interpretation,* 49–51.

This, indeed, seems inevitable, despite the protestations of Weil herself. In her last letter to Father Jean Marie Perrin she exhorted him to judge her writings irrespective of her person. People, she protested, praised her for her intelligence rather than asking whether she was *telling the truth*. A residual Cartesian understanding of discursive, impersonal truth is reinforced by a metaphysics that perceives individuation as a distortion and that allows reality to become manifest in its universality by eliding the particularity of the self.

Yet Eliot was surely right that Weil's work cannot be properly understood apart from her personality. The work is not only contingently but essentially fragmentary. The piecemeal way in which it was first published only adds to the apparent discord of its many elements. Its value consists in great part in Weil's refusal to force contradictions into formal agreement that would involve ideological closure. The work coheres, as I also hope to show, in her lived and reflected experience. But there is more to the thought than the existential integrity of the thinker. There is a systematic body of work that deserves attention as doctrine, not only as testimony. There is a danger of allowing the extraordinary life to overshadow the work.

As a corrective to the temptation to read Weil in the manner of the lives of the saints, Miklos Vetö's exemplary doxographic study is now at last available in English. By concentrating on the late, mature phase of Weil's religious thought and its sources in the philosophical tradition he produces a conceptually coherent metaphysical system. Paul King's attempt to impose conceptual order to Weil's political thought is less successful, for he seeks to relate categories such as "work," "art," and "politics" as though each had an intrinsic, constant, and unambiguous meaning. The resulting contradictions cannot be surmounted at the level of analysis at which they arise. An earlier chapter devoted to Weil by Roy Pierce conveys a livelier and more accurate idea of her political thought.[15]

It is the merit of Peter Winch to have shown that Weil needs to be taken seriously not only as a religious and political thinker but also as a philosopher, in the Anglo-Saxon understanding of the word, which tends to privilege the theory of knowledge. Winch brings the later Wittgenstein to bear on his analysis of Weil, and he traces her gradual

15. Vetö, *The Religious Metaphysics of Simone Weil;* King, "The Social and Political Thought of Simone Weil"; Pierce, "Simone Weil: Sociology, Utopia and Faith."

move away from Cartesian dualism and rationalism. He underestimates perhaps the importance of Weil's wrestling with the Marxian tradition, and he has little to say about the religious inflection of her thought.[16] The self-imposed limits of his analytical approach allow Winch to develop a coherent and suggestive presentation of Weil's thought, and of the light it casts on the nature of human understanding, under headings such as "language," "necessity," and "equilibrium." Although he does not read the work in terms of the life, he is very much aware of changes of themes and terminology over time. More important, he shows the epistemological significance of ethical experience as demonstrated in the work of Weil: if one is not just, one does not *know* what *is* a human being.

Winch has characteristically provided an introduction to the translation of Weil's *Lectures on Science*.[17] The recognition of Weil as a philosopher in the technical sense draws attention to what is perhaps the most neglected part of her work, her discussion of science. Although following its theme through the whole body of Weil's work, Betty McLane-Iles's *Uprooting and Integration in the Writings of Simone Weil* gives science its due.[18]

The dramatic and unusual pattern of Weil's life invites psychological analysis. The Harvard psychiatrist Robert Coles has made an attentive study of her "passions and obsessions." Coles acknowledges the influence of Anna Freud on the development of his analysis. He offers interesting reflections on the use by Weil of the metaphor of "hunger," on her Jewishness, on the lucidity of her analysis of power. This book provoked, however, the ire of another North American thinker, George Grant, who, in regard to Weil's curtailed sexuality and in particular in regard to her hostility to Judaism as linked to a supposed rejection of her family, in effect accused Coles of Freudian reductionism that fails to do justice to the facts of the case.[19]

The theme of Simone Weil as a woman activist, philosopher, mystic, or simply as a woman has, of course, been pursued with different

16. Winch, *Simone Weil: "The Just Balance";* as a useful balance, the reader may benefit from the familiarity with the Marxian tradition of David McLellan, *Utopian Pessimist: The Life and Thought of Simone Weil.*

17. Simone Weil, *Lectures on Science.*

18. The inclusion of this book in a series on theology and religion is indicative, however, of the dominant a priori classification of Weil in America.

19. Coles, *Simone Weil: A Modern Pilgrimage;* Grant, "In Defense of Simone Weil."

degrees of fidelity to the evidence.[20] Stephanie Strickland received the Brittingham Prize in Poetry for a long poem in the form of an alphabetical acrostic entitled *The Red Virgin: A Poem of Simone Weil.* It weaves excerpts from letters and other writings of Weil—and some other documents—together with a storied recounting of the life and the intellectual, political, moral, and religious concerns of its heroine, displaying a distinctively feminist sensibility. The title—which derives from a deprecatory nickname given Weil by the director of the Ecole Normale Supérieure—is itself telling. Does everything belong in this remarkable synthesis, including the excerpts from Gertrude Stein?[21] It is here more a matter of poetic justice than of descriptive accuracy.

Other feminist readings have been more heavy-handed.[22] A play by Terry Megan, for example, briefly produced in New York in the early 1970s is ponderously didactic and full of false notes. By contrast, Jean Bethke Elshtain has produced an admirably concise, accurate, and judicious essay on Weil and her thought, perhaps the best brief summary to be found anywhere, while paying due attention (not only biographically but also philosophically) to Weil's problematic repudiation of the body in general and of the female reproductive body in particular.[23] Elshtain calls Weil a "vexation." The lived philosophy of this extraordinary figure provokes admiration and deeper understanding, anger and frustration, but never indifference. Indeed it frequently evokes an intense personal response.[24]

---

20. Andrea Nye, *Philosophia: The Thought of Rosa Luxemburg, Simone Weil, and Hannah Arendt,* combines several themes by bringing together three Jewish women thinkers, each of whom has some claim to radicalism.

21. Strickland, *The Red Virgin: A Poem of Simone Weil,* 28. "It is a very difficult thing to have courage for something no one is thinking is a serious thing." Yet Weil herself and all who knew her never thought she and her concerns were anything but serious, even when they disapproved of her projects and views.

22. Not only in America. Dorothee Beyer, for instance, recognizes that Weil was herself no feminist and that she cannot be legitimately claimed by the feminist movement, but then tends to identify Weil's abhorrence of force with "the womanly" as opposed to "manly" self-assertion that has worked such destruction in history: *Simone Weil, Philosophin, Gewerkschafterin, Mystikerin* (Mainz: Topos, 1994), 7, 158.

23. Megan, *Approaching Simone: A Drama in Two Acts* (the introduction by Phyllis Jane Wagner is even more off than the play itself); Elshtain, "The Vexation of Simone Weil."

24. See for instance the very personal and moving remarks of Neal Oxenhandler, *Looking for Heroes in Postwar France: Albert Camus, Max Jacob, Simone Weil.*

INTRODUCTION

Objective and Method

Learn to live and to die
and in order to be human, refuse to be God.
— Albert Camus

A few years back, someone likened Simone Weil to a little candle flick-ering amid the bright lights of modern social thinkers.[1] The comparison was intended pejoratively, but the image is not inappropriate. The votive aspect of candles calls up the right associations in regard to Weil.[2] The comparison does point to a rhetorical difficulty, however: focusing the public's interest on a light that fulfills its purpose of providing illumination by spending its material substance, in the midst of so many garish floodlights powered, thanks to the marvels of technology, by the main current. Such humility does, nonetheless, reflect the nature of our author. All her life Weil sought to merge with the anonymous masses; to her, fame was a screen thrown up by the imagination, which prevents contact with the object of perception. Because Weil remains largely unknown to the broad public, there is less reason to fear such transfiguration here. Furthermore, a critical analysis of her work will hardly run the risk of creating a scandal—nor can it hope to do

1. Professor Erwin Faul, then editor of *Politische Vierteljahresschrift,* organ of the German Political Science Association, in a communication to the author.
2. "Un cierge est l'image d'un être humain" (*CS,* 322); "A candle is the image of a human being" (*FLN*).

11

so—as is claimed in a Marxist study published in France some twenty years ago.[3] This idea reflects the fact that the publication of Weil's posthumous works after the Second World War caused a sensation that has been compared to the belated effect of Kierkegaard on the German intelligentsia after 1918.[4] Albert Camus's opinion conveys an impression of the significance assigned to Weil's work: "It seems to me impossible . . . to imagine a rebirth of Europe that does not take into account the demands Simone Weil formulated in *L'enracinement*."[5]

The present work deals with Weil's political thought. The nature of the subject determines the method of inquiry. Because ideas, unlike objects in the environment peripheral to the person, are not simply given, it is not enough to describe them and classify them phenomenologically. To avoid distorting reifications of mental phenomena, it is important not only to reflect on an author's thoughts but also to rethink them hermeneutically. The hermeneutic claim explicit in this challenge does not, however, relieve us of the obligation to exercise the skepticism befitting any critical study. In what follows, my principal concern is to reconstruct those of Weil's thoughts that reveal her experience of reality. I will work within the context of a political science understood as a philosophically oriented science of order. This discipline includes the analysis of understood reality, of which political realities are an essential element.[6] My method may therefore be called an attempt to arrive at a way to interpret a mind by reconstructing it, empathizing with it. The method itself must be sketched here briefly to clarify the epistemological problems involved.

It is always a questionable procedure to view and present the work of any thinker as an abstract construct of propositions that have a "claim to truth." Such an approach to the work of Weil would, in any case, run counter to the intention of this study. The formal validity of a logical argument can, no doubt, be ascertained without reference either to the character of the person making the argument or to its substantial truth. We can even judge a virtuoso's work separately from his personality. But "existential probity"—or merely the criminal's *authenticité* that

3. Colette Andry, foreword to Philippe Dujardin, *Simone Weil: Idéologie et politique*, 9.

4. George Lichtheim, "Simone Weil," in *Collected Essays*, 458. See also Eric Walter Frederic Tomlin, *Simone Weil*, 6.

5. Camus, *Essais*, 1701.

6. On this point, see Eric Voegelin, "Was ist politische Realität?" in *Anamnesis*, 283–354 ("What Is Political Reality," in *Anamnesis*, trans. Gerhart Niemeyer, 141–213).

Sartre considered reason enough to canonize Genet—would mark the moralist. Here the *argumentum ad hominem* is indicated. The rhetorically necessary counterpart of the *argumentum ad hominem,* however, is the *argumentum a homine.* The extent to which Weil satisfied the demands of the only form of this argument that was conclusive for her through a *martyria sub specie mortis* (a witness [and martyrdom] in the face of death) may become more evident in what follows. That is why my account must end in a reflection on the death Weil accepted, even willed: a premeditated death, testifying to the authenticity of Simone Weil.

The testimony, the *martyria,* given by Weil is that of lived thinking, so that her writings cannot be properly understood without constantly linking them to their author's life and character. As François Heidsieck correctly remarks: "It is the life of Simone Weil that represents an *oeuvre de circonstance,* an answer to the entreaty of the humbled proletarian, to the entreaty of the vanquished homeland, to the entreaty of the spurned and unrecognized Christ."[7]

The book we know now as *L'enracinement (The Need for Roots)* is what Weil wrote when the Free French in London asked her for a report on possible ways to reconstruct postwar France; it is, then, a *livre de circonstance* that grew into an analysis of a civilization in crisis. The "need for roots," articulated in the thirty-fourth and last year of Weil's life, marks the end of an evolution in which death was not so much an accidental interruption as it was the logical culmination. "I always believed that the instant of death is the center and object of life."[8]

"Existential probity," however, does not extend to proving something about the ethical content of the statement—any more than the martyr's sacrifice is proof of the truth of her faith. It is merely evidence of an erotic elation that shapes consciousness, without revealing anything about the reality of that which is lovingly sought or about the ethical orientation of Eros. My attempt to probe Weil's thinking in this more comprehensively experiential sense relies on an intellectual tradition rooted in grounding political science in the philosophical breakthrough of Socratism.

The presentation can be meaningful only if it tries to group the variables around constants. But since in the case of Weil these very constants are in motion, concrete problems must be taken up over and

7. *Simone Weil,* 181.
8. *AD,* 37 (in English: *WG,* 63).

over, whenever they become pertinent to the life and work and appear in different guises under different conditions. A systematic arrangement of the material by concepts would presuppose that the meanings are constant—which is not the case with Weil. Furthermore, the sources would seem to recommend a genetically oriented study—both because of the character of Weil's writings and because of the manner in which they appeared. Let us deal first with the latter.

The bulk of the writings of Simone Weil, who died in 1943, appeared posthumously. The Catholic lay theologian Gustave Thibon published excerpts from her notebooks and letters in 1947 under the title *La pesanteur et la grâce*. In 1950 the Dominican Father Jean Marie Perrin published *Attente de Dieu,* a collection of Weil's letters to him as well as notes she entrusted to him. Beyond these books, these two men, who were most familiar with Weil's mature thinking and religious search, gave an account of their meetings with their extraordinary friend.[9] Their insights are all the more valuable in that they are based not only on her writings but also on long conversations with her, friendly and confidential. Their interpretation, however, was influenced by their orthodox Catholic viewpoint, down to the selection of texts; it was also why for a long time the intellectuals interested in Weil let the religious and "mystical" aspect of her work overshadow the political aspect. Part of this problem was relieved by the subsequent publication—now in its second edition—of Weil's complete *Cahiers.*

Thanks to the efforts of Albert Camus, the greater part both of Weil's unpublished manuscripts and of her essays scattered in a great number of periodicals have been issued in the series Collection Espoir, which Camus edited to the end of his life. After Camus's death, Simone Pétrement conscientiously dedicated herself to this mission. Some of Weil's posthumous papers, however, remained unpublished for many years.

The piecemeal publication of Weil's various works, often in selections affected by the editor's rather than the author's disposition, make a dispassionate and comprehensive view of the whole difficult to achieve. This difficulty will be overcome with the completion of the critical edition of the complete works published by Gallimard and projected for sixteen volumes under the general editorship of André Devaux and

9. Jean Marie Perrin and Gustave Thibon, *Simone Weil telle que nous l'avons connue* (in English: *Simone Weil: As We Knew Her*).

the custodian of the Weil manuscripts at the Bibliothèque Nationale, Florence de Lucy. The first volume of this authoritative edition appeared in 1988. Other volumes have followed at regular intervals.

Even when all the texts have been established and a great deal about the context of Weil's writing has been made generally available, the careful interpreter will still face difficulties arising from the author's outlook and from the form she gave to her different pieces of writing. We cannot discover any attempt on Weil's part to impose a system on her work; on the contrary, there appears a clear animus—inherited from her mentor, Alain—against systematic order. If distrust of the closed system, fear of closing out reality, appears as a rhetorical-ironic inflection in the teacher, the rejection of all systems becomes a strict existential requirement in the student's more inflexible way of thinking. If, as will be shown, in Alain's work the apparent variety suggested by the literary form of the short essay, the *propos,* plays out over long years in unvarying themes, in Weil we can discover an evolution that, over time, subjects the conceptual apparatus to considerable and often abrupt alterations. Biography and the history of publication alone cannot, therefore, account for the unsystematic nature of Weil's posthumous publications.

The form of Weil's writings also raises problems of interpretation. Only a very small percentage of the work was published by the author herself or even edited and revised with a view to publication. A few lines on something she had read, a hastily jotted note, the provisional beginnings of an idea are placed next to a polished thought, a penetrating observation, a definitive opinion. The largely fragmentary nature of Weil's corpus calls for caution on the part of the interpreter, who cannot rely on discrete, isolated statements. All Weil's writings— polemical pamphlets, mature social-philosophical projects, and reflections of highly intimate introspection—belong together, but they do not make up a closed system. Instead they appear openly composed around the single, central, searching impulse that inseparably connects life and thought *sub specie mortis.* To understand Simone Weil means to reconstruct the growth of a bold eros. Superimposing an external system on this corpus would be to misunderstand the originality of this way of thinking—that is, its relation to its origins.[10]

10. In his admirable introduction to *Oeuvres complètes,* André Devaux writes that the *evolution* of Weil's thought in its social and political no less than in its philosophical

Doxography is not my concern here. I am more interested in reconstructing a process of reflection. Its formation and growth can be understood only against the background of the experiences that occasioned and inspired it. A review by H.-M. Lohmann quite properly welcomed an anthology of Weil's "political" writings in German translation because it went beyond the religious and "mystical" writer familiar to Germans until that time by "documenting another Simone Weil: the uncompromising socialist and agitator for a radical communism that, in its moral logic and incorruptible intellectual position, comes closest to reminding us of Rosa Luxemburg."[11] He continued by stressing the current relevance of Weil's work with regard to bureaucracy and progressivism *within* socialist discussion, but not without some disparaging mention of the "objectively reactionary"—in the reviewer's eyes—nature of Weil's syndicalism and the Manichaean polarization of her line of thought. This is not the place to discuss the substantial questions raised in the concise brevity of a review. I wish merely to point out an attitude of which Lohmann's review is symptomatic— that is, treating "politics" and "religion" as separate topics in Weil's work. While Catholic writers measure Weil's precise distance from the altar, those critics who are interested primarily in her more narrowly political thought and *engagement* view her "turn to mysticism" as a phenomenon interesting merely as a peculiar psychological quirk. My work, by contrast, will attempt to relate Weil's politics to the totality of her work.

Friends who knew Weil well—among them Albertine Thévenon, the syndicalist; Maurice Schumann; and her schoolmate and biographer Simone Pétrement—have spoken of the basic consistency and inner

---

and religious aspects "involved neither reversal nor denial but rather a continuous deepening that put new elements in their proper place—elements that a relentless and unbroken experience of thought led her to integrate into her vision of the world and her understanding of man" ("Simone Weil ou la passion de la vérité," in Simone Weil, *Oeuvres complètes,* vol. 1, *Premiers écrits philosophiques,* 10). The continuity is also recognized by Winch, *"The Just Balance."* For the reception and publication history of Simone Weil in English see George Abbott White, "Simone Weil's Bibliography: Some Reflexions on Publishing and Criticism," in White, ed., *Interpretations of a Life,* 181 ff. Nevin attempts to collect the elements of a reception history in the form of a *bibliographie raisonnée* in his *Portrait of a Self-Exiled Jew,* 453 ff.

11. H.-M. Lohmann, in *Archiv für Rechts- und Sozialphilosophie* 62:2 (1976): 299– 300.

continuity of her lived thinking before and after her "conversion"—
even when, like Thévenon, they could no longer follow her into her
later phases or when, like Perrin and Schumann, they found themselves
at a great remove from her on the level of doctrine.[12]

The superb biography of Weil by her longtime friend Simone
Pétrement makes it unnecessary for me to record in detail the facts and
figures of her public life. Pétrement's work is also an invaluable guide to
Weil's intellectual development. Marie-Madeleine Davy, who devoted
no fewer than four books to Weil, deserves credit for pointing out the
philosophical derivation from Alain. She did not, however, elaborate on
this connection in greater detail, especially in relation to Weil's political
thought.[13] Along with Jacques Cabaud—Weil's first biographer—Davy
belongs to the school of "hagiographers" among the commentators.

Charles Moeller is indisputably Weil's harshest critic. His attempt
to explicate her "gnosticism" in terms of a compensation psychology
comes from a somewhat doctrinaire standpoint. *Réponses aux questions
de Simone Weil,* by Cardinal Jean Danielou and others, is primarily
concerned with ecclesiological questions, but these papers also touch
on critical problems of philosophical substance. Georges Bataille finds
fault with Weil's political position in her later writings for quite different
reasons. Philippe Dujardin attacks Weil as a figurehead for anticom-
munism, and her life is "unmasked" as the descent from youthful
"bolshevism" to subsequent "fascism." Not surprisingly Dujardin's partisanship leads him astray. For example, the central—though variable—
role played by the concept of work in her thinking is suppressed for the
sake of the ideological line of the argument.[14]

12. See Thévenon's foreword to Weil, *La condition ouvrière,* and Schumann, *La mort
née de leur propre vie: Peguy, Simone Weil, Gandhi,* 61–106, 169–89.
13. See the bibliography for Davy's works. On the subject of derivation, see also
Simone Pétrement, "Sur la religion d'Alain avec quelques remarques concernant celle
de Simone Weil."
14. Moeller, "Simone Weil et l'incroyance des croyants"; Jean Danielou et al.,
Réponses aux questions de Simone Weil; Bataille, "La victoire militaire et la banqueroute
de la morale qui maudit"; Dujardin, *Idéologie et politique.* Dujardin's argumentation
reveals several of the same shortcomings Weil charged against Lenin in a review of
"Materialism and Empiriocriticism" (*OL,* 46–47): "But it is not in this way that Lenin
seems to understand it. He does not say: such and such a conception deviates from
materialism, leads to idealism, furnishes religion with arguments; it is reactionary,
therefore false. He was not at all concerned with seeing clearly into his own thought,

A number of important aspects of Weil's thinking are taken up in the anthology edited by Gilbert Kahn.[15] This volume, which grew out of a conference held by the Association pour l'étude de l'oeuvre de Simone Weil, is particularly interesting for the stimulating contributions that discuss problems of philosophical sources, as does the longer of two papers by Rolf Kühn, and questions of gnoseology, as does the essay by Peter Winch. On the other hand, this volume fails to throw light on the political aspects.

The existing literature has so far made no effort to present Weil's political thought both in its philosophical foundations and in relation to its social and intellectual background. Weil is certainly original, and in many respects an oddity, but she is also, to a degree not yet sufficiently acknowledged, the product of her time.

The remarkable circumstance that such a representative figure as Alain served as mentor to Simone Weil adds another dimension to the search for the sources of her philosophical themes and various aspects of her political reflections. The original, personal impetus of Weil's thought is embedded in the characteristic idiom of the Third Republic. Her analyses bend back upon themselves the very terms of this language, in a twist reminiscent of the alchemists' serpent. I will show, among other things, the extent to which Weil's political thought emerges as an extreme possibility of a mentality that was prevalent in the Third Republic. Weil's critical opposition turned against an "established disorder," which practiced a political style that already included revolt and revulsion. Furthermore, Weil's reflection began at a time when, for various reasons that need not be anticipated here, the element of disorder threatened to grow increasingly virulent. The examination of the intellectual and social contexts of this reflection is therefore closely intertwined with the search for literary sources. Weil's work and France's political culture mutually illuminate each other in this constellation. The work at hand does not, however, pretend to offer an all-encompassing description of France's political culture in the 1930s and 1940s.[16]

---

but solely with maintaining intact the philosophical traditions on which the Party lived. Such a method of thought is not that of a free man" (*OLE*, 30).

15. Kahn, ed., *Simone Weil: Philosophe, historienne, et mystique.*

16. A brilliant attempt at such a synthesis is without a doubt Theodore Zeldin, *France, 1848–1945.*

Instead, it will have to be enough for us to examine the significance of some intellectual and institutional structures in their historical context. Basic problems of intellectual and political order can then be taken up in connection with this investigation. If my work presents certain central traits of political thought in the Third Republic, this is by no means to say that I have arrived at what I would consider an exhaustive description of the intellectual substance of the epoch. Even if such a thing were possible, it is not my intention here. If, for example, I claim and, I hope, render plausible the claim that Alain is representative of that intellectual climate, I nevertheless do not intend to present him as the embodiment of a particular all-encompassing spirit of a time and a people. Nor are the various elements of tradition—institutional structures and intellectual patterns—that are interwoven in the actual statements, actions, or events to be understood as a closed system. Neither the interpretation of French political consciousness in general nor the explication of Weil's work in particular must be understood as the deciphering of supposed essential chains of causality and inevitable determinations. Instead, it must be enough to demonstrate contingent relations where these are concretely manifested and, beyond this, to reflect on the theoretical problems raised by these concrete manifestations. The diverse currents and countercurrents of French and international intellectual and political thought are here taken into account only as they affect Weil's thinking.

"Contingent" does not mean "arbitrary." It can be shown her thinking is both a symptom of and a response to the crisis of the liberal system. The crisis did not engender her work, it provoked it. If, for the sake of a preliminary overview, we summarize the diverse phenomena of an intellectual, institutional, and economic nature under the customary rubric *crisis of the liberal system,* we are not prejudging the question of whether we can arrive at airtight categories of historical analysis that can be arranged by genus and species. It will be enough to start from the point where, to use Walter Benjamin's words, "whatever such names are unable to do as concepts . . . they [achieve] as ideas that do not make similar things coincide but rather bring extremes to a synthesis."[17] It is precisely Weil's eccentricity, her participation in prima facie contradictory positions—which seems to be an element

17. Benjamin, *Ursprung des deutschen Trauerspiels,* 52.

in the synthesis, or supposed synthesis, of the crisis of consciousness of the 1930s and 1940s—that strongly suggests that study of her
works be seen as the exploration of a complex and tangled intellectual
landscape.

Adequate analysis of basic problems of intellectual-political order
occasionally makes it necessary for us to place ourselves within a more
comprehensive framework of intellectual history, which stretches far
beyond the currents fashionable at the time between the wars and
which permits us to take into consideration the original or classical
manifestations and formulations of these very problems. It seemed to
make sense, for example, to treat the problem of "false consciousness"
not only in the secular reductions of Marx but also with reference to its
classical formulation by Saint Augustine, or in discussing the question
of the "holy fool," to refer to Saint Paul and Erasmus rather than
to Wagner's *Parsifal*. Given Weil's specific references to the Hellenic
tradition, consideration of texts from the classical and late-classical
periods also becomes imperative. For one, it is necessary to compare
her borrowings with the original texts; for another, such an approach
appears essential in analyzing a critique, such as Weil presents to us, of
the project of modernity as signaled by Francis Bacon.

In my attempt to portray a particular intellectual milieu, I do not
hesitate to fall back on a novel that, because it is vivid, appears more
suitable to the purpose than scholarly studies in which the price of
methodical rigor is a certain lack of expressiveness. In a different context
it seems to me not only permissible but even appropriate to cite a
newspaper article where it is a matter, not of arriving at a definitive
opinion concerning the author of the article, but of demonstrating
that views held by Weil about the institutional moorings of liberty and
the related critique of party democracy are still valid in the immediate
present and that therefore the discussion of such views is of more than
antiquarian interest.

Weil's is a sensitive personality; confronting the transformation of
grand technological achievements into instruments of dehumanization
in the workplace and then into tools of mass murder, she judges
the program of modernist domination over nature by its fruits. She
realizes that the urge to emancipation of the self is in actuality a
mania of boundless desire with a view to a metastatic change of the
human condition. In the course of time her revolutionary-syndicalist

engagement turned into an attempt to develop a social philosophy of work appropriate to advanced industrial society. She then broke through this framework as well by offering a comprehensive cultural critique, creating an opening to the ground of being. Her critique, however, could not entirely avoid all the distortions characteristic of the very object of her critique. Furthermore, the acuteness of her observations would in many cases have been more persuasive if she had paid more attention to the historical accuracy of her facts.[18] In Weil's work we encounter fundamental discussions of problems of the social and political hierarchy and debates on questions of obedience, necessity and freedom, knowledge, method, and experience. Her work continues to hold the utmost interest for dealing with problems of the world of work, industrial organization, and the ecological limits of a technological civilization, as well as the eternal problem of the humane and yet realistic structure of government. Her principal merit, however, lies in the rediscovery of the essentially dramatic rather than procedural quality of human existence behind the thicket of progressivist ideology and in laying bare the closely allied phenomenon of the delusion represented by the idolatry of immanent goods. That this gain is achieved at the cost of a flight from history and a tendency to *contemptus mundi* becomes the core of my critique of Simone Weil.

The following chapter sketches the social and political structures in France in the period between the two world wars. The second chapter attempts to describe the atmosphere of a small but influential milieu that exerted an undeniable influence on Weil. The following three chapters trace her road into the dead end of *engagement* and back again. Here the essays published by Weil herself serve as the material underlying my discussion. This section deals with Weil's relation to the various traditions of the French workers' movement, her analysis of the German crisis—which also became the occasion for her revision of her own analytical method—and her participation in the debates of the

18. Weil's brother, André, recalls a conversation with his sister that may be corroborated by many citations from her works: "She was once describing to me—it must have been in America—some historical theory, or a historical fancy of the kind that you find expressed in her late writings, and I said to her: 'This is a historical question. It must be discussed in terms of the evidence. What is your evidence for what you are saying?' She said: 'I don't need any evidence. It is beautiful, therefore it must be true'" (Malcolm Muggeridge, interview with André Weil, 679; also in *Gateway to God,* ed. David Raper, 143).

1930s, still conducted "from within" the ideological parameters of the workers' movement.

Chapters 7–12 trace Weil's meditation on her own philosophical foundations that bear the structure of her political reflection. Weil's reliance on the anthropology and epistemology of her mentor, Alain, becomes clear, since both the critical works of that period in Weil's life and those with an affirmative message are conceptualized around this philosophical core. The central text for this period—supplemented by a number of lesser writings—is the long essay "Cause de la liberté et de l'oppression sociale," which Weil completed as a kind of "testament" before her year as a factory worker in 1934. At this stage of her evolution she tried to arrive at a paradigm of the optimal free society, to serve as a measure for attempts at practical approximation to the ideal and as an instrument of social criticism. In this work "freedom" means the "realization of the person" as a deliberately acting subject in immediate opposition to a *res extensa* that is necessity, nature, and structured universe all at once. Chapter 13 describes the considerable change triggered in her reflections by the drastic experience of factory work.

Chapters 14–19 deal with the growth of Weil's political thought against the background of her experiences of transcendence on the one hand and the peripeteia of circumstances of her French homeland on the other. The aim at reform shifts from "liberation" to "taking root." The spiritual factor first inadequately symbolized as a "drive to freedom" is now transformed into an *attente,* a contemplative expectation *a vide,* which implies no temporal promise whatever, which even excludes it completely. This part of my study is based entirely on *L'enracinement,* which Weil wrote at the request of the Free French in London. However, this text can hardly be interpreted adequately without studying the wealth of introspective testimony in the diaries and letters. We find in Weil's proposals for restructuring France a shift in her political thought from concern with the structural determination of "oppression and liberty" to a quasi-Christian position, according to which the structure of the human psyche becomes the foundation of the political order.

The institutional aspects of political formation do not, however, disappear from Weil's reflections; instead, specifically in respect to being formative of an ethos, they play an eminent role. In this context Weil's repeated resort to Alain becomes interesting. The mentor's theory of institutions, which appears perhaps too loose in the earlier phase, paradoxically gains new significance once Weil has transcended the framework of his anthropology and cosmology. But Alain's student also goes beyond his theory of institutions in significant ways. In the unique situation of the Free French in London—though they wielded authority, they lacked, in contrast to an established state, any instruments of coercion—Weil sees a positively providential opportunity to bring about a way for France to "take root," even if she has no high hopes for the actual chances of success. In this context she develops at least the elements of a theory of political representation as the representation of truth. But she does not succeed in combining it satisfactorily with her doctrine of necessity. Some ambiguity remains in Weil's thought. This ambiguity arises from the fact that because of the transhistoricity of her criteria, the approach of a political order to otherworldly perfection must be conceived in terms of partaking in transcendent reality, while on the other hand everything that is political belongs to that intermediate realm of contingency that Weil's necessity-driven asceticism condemns to atrophy. The discrepancy between the purity of her ascetic postulate and the compassion that must manifest itself in the contingent middle region cannot be resolved.

My final chapter, reviewing the overall development of Weil's thought, returns to her person-centered core of experience. Our method proves to be *methodos* in the proper sense, a shared journey along the same road—we might say even, with greater etymological precision, a bridal procession, which in this case culminates in death.[19]

---

19. Henry George Lidell and Robert Scott, *Greek-English Lexicon,* new ed. (Oxford: Clarendon Press, 1940), s.v. "methodos."

ONE

The Third Republic, or the Morass

Marsh (bog). . . . Very wet terrain or terrain not quite covered by water without a drain. . . . The Marsh or the Plain, the moderate party at the Convention as opposed to the Mountain.

Littré

The Third Republic emerged from the First World War apparently strengthened. Among the Entente powers, France had borne the major burden of the war. The victory was won under a French commander in chief. The Republic had avenged the defeat of the empire at Sedan. The royalist and Bonapartist longings for a *pouvoir fort* withered away.

The Republican constitution, adopted by the National Assembly in 1875 by a mere one-vote majority, was transformed and solidified as time passed, both in the way it was applied and in the mind of the population. "The Third Republic is not 'improvised,' as is, for example, the Weimar Republic (Eschenburg), and not simply the result of a revolution in Paris, as was the Second Republic of 1848, but is truly a 'growth.' Now it has taken root and has become the political regime of French society."[1]

---

1. Rudolf von Albertini, *Freiheit und Demokratie in Frankreich,* 95. See also Jean Touchard, *La gauche en France depuis 1900,* 125. Touchard points out the frequency with which the words *défendre, protéger,* and *garantir* occurred in the rhetoric of the ruling *radicaux,* even before the war (*La gauche,* 48).

Louis-Adolphe Thiers called the Third Republic the political regime that least divided the French people. Sedan and the defeat of the Commune had immediately preceded its founding. Keeping it alive required both a balance among the interest groups that it represented—the farmers, the small and middle bourgeoisie—and continuing vigilance against threats from beyond France's borders. Thus the Republic was basically conservative; that is, it was intended to preserve the achievements of the revolutions of the eighteenth and nineteenth centuries, such as land ownership by the peasantry and civil emancipation, at the same time that it was established to work *against* the danger of reaction on the one hand and a (proletarian) revolution on the other. This dominant basic attitude is reflected in the program of the *défense républicaine,* resulting in what Roland Barthes has called *ninisme:* "ni révolution ni réaction—ni Moscou ni Rome," and the like.

When the Republic was founded, the peasantry accounted for the overwhelming majority of the population. According to the 1921 census, 54 percent of all the inhabitants of France lived in the countryside; as late as 1931 the number still amounted to 48.8 percent.[2] In 1921, of the roughly 8.5 million farmers, 5 million were working for themselves. Although migration to the cities increased after the First World War, the influx was mainly to the smaller towns, where it was still possible to lead a quasi-rural life. People tended to maintain their personal and emotional ties to the land. After a century of industrial development France essentially remained a nation of farmers, artisans, and petit bourgeois. In 1921 only 25 percent of the working population held jobs in real industry. Of these, 19 percent were self-employed, and 11 percent were heads of firms *(patrons).*[3] Of the wage earners, in turn, a scant one-sixth worked in companies with more than five hundred employees. The preponderance of industrial production, furthermore, consisted of textiles and luxury products that were manufactured more or less with artisan skills. In the economic sector, efficiency and expansion were

2. On this and what follows, see André Siegfried, *Tableau des partis en France,* 13 ff., and Georges Gurvitch, "Social Structure in Pre-War France."

3. Comparing these figures with those obtaining in England, we find: 90 percent wage earners, 6.3 percent self-employed, 3 percent "patrons" (Siegfried, *Tableau,* 16). For a more detailed description of the economic data, see Alfred Sauvy, *Histoire économique de la France entre les deux guerres.* On the dynamics of socioeconomic migration, see Touchard, *La gauche,* 93–94.

subordinated to such social goals as the position and independence of the family.[4]

The small family firm, self-supporting and aimed at the protected domestic market, remained characteristic of French industry. Technocracy, derived from Saint-Simon, remained a marginal phenomenon, standing in direct contrast to the almost universal distaste for mechanization and concentration.[5] Modern technology was not rejected outright; it was modified by traditional intellectual and social structures.[6] In the eyes of the average Frenchman, "Wealth is not a dynamic matter, connected with the general well-being, but a firmly rooted legal asset: a field, a house, a mortgage, even a purse filled with gold coins."[7] In spite of the steady increase in the number of *fonctionnaires* the bourgeoisie, which set the tone for political, intellectual, and economic life, consisted largely of "independents" and, like the peasantry, strove for self-sufficiency. "The guiding social idea, rooted down into the working class, remains the idea of an independent existence, if possible the acquisition of a small fortune that permits early retirement into private life."[8] And we should add to this all too Helvetic idyll the leisure to participate with all one's might in stirring political oratorical duels, supercharged with doctrine.

The institutions and style of the Republic expressed the desire of a great majority of individuals to be free of tutelage of any kind, permitting no one to order them around on the pretext of "government business," or to lay claim to deference (*égards*). Executive efficiency, on the other hand, was wholly suspect. The constitution of a public sphere and political participation, except as they signified affirmation of equality, were secondary. "We waste our best powers in the affirmation of that aggressive and ideological [*doctrinal*] individualism. That is the cause of the scant material yield of this democracy, which does not set material yield as its aim."[9]

The Republican synthesis positioned itself in a broad social center. Its superiority, a numerical fact, was strengthened by such institutional

4. See Stanley Hoffmann et al., *In Search of France*, 4.
5. Siegfried, *Tableau*, 40.
6. See Hoffmann et al., *In Search of France*.
7. Siegfried, *Tableau*, 226–27.
8. Albertini, *Freiheit*, 56.
9. Siegfried, *Tableau*, 226–27. See also Touchard, *La gauche*, 20 ff.

structures as the senate and the voting system. The social equilibrium on which the Third Republic, as the longest-lived French constitutional form to date, was based was, thanks to the falling birth rate, subject to only slight demographic pressure—an insignificant pressure compared, for example, to conditions in England. Politics was in no way felt to be a function of the economy: "The political sphere is autonomous and does not represent a continuation of or addition to the economic sphere."[10]

The autonomy of the political sphere permitted the particular combination of a dominant ideological and verbal orientation to the left, nourished by the prestige of the Revolution of 1789, and a social immobility and indifference to effective reform: "The contradiction in the soul of the Frenchman must not be ignored. Politically, his heart is on the left, but his pocket is on the right . . . and for all practical purposes, every Frenchman has a pocket."[11]

The politics of symbolic gestures holds great significance for the republicans' self-understanding. Anticlericalism is its most important and most striking manifestation. Radicalism, as the purest expression of this conflicted stance, not only emerges as the advocate of a social status quo of the satisfied little people; it is also the embodiment of the myth of the Great Revolution and of the civil pride linked with it. If folk wit derives the etymology of radicalism from radishes, it is impossible to imagine this root without the red skin that envelops the white (social) core.

The Third Republic has been called a fair-weather regime. This is a harsh judgment on a government that coped with the Dreyfus Affair, with Boulangism, with the Panama scandal, with the First World War, and with the inflation of the franc. The opinion is fair to the extent that the mixture of bold verbal symbolism of progress with extraordinarily moderate actions, so characteristic of the Third Republic, presupposes the autonomy of the symbolic-political sphere from the socioeconomic sphere, and this autonomy for its part requires social stability. The legitimacy of the regime was assured for as long as Robert de Jouvenel's definition remained valid: "France is a fortunate land, with a generous

10. Albert Thibaudet, *La république des professeurs,* 157.
11. Siegfried, *Tableau,* 89. On Hoffmann's thesis of the Republican synthesis as the expression of a "blocked" society, see the critical objections in Touchard, *La gauche,* 93.

soil. Politics follows the taste of individuals. It is not the condition of their existence."[12]

As long as the economic and social problems facing the great majority were such that they could be solved without government intervention on a grand scale, politics could be allowed to remain a matter of taste. The basic satisfaction among the republican consensus group could be maintained in the first half of the period between the two wars.

The time from 1919 to 1929 was defined by inflation.[13] At first inflation was accompanied by a high level of production. The upper middle class profited from the prosperity, as did the midlevel and small merchants. The trades flourished. The "new" industrial branches created new trades—automobile mechanic, electrician, and the like. Farmers' incomes and the prices of agricultural products rose. On the whole, savers were identical with groups profiting from prosperity. Thus—instead of complaining about the loss of four-fifths of the value of their savings—they were delighted when Poincaré succeeded in 1928 in stabilizing the franc. The stable social basis of the Republic was nevertheless shaken by inflation. The fundamentally defensive attitudes of the various social groups hardened. Those drawing fixed wages were inevitably the chief victims of inflation. However, the protest of the most intransigent among them—those industrial workers who had been factored out when the Republic was founded—remained strikingly weak even in the 1920s. There had hardly ever been as few strikes as during this period. The boom in the trades prevented the proletarization of larger masses. The labor movement was further weakened by the divisions that occurred in their political and subsequently in their trade-union organizations as the result of the 1920 Congress of Tours.

The structural and technological backwardness of French industry had two effects. First, it resulted in a lack of aggressive competition in the international market, leading to significant consequences for French colonial policies. Second, economic underdevelopment kept

12. *La république des camarades,* 4.
13. On this topic and what follows, see Gurvitch, "Social Structure"; Hoffmann et al., *In Search of France;* David Thomson, *Democracy in France since 1870,* chap. 5. On changes in the pact between the middle class and the state, see Zeldin, *France,* 2:1057. On the different directions of public opinion in France concerning the Commune and the Revolution of 1948, see Touchard, *La gauche,* 24 ff.

the French economy from responding sensitively to fluctuations in the world economy. Thus the international economic crisis—which marked the second phase of the interwar period—reached France somewhat later and with less devastating consequences than in, say, Germany. Instead, it lasted that much longer, especially as there was no rearmament worth mentioning to stimulate the economy.

Thus, though France did not experience the economic ruin of entire population groups, the country suffered unemployment, bankruptcies, and the perception, felt acutely by many, of the danger of losing social status. In line with the conservative instincts of the Republic, an attempt was made to counter the subsequent general insecurity by freezing the social status quo on a low level of production. One of the results was that the population became sensitized and irritated with the inadequacies of its political leadership. Mistrust began to extend to the institutions and basic principles of the Republic.

It has been said that the Third Republic governed badly but defended itself well. As far as bad government went, the judgment is surely too sweeping. Its defensive strength, on the other hand, cannot be denied. In the international climate of the day it is noteworthy that, although the Republic was seriously weakened by the international economic crisis, it was not swept away by a domestic radical mass movement—it required a foreign invasion to produce this result. This was due not only to weaker social tensions than, for example, in Germany and to the highly developed, suspicious, proud civic ethos but also to the institutional strength of parliamentary government. It was precisely some of the aspects that in another context would have to be viewed as a weakness of parliamentary democracy that proved helpful in the Third Republic's survival. One of them was the loose party system.[14] The Third Republic, no more than the similar Fourth Republic, was not, as Charles de Gaulle declared, a *régime de partis*. Quite the contrary, it was a government without effective party organizations. The lack of a right of dissolution such as that exercised by British prime ministers and the absence of "first past the post" majority suffrage in single-vote districts resulted in a large number of deputies who were not subject to serious party discipline. The outcome was, on the one hand, a chronic lack of stability in the government. On the other hand, the absence of

14. See Ferdinand A. Hermens, *Verfassungslehre,* 301–2.

party discipline in the French parliament prevented the formation of "blocking majorities" such as had paralyzed the Weimar Republic.

The French system, conceived along ultrarepresentative lines, did not, however, give the voter the power to decide, nor real choice between alternatives of the kind that might be represented by large, potentially alternating party organizations. The complex rules of the game in the "house without windows," easily misconstrued by the general public, further isolated the voter from a parliament that was itself unable to develop coherent and vigorous programs. The impulse of parliament was to control and hinder rather than empower government to carry out programmatic mandates. Even though the elections occasionally gave unequivocal results, they were distorted in this body—which between elections was completely independent—into a sequence of "interchangeable majorities" determined by the dialectic of heart and pocketbook. Maurice Duverger called this system "democracy without the people."[15]

The Third Republic was not the first to invent this way of governing. The defensive center-right/center-left coalition had been the characteristic political constellation in France since Thermidor, that is, the reaction to the revolutionary terror that resulted in the fall of Robespierre on 9 Thermidor of the year II by the revolutionary calendar (July 27, 1794). The break in continuity represented by the French Revolution could not produce a sweeping consensus that might allow the alternation of a progressive and a conservative party under commonly accepted standing rules. Social peace could be bought only at the expense of an arrangement of moderates that was inimical to participation, the perennial rule of the "middle ground," the *marais,* the morass.[16]

---

15. See *La démocratie sans le peuple,* introduction. See also Hermens, *Verfassungslehre;* Thomson, *Democracy in France,* 184 ff.

16. Duverger, *Démocratie sans le peuple.*

TWO

Opposition to the Established Disorder

Born in 1909, Simone Weil was part of a generation of French intellectuals whose differing motivations and idiosyncrasies came together in a common elation of protest. All adopted the same tone, and the same concerns united them all. The strongest and most widely shared trait of the "Spirit of the 1930s" was negativity.[1] Of course the attitude of being "against" was widespread throughout the period between the wars.[2] Once again, and paying homage to French tradition, the young intellectuals felt themselves called upon to "tear away all veils."[3] "[No] study seemed to him more important than the critique of mystification and the exposure of mendacity."[4] So thinks Rosenthal, the hero of Paul Nizan's novel *La conspiration*. No scholarly monograph can render the atmosphere of a particular intellectual milieu in the Ecole Normale Supérieure with greater precision than can this book.[5]

It is set in the period when Simone Weil attended the famous school on the rue d'Ulm, to prepare for the national examinations for high school teachers (*promotion*, then *aggrégation*). Among France's institutions of higher learning, the Ecole Normale held—and holds—a unique position. Its graduates—from Taine, Bergson, and Léon Blum to

1. Jean Touchard, "L'esprit des années 30," 100, 101.
2. Raymond Aron, *L'homme contre les tyrans,* 111.
3. See Tilo Schabert, *Natur und Revolution,* 69.
4. Paul Nizan, *La conspiration,* 61 (*The Conspiracy,* 42). See also *OL,* 173 (*OLE,* 130–31); *EHP,* 272. See further Pierce, "Sociology, Utopia and Faith," 93.
5. On this point, see David Caute, *Communism and the French Intellectuals,* 8.

Sartre, Raymond Aron, and Maurice Schumann—uniformly represent a significant contingent of the French political and intellectual elite. Since the Dreyfuss Affair, the school has always been considered, both in the minds of its graduates and in the opinion of the public, to be in the vanguard of "progressive" thought.[6] There can be no question that Weil was influenced by the *esprit normalien* and that many of her inclinations were strengthened by the spirit of the school.

Nizan's novel describes a group of students at the Ecole: "[T]hey feel themselves to be revolutionaries, they think the only nobility lies in the will to subvert. This is a common denominator among them, though they are probably fated to become strangers or enemies."[7] The basis of each one's self-esteem, which also makes him feel related to his fellow students, is the revolutionary stance—or that, at least, is what each one intends. But in fact no son of a French middle-class family is going to find it very difficult to embrace a revolutionary attitude, since it will not result in any deep crisis in his consciousness of historical continuity, no break in identity. His awareness can reach back beyond his father to his—more often than not peasant—grandfather: "nothing threatens bourgeois stability more fundamentally than this constant interchange of compensatory betrayals, which are simply the normal consequences of the celebrated stages of democracy."[8]

The bourgeoisie, whose children they are and against which they struggle, is a vague concept to these young people. Although they do not necessarily look on the bourgeois as a transhistorical type, they nevertheless tend to understand bourgeois status in anthropological, even ontological, terms, in spite of clumsy efforts to define it along economic lines. The bourgeois, living in a sham world of false values, is to them the man who has lost touch with reality: "C'est l'homme

6. See H. Lüthy, "The French Intellectuals," in George Bertrand de Huszar, ed., *The Intellectuals*, 444. See further, Ernst Robert Curtius, *Die französische Kultur*, 137. A. Diaman, "Tradition und Innovation in der französischen Verwaltung," in Gilbert Ziebura, ed., *Wirtschaft und Gesellschaft in Frankreich seit 1789*, 341: "[T]he Ecole Normale Supérieure (College for teacher training) stands unequivocally to the left and is viewed by the Communist Party of France as one of its strongholds." This statement, however, refers to the present. The avant garde has apparently become more "advanced."

7. *Conspiration*, 30 (*Conspiracy*, 17–18).

8. *Conspiration*, 18 (*Conspiracy*, 8). The passage refers to the fact that Rosenthal, the novel's central character, who is himself Jewish, lacks these roots; the same could be said of Simone Weil.

qui a perdu le sens de l'Etre."[9] He also emerges as the individual who must be destroyed in favor of "person." For Weil, as will be shown, even the category of "person" was too compact to designate real humanity. Eventually she would want to carry out the existential-speculative process of dissolution in much more radical ways, until the truly humane core of man was exposed to her view.[10] This determination to clear away the rubble, which manifests itself as antibourgeois sentiment, was certainly not limited to "left-wing" critics. Thus, the periodical *Réaction* in March 1932 declared: "We must surely know that the bourgeois has nothing to do with us. We look for the person."[11]

To express their revolutionary intent, Nizan's protagonists become enmeshed in a plot—the *conspiration* of the title. The altruism of their motive is surpassed only by the naïveté of the plan. Even the style is revealing: "Un acte d'espionage parfaitement désintéressé dans ses mobiles ou le profond *intéressement* serait d'ordre concret et métaphysique, et entièrement pur dans ses fins" (An act of espionage perfectly disinterested in its motives, whose *interest* would be of a concrete and metaphysical nature, and perfectly pure in its ends).[12] They believe they owe it to themselves, to their better selves, to attack the powers that be, and they are disappointed when the public prosecutor does not react to the provocations they unleash in the press.[13]

A number of demonstrations in which Weil took part during her time at the Ecole Normale expressed that attitude. Admittedly, these demonstrations were not unrelated to student pranks.[14] Even as a child Weil had a tendency to provocative jokes *pour épater les bourgeois*. When she was already teaching, her superiors called her on the carpet for her political activities. "I have always regarded dismissal," she said on that occasion, "as the natural culmination of my career."[15] But she

9. Emmanuel Mounier, the founder of "personalism" and of the periodical *Esprit*, quoted in Touchard, "L'esprit," 101. In his declaration of purpose for *L'Esprit* (1932) Mounier coined the phrase *désordre établi*. On this central figure of French left-wing Catholicism, see R. William Rauch, *Politics and Belief in Contemporary France*.

10. See Weil's late work, "La personne et le sacré," in *EL*, 11–44 ("Human Personality," in *SWR*, 313–39, and in *SWA*, 49–78).

11. J. de Fabrègues, quoted in Touchard, "L'esprit," 101.

12. *Conspiration*, 38.

13. *Conspiration*, 65 (*Conspiracy*, 45).

14. P, 1:131, 139 (PE, 55, 59).

15. Jacques Cabaud, *L'expérience vécue de Simone Weil*, 68 (*Simone Weil: A Fellowship in Love*, 67).

was merely transferred, and the transfer could not really be considered punishment, since there was little to choose between the two small provincial towns involved.

The glorification of workers was a natural match for the antibourgeois stance. When Weil was a student at the Ecole Normale, *ouvriérisme* had many and enthusiastic followers at the school. Although there were a number of different strains in the movement to glorify the worker, the dominant trend was congenial to her innermost nature: It was the expression of the search for contact with the sort of suffering and misery that are summed up in the word *misère*.[16] Emmanuel Mounier's proclamation is representative: "Anyone who has not felt misery ardently within himself will disagree with us in vain and will fight us unjustly."[17]

The young people of 1930 were eager to identify with the popular aspirations, to be witnesses, martyrs. No less important for these young intellectuals, who expected that contact with the common people would awaken them into real life, was the contact of the worker himself with reality, which the intellectuals mentally hypostatized into an object. Whether they came from the "right" or from the "left," they were outspoken opponents of mechanization, "rationalization," "scientific management," and the like. And of course they were crazy about the movies *Modern Times* and *A nous la liberté*.[18] The only thing that appeared to offer stability was to be hard. Nizan's young people despair in the face of the renewed prosperity of the late 1920s, which offers them no opportunity for heroism and heroic sacrifice. They long for harsher times: "What I like about Revolution, said Laforgue, is that the civilization it promises will be a hard civilization. Agreed, said Rosenthal. The age of ease is coming to an end."[19]

In 1929, joining the bourgeoisie, embarking on a career according to their parents' wishes, and thus bridling their rebellious pride had seemed

16. See Touchard, "L'esprit," 100.

17. *La révolution personnaliste et communautaire,* 312.

18. Touchard, "L'esprit," 98. For Weil, see P, 2:91 (PE, 267). On movies in general, Touchard, "L'esprit," 102. On the problem of the discrepancy between the backwardness of technical development and the acuteness of opposition to technology in France, see Raymond Aron, *L'opium des intellectuels,* 57: "Preindustrial structures are better conserved in France than in countries of the British or Scandinavian type. Thought preempts the future and already denounces the danger of a technical civilization even though the French are still far from enjoying its benefits." Aron's statement about the postwar period holds true a fortiori for the 1930s.

19. *Conspiration,* 58, 59 (*Conspiracy,* 40).

inevitable. The international economic crisis came at a convenient moment for the emotional budget of the young *normaliens*. "[T]he Wall Street crash was to reassure them; they welcomed it like news of a victory."[20] The crisis seemed not only to proclaim the end of the "age of ease" but also to provide experimental proof of the functional weakness of capitalism. The crisis seemed "scientific" confirmation of a theory: to these young people it was less the inevitable consequence of an economic analysis than the expression of "humanist" outrage. Insofar as criticism of capitalism took on the configuration of criticism of laissez-faire, the situation was not entirely free of irony; for in no other country did protectionism and state intervention play so significant a role in the economy as it did in France.[21] However, it is true that it was not until Léon Blum's popular-front government, and as a response to the great wave of wildcat strikes, that the state for the first time effectively intervened in the interest of industrial labor.[22] No more than opposition to the dominance of the machine and technocracy was anticapitalism exclusively a trait of the "left." "As a rule historians have paid too little attention to an emergent form of anticapitalism that was allied with the political right. Its intellectual roots go back to romanticism, while its followers came mainly from the countryside and the small provincial towns."[23]

And so we find, alongside actual anarchism and revolutionary syndicalism of older vintage, a *circle Proudhon* springing up under Philippe Pétain and in line with his government. Anticapitalism was part of the overall ideology that has been called the spirit of the 1930s. The international economic crisis, against the background of rising fascism and developments in the Soviet Union, clearly provided the impulse that was needed to give a common voice to the various expressions of a vaguely defined unease about the status quo. It is worth noting that many themes of the *esprit des années trente* (the spirit of the thirties) would become active both in the Vichy government and in the Résistance and Gaullism. This holds especially true for antiparliamentarianism. Robert Aron, who himself speaks from the right, put it in a way that is valid for

20. *Conspiration,* 70 (*Conspiracy,* 49).
21. See Hoffmann et al., *In Search of France,* 13–14.
22. See Georges Lefranc, *Histoire du front populaire;* George Lichtheim, *Europa im zwanzigsten Jahrhundert,* 55.
23. Lichtheim, *Europa,* 61.

the total spectrum of the rebellious young intellectuals: "We are neither right nor left—if we must of necessity assign ourselves to parliamentary categories—we are, and we repeat it, halfway between the extreme left and the extreme right, behind the president, with our backs to the assembly."[24]

Although antiparliamentarianism on the left also stresses the fact that this position turns its back on the "assembly," it is less eager to emphasize its evenhanded distance from both extremes. In the climate of France's prestige of the left, deriving from the Revolution of 1789, the Dreyfuss affair, and other events, the man of the right, *un pestiféré politique* (according to André Siegfried), who needs to establish that distance. Those who, on the other hand, are *de gauche* can boast of their allegiance.

The following quote also comes from the "right." It has the merit of vividly combining in one statement the antitechnocratic and antiparliamentary ground of the protests of the 1930s:

> The idea, like the pig, is alive when it comes to the factory—that is, parliament—on a pulley-block—that is, the party. And it comes out on the other side in the form of laws that are as numerous, different, and standardized as jellied pigs' feet, ham, and sausage. The delegates and senators sterilize their ideas and the feelings of their constituents with such perfect management methods as are imposed on the motions of the negroes of Chicago whose job it is to bleed the pigs when these reach the assembly line.[25]

Nizan's "conspirators" "tended to confuse capitalism with the grownups" *(les grandes personnes.)*[26] Their protest is directed at a social order dominated by members of their grandparents' generation rather than their parents'. In France the "lost generation" is not merely a metaphor for the intellectual disorientation of a cohort—it is a solid reality. Of the almost 8.5 million Frenchmen between the ages of twenty and forty, 73 percent were victims in the First World War. Almost 1.5 million of them died. The steady decline in the birth rates since the middle of the nineteenth century aggravated the situation to such an extent that by 1931 the percentage of the total population between the ages of

24. Quoted in Touchard, "L'esprit," 105.
25. R. Dupuis in *Ordre nouveau* 4 (October 1933), quoted in Touchard, "L'esprit," 102.
26. *Conspiration,* 70 (*Conspiracy,* 49).

thirty and fifty was the smallest of all the world's nations. Those between fifty and eighty years old, on the other hand, made up 25 percent of the total population. The traditional authority structure in France, which always favored older people, solidified into a genuine gerontocracy. "Never," wrote Henri Lefebvre, "has the conflict between generations been so sharp, so much woven with all other conflicts in all fields."[27] The young people's opposition to the "established disorder" was naturally linked to their revolt against the *vieilles barbes* (the old fogies) that headed it.[28] Nizan described the attitude of this generation of young people toward their country's authorities as follows:

> *Civil War* expressed rather well a natural state of fury, and its editors made a point of attacking . . . by name living and genuinely respectable individuals. The reasons they used to give for these indictments, though based on a great display of philosophy, were not all rigorous or valid; but when you think that France at that time, by way of great men, had President Poincaré, M. Tardieu and M. Maginot, it must be admitted that their instinct ran no risk of leading them far astray.[29]

La Guerre Civile is the characteristic title of a magazine. Publishing a magazine was the typical way these rebellious youths took action. The time around 1930 saw the establishment of countless, mostly short-lived publications. To the end, a group of intellectuals gathered as an editorial board remained for Simone Weil a model of human community, facilitating the exchange of ideas in a setting where the affinity of views did not arise from predetermined partisanship.

The readership of these magazines, never more than a few thousand for each, circumscribed the narrow scope of the agitating groups. Not that the expectations the publishers had of their periodicals were any too high: "without exaggerating the significance it might achieve, but nevertheless thinking that perhaps it would represent one segment of the thousand small enterprises of which it is thought that in the long run they change the world."[30]

27. *La somme et le reste,* 374–75.
28. See Gurvitch, "Social Structure," 536.
29. *Conspiration,* 45 (*Conspiracy,* 29–30).
30. See "Note sur la suppresion des partis politiques," in *EL,* 126–48. For Weil the fluidity of the congeniality expressed by a magazine contrasted favorably with membership in a group of rigid partisan affinity. "When one is on friendly terms with

When, at the founding of *La Guerre Civile,* one of the young men worried that the title might already be taken, another pointed out that you could not copyright civil war, it was in the public domain *(dans le domaine public).*[31] In this way the very rift of the *res publica* was proclaimed its elementary substance! By the same token a "civil war" is run as a magazine.

Enthusiasm for imagined civil wars turned into its opposite when it came to war proper. Growing up first in the climate of wartime propaganda, then in the exuberant rapture of victory, the young people of 1930 reactively understood that the "values" for which the great war effort had allegedly been waged, and all the great men who had supposedly made something of themselves during the war, were a hollow sham. They rejected these values, if for no other reason than that they were the values of the ruling old men who had not themselves fought in the last war but now—it was said—having sacrificed their sons, were prepared to sacrifice their grandsons as well. Until the German invasion Weil remained a committed pacifist. Conversely, until she experienced it at first hand in Spain, she saw civil war as a legitimate form of violence.

In part because the wartime generation was decimated, in part because victory engendered such illusions, the full psychological shock of the First World War took a decade to kick in. But then it was all the more severe, especially as the compensations of economic prosperity did not last long. Antimilitarism, antiparliamentarism, and the opposition to technocracy that in part anticipated the industrial reality in France are all aspects of the exaggerated *esprit contre* of the 1930s. In the eyes of the youth of 1930, politics in the name of abstract principles was discredited. When they were faced with the ruins of liberal–positivist radicalism (in the sense of the French *radicaux*), which had been unmasked as the established disorder, these young people were hungry for responsibility

---

the director of a journal and with those who contribute to it frequently, when one writes oneself, one knows that one is in touch with the milieu of that journal. But one does not know for oneself if one is part of it, there is no distinction between inside and outside. Further out there are those who read the journal and know one or two of the contributors. Further still, the regular readers, who draw an inspiration from it. Even further the occasional readers. But no one would conceive of thinking of saying, 'insofar as I am attached to such and such a journal I think that . . .' " (*EL,* 143).

31. Nizan, *Conspiration,* 29 (*Conspiracy,* 3).

and looked for an existential foothold. Nizan wrote: "A bad sign: there is uneasiness about the chances that the values for which we live will survive, there is a readiness for God. There is a readiness for the inevitability of the great future of communism."[32]

Many took the leap into the presumed certainty of promises of different sorts. In *Eyeless in Gaza* Aldous Huxley characterized the period as addicted to communion. Or they stylized their existentialist lack of foundation into a Promethean gesture. Others, in turn, seriously attempted to find their way out of the morass, carried along by the courage to persist in tension; among these were Albert Camus and Simone Weil. Nizan gave up membership in the Communist Party in response to the Hitler–Stalin Pact shortly before he was killed at Dunkirk in 1940; he kept his distance not only from partisan clichés, as did the characters in his novel, but also from the binding leaps into *engagement* and quick grasps for the absolute to which they are given. His search for a solid foundation is subtly woven into the plot of his novel. Rosenthal, who initiates the conspiracy, is involved in a complicated love affair, which pushes everything else in his life into the background. As a result of the "conspiracy," however, one of his friends runs into difficulties with the military authorities. Rosenthal cannot evade the effects of an action that no longer holds his interest. The act, once initiated, has consequences beyond the control of the actors. We find the beginnings of an ethics of responsibility as the modest start of catharsis.

For reasons that will become clear, the method Weil considers appropriate for the study of social phenomena is called *materialistic* and described as follows: "The materialistic method consists primarily in this: to examine all human events from the angle less of the pursued goals than of the inevitable consequences of the means to be used."[33]

Nizan's fictional characters are motivated less by an ethical sense of opposition to the status quo than by the experience of absurdity. Their stance inclines to rationalistic austerity: "They were stirred more by disorder, absurdity and outrages to logic than by cruelty or oppression, and really saw the bourgeoisie, whose sons they were, less as criminal

32. *Conspiration,* 11.
33. *EHP,* 233. See also a later passage by Weil: "Bring together people around Christian aspiration. This word is more appropriate than 'values.' For values invoke a presence, aspiration an absence, and our good is absent" (*EL,* 169).

and murderous than as idiotic."[34] We need to qualify this statement if we want to apply it to Weil; her extreme sensitivity to suffering compels us to see her in a rather different light. We can, however, say this much: she always regarded problems of an ethical nature as inextricably linked with questions of perception.

The legitimacy of the Republic is undermined. The radical construction can no longer institutionalize the *esprit contre* as its embodying principle, and this *esprit* now turns against the Republic. The objectives of the young rebels, however, are anything but anarchic. They seek to replace the established disorder with a genuine order. Despite substantive differences, Weil would have had no trouble accepting the slogan of the group called Ordre Nouveau: "L'ordre nouveau est un ordre," the new order is an order—or a command.

34. *Conspiration,* 59 (*Conspiracy,* 40).

THREE

Engagement

Two things set Simone Weil apart from the stereotype of the French left-wing intellectual. The first is her courage—that is, her uncompromising commitment to translating her beliefs into personal practice. The second is her response to the experience of wretchedness *(malheur)*, which is not self-pity along the lines of Rousseau's "pauvre Jean Jacques" but extraordinary self-mortification.[1] In her memoirs Simone de Beauvoir, who took her exams at the Sorbonne at the same time as Weil, remembers a conversation and comes to a tellingly wrong conclusion:

> [S]he declared in no uncertain terms that only one thing mattered in the world today; the Revolution which would feed all the starving people on the earth. I retorted, no less peremptorily, that the problem was not to make men happy, but to find meaning for their existence. She looked me up and down: "It's easy to see you've never gone hungry," she snapped. Our relationship did not go any further. I realized that she had classified me as "a little bourgeoise hung up on things spiritual," and this annoyed me. . . . I believed that I had freed myself from the bonds of my class.

Beauvoir also offers the anecdote that, on hearing of a devastating famine in China, Weil broke into tears; Beauvoir adds, "I envied her for having a heart that could beat right across the world."[2]

1. Lichtheim, "Simone Weil," 462, 461.
2. *Mémoires d'une jeune fille rangée*, 236–37 (*Memoirs of a Dutiful Daughter*, 252).

Weil's compassion extended to all who were degraded or enslaved, to colonized peoples, foreign laborers, prisoners, prostitutes. Besides physical suffering, *malheur* meant social humiliation and abasement of the spirit. The element of hurt pride in Weil's fundamental experience, humiliation redeemed by humility, plays a prominent part in her thinking. Thus it was that at the age of ten she suspected that the Versailles Treaty expressed the will to humiliate the defeated enemy; it was this perception, as she wrote to Georges Bernanos, that first stirred her political consciousness.

Weil's compassion was not confined to the present. It extended as well to the underprivileged of the past, to Roman slaves and the victims of the Spanish Inquisition. Their suffering cannot be eased, it can only be shared retrospectively, in memory.[3] To experience wretchedness, to understand wretchedness, is Weil's precondition for any reform: "The knowledge of unhappiness and its consequences is the essential precondition of any approach to justice."[4]

Wretchedness had different historical incarnations for Weil, but all corresponded to a basic type:

> Fortunate are those for whom the wretchedness that has become second nature is the wretchedness of the world itself in their day. Such people have the opportunity and the duty to recognize the wretchedness of the world and to contemplate its reality. That is the true redemptive function. Twenty centuries ago, in the Roman empire, the wretchedness of the time was slavery, and the Crucifixion represents its culmination.[5]

The typical sufferer is the Roman slave. The contemporary equivalent—and in this Weil is entirely an *intellectuelle de gauche*—is the proletarian: "No matter how passionately her thinking, suffused with compassion, is engrossed in the concept of 'malheur,' she nevertheless, true to the tradition of the French left, sees the incarnation of the wretchedness that destroys humankind in the proletarian and not in the Israel that is persecuted by Hitler."[6]

3. See Schumann, *La mort,* 73.
4. *AD,* 127.
5. *PSO,* 76.
6. Helmut Kuhn, "Die Philosophie des 'laisser faire Dieu,'" 593. (Unless specific English editions are cited, all translations from the German are by Ruth Hein.)

We cannot help noticing that when Weil thinks about the "wretched-ness of the world itself in our day," there is very little acknowledgment of a form of persecution that is genuinely specific to the time, branding that time indelibly; and even then it is mentioned only peripherally. Power, according to Weil's explanatory schema, is a manifestation of the law of nature that does not, it seems, allow for such anomalies. However, the explanation for what is, in the final analysis, Weil's indifference to the persecution of the Jews surely does not primarily lie in the structures of her thought system but is based on a fundamental animosity toward Judaism. "Personally, I am an anti-Semite."[7] Her biographer Simone Pétrement takes this sentence to mean that Weil wished merely to express her rejection of the sectarianism and fanaticism that might be contained in Judaism; but this is too kind an interpretation. Weil's anti-Semitism has a number of facets: it is the expression of the "inordinate appetite for her own effacement *[appétit désordonné d'abjection]*" men-tioned by Thibon in a trenchant paraphrase of Saint Thomas's definition of pride.[8] Raised in a household of freethinkers, lacking any contact with religious practices, Weil had no need of rebellion, as did such figures as Spinoza and James Joyce, to free herself from her religious community. Her criticism of Judaism cannot therefore be explained away as compensation for a discarded upbringing in strict orthodoxy; instead, it is a violent rejection, rooted in the *appétit désordonné,* of a sign of individuation. The fact that, in Weil's terms, this sign is imaginary does not change anything, since she holds that the realms of the imaginary and of evil are coextensive. In later years Weil never tired of pointing out that "he who is uprooted uproots." On the basis of this maxim, she compares the historical fate of the diaspora with the social effects of prostitution. And so, in the context of her mechanistic theory of power, she is inclined to a variation of that insidious interpretation that holds the Jews themselves responsible for their persecution. Her antihistorical attitude makes the symbolic form of Israel as the historical existence of the chosen people under God not only incomprehensible but altogether scandalous. Obsessed with the dignity of the individual as *imago dei,* she can see in Israel only a totalitarian collective gathered around an ideological idol. Her powerless God cannot tolerate the

---

7. From a conversation with Dr. Bercher, quoted in P, 2:291, n. 1 (PE, 392, n. 6).
8. Perrin and Thibon, *Telle que nous l'avons connue,* 159–60 (*As We Knew Her,* 138).

Almighty of the Old Testament. Since she cannot distinguish between undifferentiated and false consciousness—a distinction requiring at least some allowance for the historicity of human existence and the differentiation of the symbolic articulation of truth over time—the god of hosts can appear only as a cruel tribal totem, an idol of collective selfishness.

Weil did not disassociate herself from Judaism in order to escape persecution. She assumed, probably correctly, that she was not appointed to teach at a lycée because she was classified as a Jew by the Vichy government; at least she never received news of such an appointment. Her letter on this subject to the Ministry of Culture also went unanswered.[9] This characteristically provocative epistle was not calculated to smooth over her relations with the authorities. It also contains the following summary of her "non-Jewish" self-understanding, which leaves no doubt that it was in no way intended to protect her from the consequences of the persecution laws:

> The Christian, French, Hellenic tradition is mine; The Hebrew tradition is foreign to me; no text of a law can change that for me. If nonetheless the law demands that I regard the term "Jew," whose meaning I do not know, as an epithet applicable to my person, I am disposed to submit to it as to any other law. But then I want to be officially informed, since I do not possess any criterion susceptible of resolving this point.[10]

Weil's anti-Semitism is not a form of racism. But it does mark a serious defect in her theorizing and her behavior. Such a limit to a compassion that aspires to universality in a way of thinking determined by the dialectic of all or nothing must puzzle us particularly. It is merely an apologia, explaining away the implacable barriers to Weil's vocation, when Paule Bugnion-Sécretan wrote: "the suffering of the Jews can only have aroused in her the wish of sharing in it."[11] As the syntax of this sentence reveals, we have no concrete evidence that it is so. We know on the other hand that Weil was quite capable of hatred, if only toward Mussolini.[12]

9. P, 2:289–92 (PE, 390–92).
10. Quoted in P, 2:291 (PE, 392).
11. *Simone Weil: Itinéraire politique et spirituel,* 86.
12. Perrin and Thibon, *Telle que nous l'avons connue,* 137.

The representative type of the sufferer in our time is, for Weil, the member of the proletariat. She situates herself conventionally: on the left. She wrote to Bernanos: "From my childhood onwards I sympathized with those organizations which spring from the lowest and least regarded social strata."[13] Here too the controlling criterion is not oppression or exploitation but disdain. At the age of ten, under the impression made on the child's mind by the Russian Revolution at a distance and the enthusiasm and hope aroused by the Revolution in her immediate surroundings, she called herself a "Bolshevik" when speaking to her schoolmates.[14] That this was not a passing fancy is proved by her subsequent statement: "At the age of ten I was a Bolshevik."[15]

The child's emotional commitment does not, of course, mean that she consciously adopted a particular doctrine. Nevertheless, Weil retained from that period the deep conviction that only the class struggle could improve the situation of the proletariat, and she carried over a revolutionary mind-set, which she abandoned in later years only after great inner struggle.[16] In writing to her parents, she described her own political activities as *Le Communisme,* and when in 1932 she wrote to them about her disappointment that she was growing "less and less communist," this nevertheless meant that until then she thought of herself as a Communist.[17] Whether or not she was a Communist, she did nothing to dispel the impression that she was one. Even in school, but also subsequently, she carried around copies of *Humanité,* spreading the paper out ostentatiously everywhere. She frequently doodled the hammer and sickle, not only on her own papers but also in her pupils' notebooks.[18] At the Ecole Normale she was known by the nickname *La vierge rouge.* Activists, including Boris Souvarine, who met her in the early 1930s when they worked together, all attested to her communist

13. *EHP,* 220 (*SL,* 105).
14. P, 1:48 (PE, 18). On the problem of Weil's relationship to Judaism, see Kahn, ed., *Philosophe, historienne, et mystique,* chap. 3. For the pain and outrage caused among Jews by the publication of *La pesanteur et la grâce,* see especially the contribution by Rabi, "La Conception weilienne de la Création." See also G. Benesty, "La question du judaisme dans la pensée religieuse de Simone Weil," thesis, Université Catholique, Louvain, 1976.
15. Quoted in Dujardin, *Idéologie et politique,* 75.
16. See P, 1:251 (PE, 118); also P, 1:48 (PE, 19).
17. P, 1:243 (PE, 112–13).
18. P, 1:113–14 (PE, 46). See also P, 1:252 (PE, 119).

sympathies.[19] The Syndicalist leader Pierre Monatte said, "she was a communist like all the rest of us."[20]

But it is significant that all the political friends she made in that period left the party or were expelled. All of them belong to those *groupuscules* of the Syndicalist or Trotskyist "left opposition" that were not prepared to go along with the Stalinization of the Communist Party. Weil's brother, André, remembers that the draft of an application for membership to the Communist Party lay in his sister's room for a long time. But there is no evidence that the letter was ever sent.[21] The rejection of parties was, among other things, a refusal to identify with a particular party, to accept a label, and so to be inserted in an "established disorder." Because this status quo was seriously called into question as middle class, for certain intellectual circles the Communist Party assumed a special position in comparison to all other parties. After the SFIO, the socialist party, turned to parliamentarism, no matter how clumsily and awkwardly this change was made, the Communist Party seemed the only party to exemplify the intransigent revolutionary spirit, keeping an incorruptible distance from parliamentary horse-trading.[22] The left either overlooked or explained away the party's opportunistic twists and turns. After all, the party promised even more: joining it meant not only that they would be pulling themselves out of the morass by their own bootstraps but also that they would be able to summon up the desired toughness and self-denial.

> The emotional appeal of Communism lay precisely in the sacrifices—both material and spiritual—which it demanded of the convert. You can call the response masochistic, or describe it as a sincere desire to serve mankind. But whatever name you use, the idea of an active comradeship of struggle involving personal sacrifice and abolishing differences of class and race—has had a compulsive power on Western democracy.[23]

Weil considered joining the party but did not go through with it. Her libertarian convictions and the influence of Alain's integral individualism could not help but make her view critically an organization

19. P, 1:114 (PE, 47).
20. Quoted in P, 1:113 (PE, 47).
21. See P, 1:114 (PE, 47).
22. See Caute, *Communism*, 15.
23. Richard H. S. Crossman, ed., *The God That Failed,* 5.

that was noticeably controlled along rigid lines and that, in addition, was reduced more and more unequivocally to the organ of the national interests of the Soviet Union. "By the late 'twenties . . . the true nature of the Third International had emerged beyond reasonable doubt. Both the necessity of defending the internal and foreign policies of the Soviet Union and the 'Bolshevization' of the C.P.s under Stalin's inspiration resulted in increasing uniformity and conformity."[24]

For the students in Nizan's novel, for example, joining the party meant reaching for the absolute. Unlike so many of her contemporaries, who were attracted by the victory the orthodox party doctrine promised, Weil could only be repelled.

> They liked only victors and reconstructors; they despised the sick, the dying, lost causes. No force could more powerfully seduce young men who refused to be caught up in the bourgeoisie's defeats than a philosophy which, like that of Marx, pointed out to them the future victors of history: The workers destined what they somewhat rashly judged to be an inevitable victory.[25]

But it is precisely with the wretched of the earth, with the sick and dying, that Weil identified, and she harbored hope—if not in spite of hope itself, at least, presumably, without confident expectations. Her conviction that justice is always a "fugitive from the camp of the victors" was too strong to allow her to see such a prophecy as deceptive. Finally, though for Weil the Communist Party was a party sui generis, it was nevertheless a party, which means a *groupement d'opinion* and therefore incapable of more than an *action imaginaire*.[26]

All the same, Weil continued to respect the Communist Party; she did not lose this respect entirely until she experienced life in Germany shortly before the seizure of power by the Nazis.[27] Although she condemned Stalinism in conversation, she believed that such arguments were to be waged as family quarrels so as to avoid playing into the hands of the capitalists.[28] In the conflict between love of truth and *engagement*, evident here, the latter quickly had to give way to the former.

24. Caute, *Communism*, 13.
25. *Conspiration*, 60 (*Conspiracy*, 41); on reaching for the absolute, see *Conspiration*, 125.
26. See P, 1:184 (PE, 76).
27. See P, 1:114 (PE, 47).
28. P, 1:300 (PE, 142).

The October Revolution briefly allowed Leninism to seem the appropriate integration of French revolutionary traditions.[29] To the industrial worker excluded from the republican community, the success of the Revolution seemed the revenge for the painfully remembered defeats of 1848 and 1871. The Bolsheviks played a role that corresponded to that of the Blanquist idea of a self-appointed revolutionary elite. Although the special circumstances of a successful revolution in an industrially underdeveloped country revealed defects in the doctrine on which the revolutionaries relied, they also gave new impetus to the voluntarism of the French revolutionary tradition and allowed the doctrinal stress to shift from the industrial worker to Proudhon's type of worker.[30] Not least, many of those who split from the Socialist Party at the Congress of Tours in order to establish the French Communist Party were motivated not only by a refusal to compromise with bourgeois parliamentarism and democratic reformism but also by a pacifism grown virulent after the experience of trench warfare. Taking their mission from the claim to represent the revolutionary avant-garde of the world, the French revolutionaries could see that the "home of the workers" lay in the Soviet Union. Gradual disillusionment, more detailed knowledge about conditions in the Soviet Union, and the Stalinization of the Communist Party all led to defections or expulsions and—at least among some— to revision of the image of an integrative revolutionary party. From another perspective, the period between the wars becomes the period beginning with the October Revolution and ending with the Hitler-Stalin Pact. "[W]hat had a few years previously assumed the form of a logical synthesis of French revolutionary tradition now appeared almost exclusively in the guise of an alien and unsympathetic importation."[31]

Simone Weil's *engagement* took place within the context of one of France's most important traditions, rooted deep in its soil, which also most faithfully gives voice to the naive emotional protest of the masses—at least the revolutionary masses.[32] This tradition is revolutionary syndicalism.

29. See Caute, *Communism,* 12–13.
30. See George Lichtheim, *Marxism in Modern France,* 70, 19.
31. Caute, *Communism,* 13.
32. See Lichtheim, *Marxism,* 70.

FOUR

Syndicalism

French syndicalists in the tradition of Fernand Pelloutier were sensitized to the approaching so-called second industrial revolution; anticipating developments in France, they founded the periodical *La Vie Ouvrière* in 1909. That same year and for a half-century to come, the trade union Confédération Générale du Travail (CGT) came under the moderate-democratic reformist leadership of Léon Jouhaux.

The focus of Pelloutier's syndicalism was not the CGT but the Bourses du Travail. Along with their economic function, in the course of the 1890s the bourses had developed into active education centers based on Proudhon's principle of a *révolution capacité*.[1] Such a revolution, wrought by capability or talents, contrasts with a *révolution-puissance,* which, according to this doctrine, cannot itself bring about genuine improvement in the lives of workers, at best replacing one form of oppression with another.[2]

"The worker must know; he must be informed," noted the principal figure of *La Vie Ouvrière*, Alfred Merrheim.[3] The group involved with *La Vie Ouvrière* was determined to help the worker get in touch with the *vérité virile* in order to move closer to the humanistic goal of reconstructing human identity and dignity, which had atrophied in an increasingly mechanized society, with its division of labor. Creative

1. See Pierre-Joseph Proudhon, *De la capacité politique des classes ouvrières,* 1865.
2. Edouard Dolléans, *Histoire du mouvement ouvrier,* 3:13.
3. Ibid., 268.

professional education—one of the many variants of creating modern man—was described by Albert Thierry.

> It is the task of professional education—between science and labor—to restore that fullness of humanity in the city dweller which has been destroyed by specialization and the machine. . . . Industrial apprenticeship must make the city the equivalent for the artisan of what the country is, or was, for the peasant: a second nature, which—in thought and deed—creates or restores the human being in him.[4]

From the outset this pedagogy, which combines individualism and syndicalism, contains essential components of Weil's thought: first, the ideal of the manual laborer, and second, an oscillating concept of nature that facilitates great feats of mental acrobatics, as when nature, in the sense of landscape, is turned into second nature, in the sense of the formed dispositions of the human being, who in this way achieves true humanity—that is, reaches the state wherein man realizes his nature. Thierry's refusal to strive for conventional success in the world, *refus de parvenir,* acts like a premonition of Simone Weil's. So do his theoretical principles:

> [H]e believed that *ethics encompass all of life* and form the core of workers' culture. He thought that the syndicalist credo should be enlivened by a passion that is placed *at the intersection of perception and technology, where knowledge and loyalty meet.* . . . The two most powerful factors of humanity are the workers' stoicism, which marks that *elite that remains among the people in order to serve the people,* and the mysticism of work, which Albert Thierry shared with Proudhon.[5]

Le peuple is the people of Jules Michelet, standing on one side of the barricades while the "authorities" and "important people" are aligned on the other. Thierry needed only deliberately to remain among "the people"; Weil, child of the middle class, had to begin by seeking "communion" with them. Many critics never tire of trotting out the ad hominem argument of class against Weil. The Comités Syndicalistes

4. Quoted in ibid., 271.
5. Ibid., 271–72.

Révolutionnaires (CSR) was founded by the very group of *La Vie Ouvrière* gathered around Merrheim and Pierre Monatte, with the objective of combating the majority in the CGT. The "minority" group, as it was called, felt that its principles were compromised on several levels simultaneously by the policies of the CGT and Jouhaux's leadership. The participation by the great majority of labor in the war effort, in the name of the patriotic *union sacrée,* offended the international pacifism of the intellectuals around *La Vie Ouvrière.* Patriotic solidarity effected an emotional reconciliation between classes that had clashed ever since the defeat of the Commune.

Against this background the CGT tilted toward closer collaboration with the SFIO, which had grown into a democratic reform group. In doing so, it compromised the syndicalist principle of independent trade-union action. Under these conditions, the CSR contributed considerably to the split at the Congress of Tours and the establishment of the French Communist Party, as well as the Communist federation of trade unions, the CGTU, in 1920–1921. Thus, ironically, libertarian, pacifist syndicalists shared a great deal of the responsibility for Bolshevizing a large part of the French labor movement. When, however, around 1924 it became impossible to ignore the fact that libertarian-syndicalist principles were incompatible with the practices of the Communist party, such men as Monatte, Robert Louzon, and Alfred Rosmer resigned or were expelled from the party they had helped found a few years earlier. In 1925 this group, rooted in *La Vie Ouvrière,* founded a *revue syndicaliste-communiste,* titled *Révolution Prolétarienne,* to serve as an organ of the opposition.

It would be an exaggeration to claim that Weil joined this group if that were taken to mean she was in complete agreement with its doctrines. But when she left the Ecole Normale in 1931, she found a congenial *milieu d'idées* in *Révolution Prolétarienne.* Although the group she came in contact with had little direct influence even within the left, it was made up of figures whose—prevolutionary—integrity was respected on all sides and represented a genuine French branch of the revolutionary tradition. The greater part of Weil's writings published under her name during her lifetime appeared in *La Révolution Prolétarienne.* In 1931 Weil wrote to her parents from Le Puy, where she had taken up her first position at the girls' high school. She asked them for support for *La Révolution Prolétarienne,* which was in financial straits, as well as for another needy publication, *Cri du Peuple,* with which she also sympathized.

> The usefulness of the *Cri du peuple* could be argued about, for it is an organ of combat (but obviously I think it's useful, since I give them my support . . .). But as for *La Révolution prolétarienne,* the only magazine that publishes first-rate historical studies on social problems and the only independent revolutionary magazine, its disappearance would be a disaster.[6]

Even as a student at the Ecole Normale, Weil took part in an effort to translate the educational postulate of the *révolution capacité* into action. Fellow students, and others influenced by Alain, had organized a center for the immediate purpose of retraining railroad workers, to facilitate their transition to office work. At the same time, however, they also attempted to bring general culture to these workmen. This experience seems to have reinforced Weil's belief in the workers' "Aesopian" wisdom, a conviction nourished by Alain.

She expressed to the Ministry of Culture her desire for a position in a large industrial city or in a seaport. Instead she was always assigned to teach in high schools in out-of-the-way middle-class small towns: Le Puy, Auxerre, Roanne, Bourges, Saint-Quentin. Her biographers have described in detail the spectacle of her participation in demonstrations of the unemployed and in "revolutionary" rallies, as well as the expressions of outrage in the local newspaper of whatever town she happened to be in concerning the subversive activities of the refractory schoolteacher. Barely arrived in Le Puy, Weil got in touch with syndicalist leaders in Saint-Etienne, a town at least three hours away by train.[7] She immediately began to teach courses in the Collèges du Travail at the Bourses du Travail in Saint-Etienne. Like every *agrégé,* she was given an honorarium, but she regarded it as an unacceptable privilege and handed it over to the Bourses du Travail, to be used to replenish the library. Recalling the failure of the *universités populaires* before the First World War and the vehement criticism of such populist ventures from various sides, she made an effort to specify and justify her intentions.

6. P, 1:197 (PE, 85).
7. P, 1:200 (PE, 87).

"In efforts made to advance workers' culture, it is important . . . to distinguish between those calculated to strengthen the influence of the intellectual on the workers and those calculated to free the workers from this influence."[8]

She herself was brilliantly successful in popularizing classical texts—such as *Antigone*—according to her own principles, without condescension. She believed that a suffering, uneducated worker could much more easily grasp the truth of tragedy than could, say, the factory manager, since his bourgeois existence shielded him from such contact. If she had succeeded—she wrote—in making available to everyone the moving, deeply human matters that fill the pages of Homer and Sophocles, then "it must interest and touch everyone, from the manager to the uneducated worker, and this latter should be able to enter unimpeded, without feeling a sense of condescension, without becoming aware of an attempt of putting oneself on his level. That is how I understand popularization."[9]

Weil believed that the truth of Homeric epic and of Greek tragedy is identical with the wretchedness that, in her view, represents the workers' daily experience. In this the universal-human obligation of the tragic *tua res agitur* is limited to a human type that is determined by an activity highly stylized into a mode of experience: work. We can also put it the other way around—work is raised to the human *differentia*. Ancient Greece is one of those mental landscapes that in Weil's thinking are always of absolute heuristic significance, even if her discussion does not always scrupulously heed the most reliable historical and philological information.[10] Homer, Aeschylus, Sophocles, Plato, the Pythagoreans, and the Stoics appear over and over again in Weil's work, acting as a mainstay of her thinking and a component of her meditations. Only Aristotle, who admits of no neo-Platonic interpretation and seems always to have stood in the way of rash egalitarianism, was banned from Weil's canon, along with the Hebrew patriarchs. As is shown in the notebook of one of Weil's students in Le Puy, unearthed by her biographer Jacques Cabaud, in her lessons Weil called this custom-

8. *L'Effort,* Organe du cartel autonome du bâtiment de Lyon, December 19, 1931, 2.

9. *CO,* 154.

10. See P. Savinel, "Simone Weil et l'hellénisme."

tailored "Greek culture" "the abstract form of the perfect society modeled upon human nature."[11]

The ancient form remains "abstract" because, according to Weil, it could find concrete expression only in work, since in her view high esteem for labor—manual labor—is the core of any imaginable re-formed, healthy society—unlike ancient Greece.[12] The shift of political thought from the yardstick of Greek or even Hebrew origin to a social philosophy concerned with work is described by Jürgen Habermas:

> This practical necessity requiring technical solutions marks the be-ginning of modern social philosophy. In distinction to the ethical necessity of classical politics, it requires no theoretical foundation for the virtues and the laws in an ontology of human nature. If the theoretically based point of departure of the Ancients was how human beings could comply practically with the natural order, then the practically assigned point of departure of the Moderns is how human beings could technically master the threatening evils of nature.[13]

If, responding to the actual or supposed bankruptcy of a technical-rational society, Weil goes to great lengths to make the Greek criterion —accordance with nature—binding on the contemporary world, she is also eager to preserve the dignity of labor, even to shift it thereby into the proper light. Although she wants to restore the primacy of the ethical norm, she is determined to ground it in a practical, mechanical natural law. Now to the extent that labor, as an action "mastering natural evil," comes to grips with the necessary and unyielding natural order with which the subject is confronted, it effects—better still, it *is*—perception. But work is also the acceptance of practical necessity, it is *pathos*—that is, a mode of receiving the imprint of the reality it engages—it is experience. The transformation of active practice into passive experience is the transubstantiation of practical compulsion into ethical necessity. The concept of labor is the speculative bridge by means of which this transition is effected.

Weil's anti-Aristotelianism—as well as her anti-Semitism—places her in the tradition of modern revolt against authority. Rome is another

11. Cabaud, *L'expérience vécue*, 57 (*Fellowship in Love*, 56).
12. *E*, closing sentence (*NR*, 302).
13. *Theorie und Praxis*, 22 (*Theory and Practice*, 50–51).

one of Weil's bêtes noires. These dislikes manifest themselves as a more intensive variant of French-republican laicism. The Old Testament, Thomas Aquinas, and Rome stand for all historical, systematic, and institutional aspects of the Church. Weil rejects them all the more vigorously as she moves from respectful toleration of the sacramental and mystical elements—those that can be interpreted to the highest degree in individual terms—to placing them at the core of her spiritual life. Both in her admiration for Greece and in her political *engagement* Weil is part of the minority and the opposition. "To be a Hellenist and despise the Romans is an exception in France, if not an oppositional stance. Today it is occasionally found among politically left-wing academics, who see the Roman idea as the support of governmental and clerical authoritarian thinking, while Greece (Archimedes) signifies for them the haven of unhampered research and independent thinking."[14] The declaration of loyalty to the Hellenic heritage occurs against a political background in which the exaltation of Latinity sometimes serves as the basis of claims of racial superiority and the usurpation of the symbolic power of Rome by such right-wing figures as Charles Maurras: "Je suis romain, je suis humain: deux propositions identiques."[15] A sensibility deformed by the politics of symbolic gestures fails to penetrate intellectually and recapture historically the symbols of the past. It is unable to liberate them from the many layers of ideological accretions and adopts instead an equally associative and emotionally burdened counterstance.

However this may be, Weil was so taken on the one hand by the blazing light of Greek literature and on the other by populist egalitarianism that she wished to see Greek introduced as a compulsory course in *all* the schools in what she envisioned as the best possible France of the future.[16] In an article written for the newspaper of the construction workers' union of Lyon, she called on the workers to take up the entire inheritance of past generations. Taking possession of human culture is especially important: "Indeed, this act of taking possession *is* the revolution."[17]

14. Curtius, *Die französische Kultur,* 86.
15. Quoted in ibid., 116.
16. *Ep,* 298 (*NR,* 236–37).
17. Quoted in P, 1:202, and in Cabaud, *Simone Weil: Die Logik der Liebe,* 48 (PE, 88; Cabaud, *Fellowship in Love,* 51: "For the whole essence of the Revolution consists in entering into this heritage").

Taking possession of culture in this way, and in particular the ability to use language, comprises for Weil the realization of a liberating *révolution capacité*. In the same spirit she adopts Marx's statement about overcoming the debasing separation of intellectual and manual labor:

> In Marx's eyes, perhaps the most important conquest of the pro-letarian revolution should be the abolition of what he called "the degrading division of work into intellectual and manual work." The abolition of this degrading division can and must be achieved, and we must prepare for it now. To this end we must, first of all, give the workers the ability to handle language and especially the written language.[18]

The bourgeois represents the transhistorical type of man who gains his living by persuasion, by exerting influence in the human-social sphere. Facility in handling words also creates hierarchic power rela-tionships by the use of mystification.[19] For Weil it is not a matter of dismissing cultural achievements as "bourgeois"; she is concerned with breaking one caste's monopoly on the power of words.[20] Given the humanistic growth toward independence in the workers' lives on the one hand, as well as the demystification of thinking through contact with the *vérité virile* of work on the other, the intellectual, according to Weil, is assigned a service function. She is always intent on diverting not only the reproach but also the real danger of elitist perversion of a populist program of enlightenment as advocated by Proudhon: "To lead man by his head and his hand to the philosophy of work, which represents the triumph of liberty."[21]

Partly out of principle, partly because of local conditions wherever she was teaching, Weil joined teachers' unions; one union was affiliated with the CGT, all others were under the CGTU.[22] She fought as hard as she could for the unification of the labor movement, even though she saw the validity of some of the grounds advanced by each umbrella or-ganization for standing apart. Thus she welcomed the uncompromising class-war attitude of the CGTU even as she condemned of its close ties

18. P, 1:202 (PE, 88–89).
19. This is in line with Alain's teachings. See for example *Politique*, 107–8.
20. See P, 1:202–3 (PE, 89).
21. Dolléans, *Histoire*, 270.
22. P, 1:327 ff. (PE, 161 ff.).

to one party—the Communist Party.[23] Conversely, she felt comfortable
in the tradition of independent union action, which was still alive in the
CGT, while she disliked the reformist moderation of this organization.
It would be idle to discuss in detail the sectarian struggles in the French
trade union movement and Weil's position in each instance, especially as
Simone Pétrement has described this aspect of her activities exhaustively
and in chronological order. We should, however, note that the debates
both within each union and among the various trade unions were
increasingly affected by events abroad, including the rise of fascism
in Europe and the growth of the Communist Internationale. Weil's
last significant act in relation to syndicalism was her participation in the
CGTU congress that took place in September 1933 in Paris's Huyghens
Stadium.[24] The congress was firmly controlled by spokesmen for party
orthodoxy, skilled at silencing any voices raised in opposition; they
vilified and intimidated the dissident delegates, Weil among them. In
particular, she was prevented from reporting on events in Germany,
which she had observed at close hand, because her publications made
it clear that she refused to reinterpret the mistakes and defeat of the
German labor movement along party lines to make them appear as
carefully considered actions and victories. "When . . . Simone Weil's
prognoses became reality and Hitler seized power . . . Simone Weil, the
Ecole Emancipée, and the Fédération Unitaire were accused of kicking
the victims of Nazism."[25] A month after the congress, Weil published
an unsigned report. In it she wrote:

> The true character of the congress was fully revealed when, after
> the session ended, Charbit and Simone Weil were brutally pre-
> vented from distributing appeals in the street for solidarity with
> German comrades, victims of Fascist terror, who did not belong
> to either of the two main Internationals. Such things would be
> impossible in a real trade union organization. But the C.G.T.U. is
> an outright appendage of the Russian state apparatus.[26]

But the Bolshevik turn of the CGTU was not the only thing that
discouraged Weil. Now that she had experienced the revolutionary

23. See P, 1:194 (PE, 83); Marie-Madeleine Davy, *Simone Weil,* 98.
24. See P, 1:357 (PE, 179).
25. Gilbert Serret, *Le syndicalisme dans l'enseignement,* 3:226.
26. *L'Effort,* October 28, 1933; quoted in P, 1:358 (PE, 180).

syndicalism of her friends in Saint-Etienne from the "inside" for a little more than two years, it seemed to her inadequate and dogmatic.[27] In February 1933 she wrote to her friend Urbain Thévenon: "This is the moment above all—above all for the young—to start seriously reviewing all ideas, instead of adopting 100 percent any prewar platforms (prewar C. G. T. or Bolshevik party), at the present time when *all* workers' organizations have *completely failed*."[28]

She would cast her lot one last time with a syndicalist organization when during the Spanish Civil War she enrolled in the militia of the Catalan CNT. Disillusioned by this experience as well, she wrote to Bernanos: "From my childhood onwards I sympathized with those organizations which spring from the lowest and least regarded social strata, until the time when I realized that such organizations are of a kind to discourage all sympathy."[29]

Weil hoped that the trade unions would serve as agents for a revolution that could not only seize the bureaucratic and military machines but smash them as well. She thought that she could assign this function to the trade unions because the unity of their members was brought about "not through the imaginary ties created by the community of opinion but through the real ties created by the community of their productive function."[30]

After three years as a militant syndicalist, Weil acted on her perception of the movement's structure and course of action on the one hand and her analysis of the contemporary crisis on the other. She felt she had no choice but to abandon, if not her revolutionary hope, at least her conviction that the trade unions could be the embodiment of this hope.

> The problem is: to find some way of forming an organization that does not engender a bureaucracy. For bureaucracy *always* betrays. And an unorganized action remains pure, but fails.
>
> The "revolutionary syndicalists" are against bureaucracy, I know. But syndicalism is itself bureaucratic! And even the revolutionary syndicalists, discouraged, have wound up by coming to terms with the bureaucracy.[31]

27. P, 1:311 (PE 151).
28. Quoted in P, 1:309 (PE, 148–49).
29. *EHP,* 200 (*SL,* 105).
30. *L'Effort,* January 2, 1932, quoted in P, 1:184 (PE, 77).
31. Letter to Urbain Thévenon, quoted in P, 1:312 (PE, 150–51).

Given these circumstances, Weil felt compelled to reject any responsibility in organized revolutionary acts, although she did not resign her principled solidarity with the workers' movement, whenever it became manifest as the spontaneous protest of the masses. On March 20, 1934, she wrote to Pétrement:

> I have decided to withdraw entirely from any kind of political activity, except for theoretical work. That does not absolutely exclude possible participation in a great spontaneous movement of the masses (in the ranks, as a soldier), but I don't want any responsibility, no matter how slight, or even indirect, because I am certain that all the blood that will be shed will be shed in vain, and that we are beaten in advance.[32]

Alain had chosen to spend the First World War as a simple soldier, and he had turned the experience into a symbol of physical obedience without spiritual subservience. Weil did all she could to take part in the actions of her male fellow students at the Ecole Normale; they had declared that they wished to meet their military obligations alongside the rest of their simple compatriots, in a kind of community of oppression, but would not, as was customary among students of the Ecole, let themselves be trained as reserve officers. For Weil, the revolutionary struggle was not so much hopeless as it was compromised by its potential leadership cadre. On the level of the spontaneous sacrifices of its "simple soldiers," the battle nevertheless retained its dignity and commanded solidarity. Because of this ambiguity Weil felt obligated to participate but at the same time to reject the responsibility that goes along with any leadership role.

From that time on, Weil was intent on keeping her distance from all political activity save theoretical research. On October 1, 1934, she took an unpaid leave of absence "for personal studies," to start working on December 4 of the same year at an unskilled factory job.

32. Quoted in P, 1:401 (PE, 198).

FIVE

Trotsky and Germany

In the summer of 1932 Simone Weil traveled to Germany because she thought that was where she would be able to witness the alternative between fascism and revolution in its most acute form—an alternative facing the entire world, she believed, given the economic crisis. What made her decide to gather information at the source was no longer the intensity of the crisis. She was more concerned with figuring out what a victory of one or the other side would mean for the international balance of power:

> [T]he life of the German workers is of vital importance to us as well. For, in the breakdown of the capitalist economy that is threatening to wipe out the gains of the workers in the democratic countries and even in the USSR by a wave of reaction, our greatest hope lies in the German working class, the most mature, the most disciplined, the most educated in the world; and especially in the working-class youth of Germany.[1]

Weil saw the events she observed in Germany in the light of an either-or prognosis, which she had adopted from Trotsky. We can sense a projection of the Leninist expectation of 1919 that the European proletariat, with the German proletariat in the vanguard, would follow the Russian example and that the detonation of the October Revolution

1. *EHP,* 150 (*FW,* 100).

would ignite the European powder keg that was assumed to exist and cause it to explode.[2]

> But according to Trotsky, that is the place where the problem will be solved for the whole world. In any case, there can be no argument that the German revolution, establishing connections with the Russian Revolution by way of Poland and conferring new impetus on it, would form an extraordinary revolutionary force. On the other hand, German fascism, by making common cause with Italian Fascism and the counterrevolutionary Danube countries and by supporting the fascist currents already apparent in various European countries and in the United States, would be a threat to the whole world, including the USSR.[3]

Weil never voiced any great hopes for the probability of revolution in Germany. She merely noted that both fascism and revolution in Germany would have worldwide repercussions. A successful German revolution, she believed, would also affect the Soviet Union, bestowing a "new impetus" on the Russian Revolution. Here, too, she agreed with Trotsky that the Soviet Union represented a bureaucratic derailment of the revolution, although her radical-democratic demands went much further than those of the organizer of the Red Army. Nevertheless, at this time, in spite of all doctrinal differences, Trotsky was her ideal of the man of courage. Although later she would revise this judgment, it deserves to be cited, because it sums up her image of the ideal man of action. In a review of the French translation of *What Now* she wrote:

> In the midst of confusion, of universal discouragement, it was only the man sent into exile, the man defamed in every country by every party—the few friends in Russia who have remained loyal to him are almost all dead, deported, or imprisoned—who has been able to maintain courage, hope, and a heroic clearsightedness—it is his special trait. This essay once again expresses the capacity, peculiar to the true man of action, to examine all the elements of a given situation calmly, one after another, and to pursue his analysis to the end, concentrated entirely on the immediate action and managed with immaculate theoretical candor.[4]

2. George Lichtheim, *Kurze Geschichte des Sozialismus*, 212.
3. *EHP,* 117.
4. Ibid.

Persecuted, isolated, rejected, and yet—or perhaps for that very reason—courageous, hopeful, clear-sighted, his candid theoretical analysis directed straight at praxis, this Trotsky combines all the virtues of the earlier "heroic" phase of Weil's theory of man.

Weil shared Trotsky's evaluation of German Social Democracy, which was intended to explain its alleged cowardice and treacherous assimilation to, even support of, the capitalist state as the reason the German revolution, announced since 1919, failed to materialize.[5]

Overcoming the split among German workers by reuniting them "at the basis" would result in their absorption by the Bolshevik Communist Party of Germany, an eventuality Weil considered not only illusory but also disastrous.[6] In clear contrast to Trotsky, she was not persuaded that a German Communist Party cleansed by a (Trotskyite) "left opposition" could successfully serve as a bulwark of revolutionary forces. She attributed such an expectation to Trotsky's "superstitious devotion" to the party. But she did adopt his analysis of the crisis: "The current stage of the capitalist regime—most analyses of the bourgeois economy lead to this conclusion—can be reconciled neither with economic liberalism nor, consequently, with bourgeois democracy."[7]

The "capitalist regime" remains an impenetrable symbol. Whatever it is meant to designate precisely, it is unreconcilable, "even according to bourgeois economists," with the liberal economic system, whose function appears to be bourgeois democracy.

> The economic crisis raises the question with greater acuteness. Normal police methods are no longer adequate to keep capitalist society in check. This is the hour of fascist tactics. "Using the fascist agency, capital mobilizes the masses of the stultified petit bourgeoisie, the bands of the degraded, demoralized lumpenproletariat, and all the innumerable human beings who have been thrown into despair and misery by that same finance capital."[8]

The radicalization of the population brought about by the economic crisis and more particularly by widespread unemployment is the last hope for the creation of a revolutionary situation in Germany—a

5. Ibid., 119 (see also Lichtheim, *Sozialismus,* 220).
6. *EHP,* 119–20.
7. Ibid., 117.
8. Ibid., 117–18.

situation that would reflect all the slogans Trotsky had uttered since the success of the October Revolution. The same radicalization, however, also provides fascism with its best opportunities to make inroads. According to this interpretation, fascism in its turn is merely a tool of economic capitalism, in whose hands it tries to place all institutions of government, leadership, and education. Weil, too, started with the cliché of fascism, a movement based on the confusion of the disconcerted petit bourgeoisie and conducted in favor of "finance capital."[9] She went to Germany believing, "Thus everything is imperiled all at once: not only the working class, but also the achievements of the liberal bourgeoisie and culture in general."[10]

On her arrival, Weil discovered that the intensity of the crisis in Germany was such that social problems had penetrated deep into individuals' personal sphere. While in France problems of the social structure were still debated only in a subsector of national life, which was called "public"—newspapers, political meetings—in Germany the most intimate decisions and personal perspectives were already directly related to the "framework of society," the network of economic and political relations.[11] It was the crisis that seemed to *create* that dependence of the individual (Weil does not say of consciousness) on society that revolutionary theory talks about. In this theory society is understood as the system of economic relations. In normal times, Weil believed, such a statement had only theoretical meaning. Under the conditions of depression and unemployment, however, it was a fact of life.[12]

> For almost every German, at least in the petty bourgeoisie and the working class, prospects, good or bad, that concern even the most intimate aspects of one's own life are immediately formulated, especially if one is young, as prospects that concern the future of the regime. Thus the amount of a people's energy that ordinarily is almost entirely absorbed by various passions and the defense of private interests is, in present-day Germany, brought to bear on the economic and political relationships that constitute the very framework of society.[13]

9. See Lichtheim, *Sozialismus,* 224.
10. *EHP,* 118.
11. Ibid., 128, 148 (*FW,* 99).
12. *EHP,* 126.
13. Ibid., 128, 148 (*FW,* 98–99).

The crisis blurred the boundary between the private and the public spheres. It is worth noting that Weil was thinking of the duality of French social life when she examined this split between carefully guarded domestic and private happiness, *le petit bonheur,* on the one hand, and the public activities of the politics of symbolic gestures on the other. She ascribed the absence of such a duality in the attitude of the German worker families she met entirely to the severity of the crisis. She did not consider that such a blurring might have deeper roots in Germany. The crisis was painful, but, in that it laid bare the "naked reality" of modern society, it was healthy: "The crisis has shattered everything that prevents man from freely asking himself about the problem of his own destiny—that is, habits, traditions, firm social relations, security, any expectation of the future."[14]

The norm shattered by the crisis was, according to Weil, mendacious. The crisis revealed the falsity of the norm in that it barred all paths of man's "imaginary"—that is, false—self-realization and constitution of identity. This is a recurring theme in Weil's thought: reality is revealed at the moment when the empirical self is powerless and the blinders of the "imaginary" are removed. But at the same time the tabula rasa is connected with hopelessness and lack of expectations. Such a situation is tragic in that weakness as such cannot make its way in the world. In order to realize its truth, it must grow powerful. But in the process, a lie distorts it immediately and inevitably. This is the speculative background against which Weil planned to explore the conditions of possibility for revolutionizing a society, using the example of Germany.

She would have considered that deliberately increasing the misery of the underclass in order to provoke a revolution was not only criminal but also yet another factor of false consciousness. During her stay in Germany, Weil gained the impression that whereas the German workers were not at all prepared to capitulate, at the same time they were in no position to fight in any meaningful way. Her criticism was directed at the organizations of the workers' movement, her praise at the workers themselves. Her conviction, reinforced by Alain, that *le peuple vaut mieux que ses maîtres* (the people is worth more than its master) grew into genuine enthusiasm for the German working youth: "[O]ne cannot

14. *EHP,* 126.

imagine anyone more courageous, more lucid, or more fraternal than the best of them, despite this life."[15]

Weil never grew tired of expressing enthusiasm for the young German workers' love of sports and of nature, for their love of music and literature.[16] The contact with nature is of great significance, as the experience of necessity, as natural beauty, or as athletic control over one's own body. Weil's mind-set combines a Rousseauian romanticism and the ideal of Stoic discipline, allowing her to turn the German working youth into a prefiguration of the emancipated socialist *uomo universale*. By using her shifting concept of nature, she tried to legitimate her wishful thinking about these young people, who vicariously stood for all the people who, though suffering, were yet buoyed by hope. She admired most of all the way these young people remained steadfast as they became disillusioned, the fact that "the best" among them were not inclined to give themselves over to compensatory raptures. "They are not trying to forget; they are not complaining; in this hopeless situation they are resisting every form of despair. In general they are trying—some with more energy than others, and the best wholly achieve it—to build a fully human life within the inhuman situation in which they have been placed."[17]

Evidently, as it turned out, there were not very many of these best. Nevertheless, Weil was convinced that if these young people could survive the fascist onslaught, they would represent the brightest hope for the future of Europe.

Weil's praise was by no means limited to the young. She saw them merely as the flower of the "German working class, which, as we saw, seemed to her the most cultured, most disciplined, and most mature working class in the world."[18] How does it happen, then, that this "most advanced, best organized proletariat in the world" did not seem able to take up the battle against fascism, much less bring about the revolution?

In the economic crisis every single act of rebellion runs up against the rigidity of the social structure. Why is it, then, that the dormant energy—which, given these circumstances, can no longer be absorbed in private interests—does not change into revolutionary vigor? Weil

15. Ibid., 150. (*FW,* 101).
16. *EHP,* 127.
17. Ibid., 150 (59; *FW,* 101).
18. *EHP,* 150.

elicited several factors. The problem of transforming the social order as well as the means of production confronts a working class that is not homogeneous and that, for this reason, is incapable of concerted, effective action.[19] "Thus, even though the crisis forces almost every German worker or petit bourgeois to feel, at one time or another, that all his hopes are being dashed against the very structure of the social system, it does not by itself group the German people around the workers determined to transform that system."[20]

The great number of office workers—who, as a consequence of the "terrible expansion of capitalism in the period of prosperity," had come to make up a very considerable segment of all wage earners and the unemployed—presented, in Weil's view, a serious weakness in popular solidarity, since on the one hand they were not much inclined to join ranks with the factory workers and, on the other, they "were incapable of taking their fate into their own hands, by the very nature of their professions." The use of hands as a metaphor is characteristic of Weil's basic attitude. Nevertheless, there is fundamental and historical accuracy in her psychological observation that those who have fallen out of their class or who are threatened by such a fate are not inclined to join ranks with the class to which they have sunk. Weil considers that the proletariat is assigned, not necessarily a historical, but certainly an ontological role: it is in touch with reality; she therefore feels the subjective claims of those who have fallen socially to be in the most trenchant way imaginary—that is, evil. It thus becomes clear that Weil shared the vulgar Marxist prejudice against the tertiary sector of the economy. In the massive expansion and renewal of industrial powers since the First World War she saw only the result of a terrible extravagance; according to her interpretation, this process could not help but lead to a devastating growth in the number of office workers, to overproduction, and therefore to the crisis. She would have considered the idea of alleviating unemployment through deficitary economic policies to be sheer madness, though she would not have been alone in this view in 1932 (or indeed, again, in 1995).

The workers still employed in manufacturing, Weil notes, are prepared to remain loyal within the framework of the regime because

19. *EHP,* 128, 148 *(FW,* 99).
20. *EHP,* 129, 149 *(FW,* 100).

they have something to lose—their jobs. Their fighting spirit *in* the workplace, in turn, is dampened by the threat precisely to this workplace, itself conditioned by the large number of the unemployed.[21] The result is a vicious circle. The crisis that brings about the—potential—revolutionary situation also and for the same reason paralyzes the principal representatives of the revolutionary spirit—the highly skilled workers who under normal conditions are indispensable to industry and therefore can afford a revolutionary attitude in the awareness of their independence:

> In times of prosperity, the revolutionary movement generally depends mainly on the strongest part of the proletariat, on those highly skilled workers who feel that they are the essential element in production, know that they are indispensable, and are afraid of nothing. A crisis radicalizes the unemployed, but it also allows the bosses to drive the revolutionary workers out of the system of production, and forces those who are still in the factories (who are all, even the most skilled, afraid of losing their jobs) into a submissive attitude. Thereafter, the revolutionary movement relies on the weakest part of the working class.[22]

This movement, set in motion by the crisis, is a concrete manifestation of the dialectic of weakness and strength mentioned briefly above. "Spontaneous struggle has always proved itself to be ineffective, and organized action almost automatically secretes an administrative apparatus which, sooner or later, becomes oppressive."[23]

The third potentially revolutionary group, the unemployed, are demoralized by their unemployment. All the virtues that must develop in the course of work, according to Weil, wither in conditions of enforced leisure, of deprivation, of dependence on others. Once again Weil tries to explain a specific psychological situation by recalling a philosophy of work.

> This life of idleness and poverty, which robs skilled workers of their skill and the young of any possibility of learning a trade, which deprives the workers of their dignity as producers, which after

21. *EHP,* 149 (*FW,* 100).
22. *EHP,* 168 (*FW,* 120).
23. *OL,* 35 (*OLE,* 21–22).

two, three, or four years finally leads—and this is what is worse—
to a sort of sad tolerance—this life is no preparation for assuming
responsibilities in the whole system of production. Thus the crisis
constantly brings new ranks of workers to class consciousness, but
it also constantly pulls them back again, as the sea brings in and
pulls back its waves.[24]

These weaknesses at the foundation can be remedied only by strong
organization, but this too is fraught with problems.

[C]onversely, an uprising of the masses left in the factories is
the only thing that can really endanger the bourgeoisie. The
existence of a strong revolutionary organization, therefore, is a
nearly decisive factor. But for a revolutionary organization to be
said to be strong, the phenomenon that reduces the proletariat
to impotence in times of crisis must not be reflected in the
organization, or reflected in it only to a very slight degree.[25]

Weil examined the organizations of the workers' movement according to this criterion. These organizations did not appear to be
in a position to stem the dissolution of demoralized individuals and to
conspire in effective action. To explain the failure of the organizations
to herself, Weil investigated the internal structure and the relations of
the "revolutionary" parties to each other under the conditions created
by the crisis. In her view, the starting points of organizational action lie
on the one hand in the emotional reaction of the masses to the crisis
and on the other in the existence of pockets of the population both
capable and determined to act. Among the former are a sentimental
attachment to the current regime, which need not stand in the way
of a free-floating longing for change. The individual social elements
that, according to Weil, were potentially capable of methodical action
are the—deliberately—revolutionary section of the proletariat and the
haute bourgeoisie.[26]

The polar opposites represented by the protagonists in a potential
"methodical action" correspond to the polarity of the perspective
on the future, "fascism or revolution," adopted as the basis of the

24. *EHP,* 148–49 (*FW,* 99). See also *EHP,* 150 (*FW,* 101).
25. *EHP,* 168 (*FW,* 120).
26. *EHP,* 129–30.

analysis. We sense here a clear aversion to an intermediate realm, which appears unreal and which also includes the "formal" representative institutions. In this "imaginary" no-man's-land, according to Weil, there are only games of opinion and self-deception. It becomes clear that concrete analysis using Trotsky's schema represents an exemplary reflection of Weil's ontological-anthropologic dualism. The Social Democrats were circumspect people, wrote Weil, concerned lest they forfeit their achievements. She appreciated the Social Democrats' accomplishments "within the framework of the regime" in regard to social security, training, workers' education, and the like. In the SPD, however, Weil saw, merely the parliamentary arm of the well-established reformist trade unions, whose "conservatism" was further strengthened by the fact that the Social Democratic trade-union members, who represented the great majority of organized labor, had for the most part held on to their jobs. The main points of the criticism of Social Democracy were its adaptation to the bourgeois state externally and the internal bureaucratic trend to oligarchy. Weil underestimated the role of Social Democratic revolt as the organ of representative-democratic aspirations; the realization of such aspirations seemed guaranteed by the Weimar Republic, and though Weil, the French *citoyenne,* may have considered them illusory, she also saw them as fulfilled. The "bonzes," or high functionaries, of the trade unions seemed to her an extension of governmental bureaucracy pure and simple; as such, they represented coopted elements of the repression mechanism. She perceived the guiding principle of the Social Democratic leadership to be anxiety about preserving their organizations, effectively preventing any and all risk taking. "It is a matter of . . . avoiding any battle that would raise the question of 'revolution or fascism'—a battle that would always end in destroying the reformist organizations." The regime must not be put in jeopardy. But in that case, how is an antifascist struggle conceivable? "Fight? For the Weimar Republic?!"[27]

To fight for such an insipid cause was evidently inconceivable. The Communists, in turn, seemed at first glance to represent a considerable revolutionary force. They drew on a living revolutionary tradition and could take their bearings from the years 1919–1920 and 1923, unlike the French revolutionaries, who had to reach all the way back to

27. Ibid., 133.

1871. Communist activity in social-service and sports organizations, she reasoned, was complex. In reality, according to Weil, the Communist Party showed significant weaknesses and errors. The weaknesses were connected with the recruiting of party members. Most members were recently enrolled and, in contrast to those with jobs, who remained loyal to the Social Democrats, were generally unemployed. Thus the split between employed and unemployed workers was intensified by differing party loyalties. Out of work, the Communist workers lacked all access to the sites of production, and their revolutionary activities were of necessity limited to agitation among adherents of other parties. "The vanguard of the German proletariat is on the whole composed of men who are truly dedicated and courageous, but for the most part they are devoid of experience and political education, and almost all of them have been thrown out of the production process, out of the economic system, condemned to a parasitic existence."[28]

But Weil saw in the Communist Party not only weaknesses but also errors—more precisely, vices.[29] Using vivid examples drawn from current events, she documented for the readers of *Ecole Emancipée* and *Révolution Prolétarienne,* first, the hypocrisy of the slogan concerning the united front of all revolutionaries "from below"; second, the nationalism manifest in referring to the Social Democrats as "national traitors"; third, the perfidy and shortsightedness of forming a united front with the National Socialists so as to fight against the Social Democratic comrades, who were being slandered as "social fascists" and singled out as the "main enemy." The Berlin transport strike furnished excellent examples of this attitude. Not last she denounced the dictatorial leadership methods within the party and the sacrifice not only of the interests but also of the intelligence and truthfulness of the workers' movement in favor of the protean dictates of policies forged in Moscow.

Arthur Koestler, who was a member of a cell in Berlin at the time, left us a vivid picture of the shadow play of Communist agitation during the last days of the Weimar Republic. He wrote about the defeatism that pretended to feel assured of victory, of the abject obedience to the commands of Soviet foreign policy and Stalin's methods of forcing everyone to toe the line, of the "dialectical" surmounting of contra-

28. Ibid., 174 (*FW,* 126).
29. See also Lichtheim, *Sozialismus,* 220.

dictions with "principles" previously proclaimed that set in with each new directive. "The days of the Weimar Republic were numbered, and each of us members of the German CP was earmarked for Dachau, Oranienburg, or some other garish future. But we all moved happily through a haze of dialectical mirages which masked the world of reality. The Fascist beasts were Fascist beasts, but our main preoccupation was the Trotskyite heretics and Socialist schismatics."[30]

The picture Koestler drew from his critical memory is almost identical with Weil's contemporary analyses. The only difference is that she does not seem to have grasped the full extent of how bizarre the situation was. For one, since she had never joined the party, she was never directly confronted with the necessity of becoming one of the "virtuosos of Wonderland croquet."[31] For another, her low sensitivity threshold made even a lesser evil appear unacceptable to her; as a result, at times, because she became critical at such an early juncture, her criticism did not go far enough. She discovered that the only hope for a revolution in Germany lay in a spontaneous action of the masses. But her assurance is slight indeed: "If factory workers and the unemployed decide to rise in unison, the working class will emerge in its full strength, with far greater brilliance than it did in Paris in 1871 or in St. Petersburg in 1905. But who can say whether such a struggle would not end in a defeat, such as has put an end to all spontaneous uprisings up to now?"[32]

Révolution Prolétarienne edited out the final sentence, to Weil's great annoyance. The editor, she felt, had committed an act of deception, an offense against solidarity. At this time Weil was close to the radical democratic positions of Rosa Luxemburg, and like Luxemburg, she saw that the Russian Revolution had spawned the establishment of a bureaucratic ruling class. Weil adopted the interpretation of Stalinism as a bureaucratic distortion of socialism—an interpretation that, in spite of all of Stalin's "purges" (which were tantamount to liquidation of the Russian bureaucracy), managed stubbornly to persist among the anti-Stalinist splinter groups.[33] Furthermore, there can be no doubt whatever that she warmly welcomed the Soviet Communist aims, even as she held a very pessimistic view of the possibility that they would be realized,

---

30. Koestler in Crossman, ed., *God That Failed*, 29.
31. Ibid., 42.
32. *EHP,* 142. See also a similar statement in P, 1:296 (PE, 139).
33. See Hannah Arendt, *The Origins of Totalitarianism,* 319, n. 27.

especially as she was painfully aware that the Soviet Communists were devoid of substantive ideas.

The 1933 seizure of power by the Nazis gave Weil the ultimate proof that it was time to abandon her basic Trotskyite premises, which she had extended *ad absurdum* in her concrete analysis. This was certainly true for the Trotskyite concept of fascism as the bourgeoisie's last trump card. "There exist small groups of high financiers, big industrialists and reactionary politicians who consciously defend what they take to be the political interests of the capitalist oligarchy; but they are as incapable of preventing as they are of arousing a mass movement like fascism, or even of directing it."[34]

She had occasion to note that these groups at times assisted and at other times fought against fascism and that they had tried in vain to turn it into a docile instrument and finally themselves surrendered to it. If, in the presence of an exasperated proletariat, they thought fascism to be the lesser evil, it was never a card they could play. The manner in which Hitler dismissed Alfred Hugenberg was, she thought, significant in this respect.[35]

Similarly, Weil did not admit that the Soviet state, which had not withered away but was more powerful than ever, was, as Trotsky would have it, merely a deformation, nothing but an anomaly of a workers' state: "Descartes said that a clock that runs imperfectly is not an exception to the law of clocks but is a different mechanism, obeying its own laws."[36] In the same way the Stalinist regime obeyed the rules of its own mechanism, which was not, as would befit a workers' state, the democratic organization of the working class, but the centralized administration of the totality of the country's economic, political, and intellectual life.

Trotsky responded to Weil's publications and those of other dissidents in a pamphlet entitled *La Quatrième Internationale et l'URSS,* which was published on October 13, 1933. An extract from this text appeared that same day in *La Vérité.*[37] In it Trotsky wrote, "The Left Opposition did not have to wait for the discoveries of Urbahns, Laurat, Souvarine, Simone Weil, and others before declaring that bureaucratism, in all

34. *OL,* 17 (*OLE,* 6).
35. *OL,* 17 (*OLE,* 6–7). On Trotsky's interpretation of fascism, see *EHP,* 118.
36. *OL,* 169.
37. *CO,* 170.

of its manifestations, corrodes the moral texture of Soviet society, engendering a sharpened, legitimate discontent among the masses and entailing great dangers."[38]

Trotsky's argument that the bureaucracy was not a new class of exploiters was based on his premise that it did not quite satisfy the "scientifically determined" concept of class. The bureaucracy, he claimed, was not a separate ruling class, not in the Soviet Union nor in the capitalist countries. With this he shifted the argument about the dominance of one group to one about whether such a group could be properly defined as a "class." Even after he had lost the match, practiced Wonderland croquet player that he was, Trotsky defined the Stalinist apparatus "dialectically": "Today, when there is no longer—or when there is not yet—a Marxist leadership, it [the apparatus] defends the dictatorship of the proletariat in its own way. But its methods are suited to promote the victory of the enemy in the near future. Anyone who has not understood this dual role of Stalinism in the USSR has understood nothing." Concerning Weil herself, Trotsky wrote that she belonged to that category of "melancholy revolutionaries" who live on the interest of capital made up of memories. "Despairing over the unfortunate 'experience' of 'the dictatorship of the proletariat,' Simone Weil has found consolation in a new mission: to defend her personality against society. A formula of the old liberalism, refurbished by a cheaply bought anarchist exaltation."[39]

Trotsky's analysis has a polemical tone, but basically it is to the point. Weil would no doubt have rejected the word *personality* because of its contingent connotations. However, she surely felt the imperative of defending the integrity of the *esprit* against the illusions and corruptions of the social sphere. "We want to posit the individual and not the collective as the highest value."[40]

In the summer of 1933 Weil made it possible for Trotsky to hold a meeting in an apartment belonging to her parents that happened to be vacant at the time. They met on this occasion and quarreled about Trotsky's role in the Kronstadt uprising.[41]

---

38. Quoted in P, 1:355 (PE, 178); Dujardin, *Idéologie et politique*, 114.
39. Quoted in P, 1:355 (PE, 178).
40. *OL*, 38; see also *OL*, 32 (*OLE*, 20).
41. See P, 1:383 (PE, 187–88).

SIX

Renouncing Revolution

For Simone Weil revolution was never an end in itself, an intoxicating fantasy; it was merely a means for arriving at optimal social conditions. Like all methods, she judged it not only by its professed aims but also by its unintended, unpredictable, but inevitable consequences. "The revolution is a *job,* a methodical task that the blind or people with blindfolded eyes cannot perform. And that is what we are at this moment."[1]

Yet, she argued, the revolution was everywhere proclaimed not as a solution to existing problems but as a kind of miracle that relieves us of the necessity to face problems; in the last analysis, as a blind frenzy of activity. The revolution seems possible only as a *divertissement,* not as methodical work with a clear vision of aims and side effects. Weil firmly distanced herself from a revolution that could serve only self-forgetfulness, flight from ennui. She referred to a review, written by Georges Bataille, of André Malraux's *Condition humaine* and deplored the fact that the reviewer singled out the negative aspects of the book for praise: "We would have to know . . . whether the revolutionary spirit should be considered a kind of disease. What creates the basis of the novel and the unity of all of its characters . . . is the idea of diversion, in the sense that Pascal used this term, that is, the idea that man cannot become aware of himself without intolerable an-

1. Letter to Urbain Thévenon, quoted in P, 1:312 (PE, 151).

guish . . . and so plunges into action in order to lose consciousness of himself."[2]

Having traveled to Germany to verify empirically the premises of Trotsky's analysis of the crisis in general and the rise of totalitarianism in particular, Weil returned home convinced that the premises amounted to nothing more than clichés that were not made more true by repetition.[3] The naive or cynical concealment of reality, the attempts at deception and self-deception, perhaps the will to pass off the hopelessness of the revolutionary aspirations in Germany as historical promise, defeat as victory—these happen by setting up a blind made up of clichés. In the context of the debates current in her circles, Weil believed that Marxism, too, played the role not so much of a living doctrine and productive method as of an eristically applied dogmatic commonplace: "As for ourselves, Marx represents for us, at best, a doctrine; far more often just a name that one hurls at the head of an opponent to pulverize him; almost never a method."[4]

Weil felt that "scientific socialism" had been reduced to a dogma, just as had all the results obtained by modern science, in which everyone believes the conclusion without understanding the methods by which it was reached.[5] The illegitimate appeal to Marx's authority thus became for her an expression of that dominant way of thinking that a liberating discourse should aim to defeat. The revolutionary theory that proposes to overcome alienation falls apart itself; a construct of dogmas separated from its methodological preconditions, it deteriorates into one of the most acute forms of disjunction, which cannot be distinguished from the loss of reality.

Here Weil connected her criticism of the contemporary doctrinal wars with her fundamental condemnation of a specializing, alienating, mystifying science, which makes it impossible to reconstruct *more geometrico* and thus to overcome the "debasing division of labor." Such a battle of the dogmas, blocking the way to its own objectives, does not deserve to be called either science or theory. If, Weil wrote, Lenin is correct when he stated that without a revolutionary theory there

2. Quoted in P, 1:424 (PE, 209). (The first sentence does not appear in the translation and has been translated here from the French.)
3. See *OL*, 17 (*OLE*, 6).
4. *OL*, 40 (*OLE*, 25).
5. See *OL*, 60, 185 (*OLE*, 39–40, 140).

can be no revolutionary movement, we must also accept that there is practically no revolutionary movement at present.[6] "We are living on a doctrine elaborated by a great man certainly, but a great man who died fifty years ago. He created a method; he applied it to phenomena of his time; he could not apply it to phenomena of our own time."[7]

Weil clung to Marxism as a revolutionary critique of nineteenth-century bourgeois society and of capitalism as the concomitant economic system. But in her view events were such as to render inadmissible the projection of the results of that analysis to her own present. The methods of Marxism continued to guide her in many ways, but the object of its concrete analyses, the society of its day, no longer existed. Lenin's slim pamphlet on imperialism as well as a number of German tracts exhausted, according to Weil, all Marxist attempts to keep pace with the new forms of capitalist oppression. These works, too, related to events of the prewar period.[8] "[W]e must recognize that the two economic categories established by Marx—capitalists and proletariat—are no longer sufficient to grasp the form of production."[9]

The traditional categories did not allow Marxist commentators to do justice to the phenomenon of totalitarian elites, whose position of power is independent of their social origins.[10] When they are confronted with newly formulated problems, the Marxists, instead of recalling the sources, engage in mythmaking to explain away the phenomena that do not fit into the dogmatic schema: "In the communist daily press, the division into classes which, in Marx, was meant to explain political phenomena by relationships of production, has become the source of a new mythology; the bourgeoisie, in particular, plays in it the role of a mysterious and maleficent divinity, which brings about the phenomena that are necessary to its purposes, and whose desires and subterfuges explain almost everything that happens."[11]

The literature that claims to be exacting is not much better in this regard. Having lost touch with reality, the Marxists must fabricate "camouflage tactics" for the bourgeoisie, which has been deliberately

6. *OL,* 40 (*OLE,* 26).
7. *OL,* 39 (*OLE,* 25).
8. See *OL,* 39, 166 (*OLE,* 25, 125).
9. *OL,* 42 (*OLE,* 27).
10. See Lichtheim, *Marxism,* 157.
11. *OL,* 166–67 (*OLE,* 126).

stylized into a historical actor; in this way they can avoid giving up their stereotype. Instead of trying to develop a set of analytical tools appropriate to the new conditions, the various revolutionary groups, each in its own way, harbor nostalgic feelings for the good old days before the war, when you still knew what was what.[12]

The negation of prognoses by facts reflects on the methods themselves and leads to uncovering internal contradictions: "[I]t is not by comparison with the facts, but in itself, that I consider Marxist doctrine to be defective."[13] Not only because external conditions changed in the course of time but also because of its internal deficiencies and inconsistencies, Marxism, according to Weil, cannot meet the task assigned to it: to be revolutionary theory. It is not necessary to wait for results to uncover these inconsistencies. Weil wrote that, even when she was very young, on first reading *Das Kapital,* she noticed a number of contradictions.[14] On the other hand, we have seen that she made an initial effort to understand the German crisis by using the categories that in her mind were part of the Marxist canon.

How can we account for the fact that, within the context of her revolutionary *engagement* and journalistic activism, Weil adopted categories that in her own mind were full of internal contradictions as well as contrasting sharply with the philosophical—especially anthropological and epistemological—ideas she had developed as early as her days of studying under Alain and, as her students' notebooks prove, had never abandoned? She herself described the phenomenon as the misguided lack of confidence of a young person before the "great minds" that had embraced Marxism. Her case is a concrete example of a false belief in authority. "How many young minds are not thus led, through lack of self-confidence, to stifle their most justified doubts?"[15]

Once her honest efforts to apply the Marxist schema had proved to Weil that it was factually false, her suspended doubts were reaffirmed. Although she had previously set those doubts aside out of reverence for the authoritative figures of the leftist milieu, they had first occurred to her with respect to the theoretical coherence of Marx's design. She saw herself compelled to work out with the greatest possible precision the

12. See *OL,* 167 (*OLE,* 126).
13. *OL,* 195 (*OLE,* 147).
14. *OL,* 194 (*OLE,* 147).
15. Ibid.

inadequacy of the interpretational scheme. In this effort, in the course of time, she shifted increasingly from attempting to extract a Marxian purity in the face of a Marxist coarsening to a fundamental critique of Marxism. Starting from Cartesian and Kantian anthropological and epistemological premises, she would attempt to undertake an analysis of political reality, which led her to a philosophy of work. One of the results of this analysis was the insight that the course of writing in the immediate future would be determined not by a revolutionary emancipation of the proletariat but by the war that, as she believed, would bring about the opposite of all the presumptive promises of liberation. "Twentieth century: war has replaced profit as the dominant motive [of human behavior]."[16]

Her retreat from syndicalist *engagement* was accompanied by a return to her own analytical frame of reference, which no longer deferred to the prestige of the "classics" of socialism. Weil developed this conceptual frame in a long essay, which she wrote as a sort of "testament" before starting on her year of factory work in the heavy-metal industry of the Paris region in 1934.[17] The analysis presented in "Reflection Concerning the Causes of Liberty and Social Oppression"[18] and in the supplementary shorter texts entails a sustained critical discussion of Marxism. But Weil's greatest debt was doubtless to the doctrines of Alain.

16. *EL,* 175.
17. See P, 1:432, 2:7 (PE, 216).
18. *OL,* 55–162 (*OLE,* 37–124).

SEVEN

Philosophical Beginnings
Alain

Like most representatives of the "spirit of the thirties," Simone Weil, too, was a *philosophe*.[1] In concrete terms, this means that she chose a course of study that certified her to teach philosophy in secondary schools. In a country whose culture is molded by literature, where the writer, the *moraliste,* enjoys much greater respect and a higher standing than the philosopher—not to mention the professor of philosophy— this was a break with tradition.[2] This break indicates that the political professionals and the form of government were not alone in losing the faith of the people; the traditional guardians of the national conscience, the keepers of the grail of the *esprit,* the writers, were also accused of breaking faith, of engaging in the *trahison des clercs.*[3] "France has no peer in her high regard for intellectuals as a class. Not only do French intellectuals regard one another as the guardians of an elevated vocation, the vocation of the *esprit,* but society has tended to value them on their own terms."[4]

In hindsight, Proust, Gide, and Valéry—who by 1930 were either dead or had passed the zenith of their creativity—appear to be not so

1. See Touchard, "L'esprit," 98, n. 43.
2. See Lüthy, "The French Intellectuals," in de Huszar, ed., *The Intellectuals,* 444; Curtius, *Die französische Kultur,* 77.
3. This phrase is the famous title of a work by Julien Benda; see Lichtheim, *Marxism,* 90–91.
4. Caute, *Communism,* 11.

much pioneers as the last to relate to the "classical" French tradition, doing so as its liquidators.[5] *Litterature engagée* would try in vain to fill the vacuum thus created. Moreover, the experience of a void spurred on philosophy. "In France, philosophy has always become a concern of the entire culture only when it appeared not as pure philosophy but as worldly wisdom or as the lever of political emancipation or as paving the way for new social forms or as the ally of natural science."[6]

Of course in school and at the university, Weil attended lectures by a number of philosophers, among them Le Senne and Leon Brunschwicg, but she acquired the most important part of her schooling in philosophy from Alain. Although it cannot be said that he served as Weil's inspiration, the tools she gradually sharpened to explicate her own experiences derived from his philosophy. Her work, even where it surpassed that of the master—be it in her revolutionary stance or subsequently in her access to the transcendent—remained structurally related to his. Under his influence Weil's epistemological as well as moral impulse took on the contours of an anthropology and cosmology that encompass the treatment of the political realm.

The unassuming secondary-school teacher Emile Chartier, better known by his pseudonym Alain, was already teaching before the First World War, but he exerted his greatest influence on a considerable part of France's young intellectuals during the years between the wars.[7] Alain deliberately refused to systematize his thoughts. In his striving for a "politics of understanding *[entendement]*," he rejected any "trap of reason":[8] a system. He mainly made use of the *propos,* a literary form characteristic for him: short, associative meditations provoked by something read or actually experienced. A huge number of such

5. See *EL,* 18–19 (*SWA,* 57). On the entire question, see H. Stuart Hughes, *The Obstructed Path: French Social Thought in the Years of Desperation, 1930–1960,* chap. 1.

6. Curtius, *Die französische Kultur,* 75.

7. For Alain, see S. Dewitt, *Alain: Essai bibliographie;* André Bridoux, *Alain, sa vie, son oeuvre;* André Maurois, *Alain;* H. Mondor, *Alain;* Marie-Thérèse Sur, "Alain et la théorie démocratique." In addition, see the special issues of *Mercure de France,* December 1, 1950, and *Revue de métaphysique et de morale,* April–June 1952, as well as the *Bulletin* of the Association des Amis d'Alain. Among the larger French public the name of Alain evokes the title of one of his collections of *propos: Le citoyen contre les pouvoirs* (The citizen against the powers). The name of the work by Aron, *L'homme contre les tyrans* (Man against the tyrants), is a direct critical allusion to it. In Aron, see in particular the chapter "Prestige et illusions du citoyen contre les pouvoirs."

8. Alain, *Politique,* x.

propos were published in local radical periodicals, until an organ was expressly created for them in the magazine *Libres Propos*.[9] This magazine also took Weil's earliest published writings.[10] Younger friends, Alain's pupils, occasionally published collections of *propos* in book form. In accordance with the master's wishes, they hardly ever deviated from purely chronological order, precisely because of the occasional nature of the pieces; they considered the chronological arrangement the closest approximation to "a lack, or rather . . . a rejection, of any systematic order, even any premeditated order, and *a fortiori* any subsequently imposed order."[11]

As a rule, systematic summaries of Alain's ideas by commentators who are well disposed toward him are accompanied by respectful apologies.[12] The marked dislike of any form of systematization is nonetheless accompanied by an astonishing permanence of themes over several decades. These themes dominate not only Alain's writings but also his teaching. Alain, who is described by all who experienced him as an extraordinarily attractive figure, affected the younger generation as a teacher even more than as a writer. Not only the students enrolled in his courses at the Lycée Henri IV but also students at other institutions came to attend his lectures. Because he was a professor of philosophy at one of Paris's elite schools, whose upper grades (*première supérieure*, called *khâgne* in student slang) then as now prepared students for admission to the *Grandes écoles*, in this highly centralized country a large number of the rising intellectual elite of France automatically passed through his hands. That is where Weil encountered him as well.[13] He, in turn,

9. "Radical papers that lacked money and that well-connected people preferred to ignore," Alain himself said in ibid., 1. More than three thousand *propos* appeared in the *Dépêche de Rouen* alone. In spite of Alain's emotional statement about impoverished magazines, the importance of the radical provincial press must not be underestimated, as the national influence of the *Dépêche de Toulouse* sufficiently demonstrates. It is quite true to style that the principal organs of radicalism, nourished by the *esprit de clocher*, were published in the provinces.

10. "De la perception ou l'aventure de Protée," *Libres Propos* (Nimes) 5 (May 20, 1929): 237–41; "Du temps," *Libres Propos* 8 (August 20, 1929): 387–92. During the 1930s Weil continued to publish in *Libres Propos*, along with her submissions to syndicalist journals.

11. Michel Alexandre in Alain, *Politique*, ix.

12. There is also the tact that allows Pétrement to conclude, "In fact, Alain did indeed have a doctrine, whether he wanted to or not" (P, 1:72; PE, 31).

13. See P, 1:chap. 2 (PE, chap. 2); Cabaud, *L'expérience vécue*, 22–23 (*Fellowship in Love*, 26–27); Marie-Madeleine Davy, *Introduction au message de Simone Weil*, 25–26.

recalled her as "surpassing most of her contemporaries—surpassing them by far"; he survived his student, forty years his junior, by eight years. He combined his praise with a reference to affinities in their way of thinking. Reading one of her late political writings, he was reminded of himself.[14]

French philosophy was shaped by Descartes. At any time the great majority of the French can be united under the name of Descartes. There are hardly any ideologies that do not claim him. "A loud 'We Cartesians' in the tumultuous National Assembly brought about a moment of solidarity, since it calmed the notables and honored the activists. Cartesianism was put forward equitably against the obscurantism of the right, the confusion of the center, and the dialectics of the left."[15]

For three centuries Descartes remained the patron saint of French thought. His style not only satisfied literary taste; it shaped it to a considerable extent. Thus his work could be influential in a way that could not be achieved by, say, Auguste Comte with his convoluted French. In popular culture Descartes became a symbol for clear, unprejudiced thinking that defies authority. The name of the "lawgiver of reason" legitimated a presumed clear and distinct understanding characteristic of Gallic genius.

> [W]e can even say that this vulgar Cartesianism has been the greatest obstacle to the unfolding of a genuine philosophical spirit in France. . . . That is why today [1930] the efforts of all serious thinkers in France are directed to exposing Descartes's philosophy again in its pure form, to wresting it from the domain of popular philosophy, and to setting it in its rightful place in the context of the great, little-known achievements of French thought.[16]

This purification seems all the more important as Cartesianism becomes the common denominator of self-understanding in a society that makes no attempt to separate culture in the narrower sense from science and political action, considering them instead to be closely interrelated.[17] And so it is not surprising that Weil's thesis was titled

---

14. In *La Table Ronde* 28 (April 1950): 47.
15. J. Kayser, "Le radicalisme des radicaux," 71.
16. Curtius, *Die französische Kultur*, 77, where he also discusses Marechal Foch as the embodiment of the Cartesian spirit.
17. See Hughes, *Obstructed Path*, 4.

"Science and Perception in Descartes."[18] Although for the record her dissertation supervisor was Leon Brunschwicg, the work is quite clearly influenced by Alain—which may be why it was given a low grade.

Alain was a Cartesian in the sense that he not only accepted Descartes's dualism as the truth but went further to raise it to the absolute criterion of those philosophies that "can be trusted [se fier]."[19] That he named Plato in the same breath with Descartes can be ascribed to a most peculiar view of Plato, which Weil adopted as well: "Plato and Descartes are two incarnations of the very same being."[20]

Weil's predilection for Cartesian dualism as the sign of "true" philosophy is very plainly revealed in her teaching, which is available to us thanks to the publication of the college notebook of her onetime student, Anne Reynaud.[21] In Alain's work, as in Weil's, dualism was the indication of "critical" philosophy, as opposed to ontology and ideology, protection against creating a closed system. Alain's refusal to present his work in systematic form, his use of the format of the *propos,* is part of this attitude. After reading her essay "Reflexions sur les causes de la liberté et de l'oppression sociale," he wrote to Weil: "Your example will encourage the generations who are disillusioned with ontology and ideology. Criticism is waiting for its workers."[22] Coming from Alain's pen, the word *workers* is not a loose metaphor, since for him the trade, the métier, was the basic form of reasonable activity, no more, no less.[23] And so Alain praised Weil's essay on parties, which we will discuss at greater length below, because, he said, it was written "as with a workman's pickax."[24]

Along with Descartes and Plato, Weil considered Kant, Alain himself, and his teacher Jules Lagneau to be true philosophers. Conversely, Aristotle was for her the prototype of the systematic ontologist, a concept in which she seems to take up the tradition of French neo-Augustinianism in its opposition to scholasticism and Thomism. Later, Husserl was added to the true philosophers.[25] At the same time, because

18. *Sur la science,* 11–99 (*FW,* 21–88).
19. Quoted from "Extraits," in Bridoux, *Alain,* 99. See also P, 1:83 (PE, 38).
20. *Leçons,* 217 (*Lessons,* 219).
21. *Leçons,* 10, 99, 117, 192.
22. *OL,* 8.
23. See Bridoux, *Alain,* 34.
24. In *La Table Ronde* 28 (April 1950): 47.
25. Miklos Vetö, *La métaphysique religieuse de Simone Weil,* 10.

in Weil's estimation Descartes was not always motivated by selfless love of truth but by vanity, he is said to distort his sequence of thoughts so as not to jeopardize his renown of originality—that is, from *amour de soi*—and he must therefore be expelled from the inner circle of genuine lovers of truth, even if he remains a valuable master in many things; as she wrote: "Descartes himself admits having done this [deliberately smudged the argument] in his *Géométrie*. Which proves that he was not a philosopher in the sense in which this word was understood by Pythagoras and Plato—a lover of divine Wisdom. Since Greece disappeared there hasn't been such a thing as a philosopher."[26] But such formulations mark the break in Weil's rationalistic worldview that seems to have been caused by the experience of factory work. The aspect of Descartes's thought Weil finds to criticize is not his dualism but the existential dishonesty into which he was seduced by his desire for fame. After the breakthrough, she was able to express the philosophical function of contradiction more clearly: absence of contradiction is not sufficient proof of truth, since it cannot establish the reality of the premises. Rather, on the level of discursive reason, a contradiction can point beyond the discursive mode of apprehending reality. The "legitimate use of contradiction" by Weil is a variation of the *credo quia absurdum*.

> [C]ontradiction, as Plato knew, is the sole instrument of develop-
> ing thought. But there is a legitimate and an illegitimate use of
> contradiction. The illegitimate use consists in combining incom-
> patible assertions as if they were compatible. The legitimate use
> consists, when the human intelligence is faced with the necessity
> of accepting two incompatible truths, in recognizing them as such,
> and in making of them as it were the two arms of a pair of pincers,
> an instrument for entering indirectly into contact with the sphere
> of transcendent truth inaccessible to our intelligence.[27]

Just as Alain made dualism the criterion for "trustworthy" philosophies, Weil believes the "contradiction pincers" to be useful as "perhaps . . . a criterion for discerning which religious or philosophical
traditions are authentic."[28]

26. *E*, 218–19 (*Ep*, 323; *NR*, 257).
27. *OL*, 208–9 (*OLE*, 159).
28. *OL*, 209 (*OLE*, 159). On the significance of methodical doubt for Alain and for Weil, see Davy, *Introduction*, 38.

"Transcendent truth," a phrase belonging to the late stages of Weil's thinking, indicates the independent reality of what can be perceived only by a faculty beyond intelligence—that is, beyond discursive reason. In the earlier phases of her thinking and in Alain's work, this aspect of truth does not emerge. Truth or truthfulness, Reynaud's notebook reads, "It is not virtue which proceeds from God, but God who proceeds from virtue."[29] The similarity of structure testifies to the continuity linking the earlier with the later phases of Weil's thought.

For Alain, the controlling human faculty, ruling discursive reason, was will—but will that must first be willed: *vouloir vouloir,* Alain stated, and he frequently gave this will to will a name that could not help but appeal strongly to his pupil. He called it *courage.* "In a thousand shapes, even under the name of religion, we can observe how courage finds it object and its proof. Nevertheless, whether it is life to come, the future of the species, the realm of reason and justice, the object is always merely an image *[imaginaire],* and it is courage that supports it all. . . . By its nature will is constituted in such a way as to prove itself."[30]

And Weil: "The will is what understands (grasps), it is not an object of understanding (is not grasped)."[31] Will justifies itself, and accordingly, in Alain, the adjective *volontaire* predicates the will *per definitionem.* Alain sought to combine the Cartesian *ego cogitans,* which reassured itself in itself, with the *volonté* of Rousseau—that is, to lead perception and action back to the same starting point, removed from Pyrrhonist doubt. This is also the tone of early Weil: the phrase *Je veut donc je suis* (I will, therefore I am) appears in her thesis.[32]

The principal doctrine to be wrested from Descartes is, for Alain, the courage to endure an antinomy. "Thus we take from Descartes the courage necessary to firmly hold two ideas, without first knowing how they fit together, without rushing to sacrifice either of them."[33] Subsequently, when in Weil's thought the active, self-justifying will is displaced from the summit of the order of the human soul by an expectant readiness to receive, *attente,* the philosophical method of just such a form of courage is described. Specifically, it consisted "in clearly

29. *Leçons,* 194 (*Lessons,* 183).
30. Bridoux, *Alain,* 103.
31. *Leçons,* 219 (*Lessons,* 204).
32. See the excellent discussion in Winch, *"The Just Balance,"* chap. 2, "The Cartesian Background."
33. Bridoux, *Alain,* 99.

conceiving the insoluble problems in all their insolubility and then in simply contemplating them, fixedly and tirelessly, year after year, without any hope, patiently waiting *[attente]*."[34]

What here is cited as a general hermeneutic rule relates preeminently to two ideas: moral freedom and natural necessity. The antinomy, which according to this understanding forms the poles of the human condition, may not be resolved by explaining away one of the terms or by subsuming one term in the other. Courage as the cardinal virtue of a philosophy that understands itself not as *vana et peritura curiositas* but as a life discipline means that both "idealistic" and "materialistic" reductions of the existential tension must be avoided. "So, the first thing to be sought is freedom."[35]

Weil describes letting oneself be driven by pure chance as the "sin of sins, the sin against the Spirit."[36] Not to summon up the courage required by the will to will also means giving oneself over to a slothful understanding of necessity, letting oneself be driven by chance. "Fundamentally it may be . . . that the concept of liberty, because of a lazy *[paresseuse]* idea of its opposite, necessity *[nécessité antagoniste]*, is overlooked by almost everyone. It is also clear that practical liberty often does not take hold because what stands in its way is not initially perceived in the full measure of its insuperable power of resistance."[37]

Alain turned against a theory of perception—that is, of contact with reality—as the imprint of external reality acting on a passive subject. Rooted in the tradition of the French moralists, he also rejected an introspective science of psychology. Following him, Weil wrote to one of her students in 1933, "As far as psychology is concerned, Stendhal and Balzac are far better than university professors."[38]

The rejection of psychoanalysis is not a special trait of Alain's mode of thought; it was characteristic of French culture as a whole until 1940. To the extent that Freudian doctrine was adopted in France at all, it was typically modified; Gaston Bachelard, for example, introduced voluntaristic elements.[39] For Alain, the passions are simply bodily functions.

34. *CS,* 305 (*FLN,* 335).
35. *Leçons,* 193.
36. Ibid., 114.
37. *CS,* 114.
38. Quoted in P, 1:350.
39. See Lichtheim, *Europa,* 311 (*Europe in the Twentieth Century,* 176); Hughes, *Obstructed Path,* 9.

To make his point he chose his examples with the greatest caution: not anger or jealousy, but weariness: "The impulses of feelings [humeur] are not thoughts, weariness is not a thought. There are actualities in the world that I can resist, that I can fight, or that I can give in to, as I surely must always do in regard to things."[40]

Like her teacher, Weil denied the unconscious as being a psychological phenomenon and spoke of everything that was not *conscience* as an aspect of the body, using the French word that means both consciousness and moral conscience. The intellectual and ethical virtues are thus closely connected.[41] The point of departure for man is not ignorance but error, Weil states in her dissertation.[42] For Alain, only those things rooted "in the clearest, the most definite, the best controlled part of our thought" belong in the sphere of human thought. Everything else is "noises of nature [bruits de la nature]."[43] Everything that is not pure thought and resolute will belongs to psychology, is physicality or its direct emanation—that is, in the sense of this doctrinal scheme, extension. Even altruism must, according to Weil, be reprimanded whenever it appears not as a rational obligation but as an emotion. "Any ability [facultés] which is not directed towards conscious thought (even philanthropy) must be condemned."[44]

By disputing that the dignity of a *pensée* pertains to emotionally tinged notions and intending to deal with them as "things," Alain seeks to subject them to will: "I force them [the passions] into the field of action of my will; I treat man as a thing; in doing so, I by no means despise him; on the contrary: I refuse to view something as pertaining to him that is foreign to him and imposed on him from the outside."[45]

Liberty is self-control, and this relation is explained as a double exercise of power. Weil told her students, "Duty towards oneself is to be free, that means (a) to rescue the mind from being overcome by the body; (b) to put the body under the control of mind."[46]

Alain takes from the Stoa the idea of a hegemonic *ratio* that does not—as it does, for example, in Plato—inform the soul in the mode

---

40. Bridoux, *Alain,* 73.
41. *Leçons,* 82–92 (*Lessons,* 92–98).
42. *Sur la science;* see also *EL,* 139: "Le mensonge, l'erreur—mots synonymes."
43. Bridoux, *Alain,* 74, 72.
44. *Leçons,* 209 (*Lessons,* 196).
45. Bridoux, *Alain,* 72.
46. *Leçons,* 191 (*Lessons,* 181).

of participation, but is radically distinct and *opposes* man's physically and mentally determined passion and *controls* it. "The Stoics, who are among the best teachers, had a clear and expressive word for the soul and the spirit; they called it 'government' *[gouvernement]*; following our pleasant folk custom, I would prefer to call it 'guidance' ('steering wheel') *[gouverne]*. Your steering wheel: your inner life."[47]

The analogy with a radical concept of government vis-à-vis the rulers and the ruled is obvious; but here, because it is acted out within the individual, Alain regards rule as legitimate, even as an ethical obligation. The analogy to the Platonic actualization of reason and the corresponding harmonious dispensation of the soul is in Alain a *kratos,* a power, a state, and not *arché.* The adoption of Stoic psychology is accompanied in Weil by the genuinely Stoic distinction between things that depend on us and those over which we have no influence.[48] As Weil adopts the concept, Descartes's courage is closely related to the Stoics' resoluteness: it matters little for human dignity whether the actions in themselves are easy or painful, or even whether they are crowned by success.[49] "We can easily accept the fact that the results of our actions are dependent on accidents outside our control; what we must at all costs preserve from chance are our actions themselves, and that in such a way as to place them under the control of the mind." For "pain and failure can make a man unhappy, but cannot humiliate him as long as it is he himself who disposes of his own capacity for action."[50]

This self that Alain endeavored to protect from any contamination is, using Kantian terminology, not an empirical but a noumenal self. In her early phase Weil made a distinction between a noumenal *je* and an empirical *moi.*[51] She wrote: "In all circumstances, to be a man, is to know how to separate the 'I' and the 'self' *[le "je" et le "moi"]* . . . do not confuse yourself with your thoughts . . . the actual "I" *["je"]* cannot be found in any passion."[52]

As Alain saw it, though the will is not all-powerful, it is, within given limits, the creator or at least the master builder of the human soul: "The

---

47. Bridoux, *Alain,* 244.
48. See Aimé Puech, foreword to Marcus Aurelius, *Pensées,* ed. and trans. A. I. Trannoy.
49. *OL,* 115 (*OLE,* 85).
50. *OL,* 118, 115 (*OLE,* 88, 85).
51. Vetö, *Métaphysique religieuse,* 25, n. 22.
52. *Leçons,* 205–7 (*Lessons,* 193).

soul never exists in order to discover or describe. Its entire purpose is to make or to make new. Granted, we are not what we will, but we are nothing without having first willed it."[53]

This means, to begin with, merely that the soul is not an object in the same way as the things of the external world, that it cannot be discovered like an unexplored island that already exists before it is discovered: thinking about the soul—better yet, to think the soul—is part of constituting the "object." It also means that the soul cannot be arranged if the endeavor of arranging it is not willed. Here the will is assigned a position that exceeds the predisposition to search for truth and virtue that Aristotle called *prohairesis*. The role of will is perhaps even more prominent in Weil's version:

> Man is a limited being to whom it is not given to be, as in the case of the God of the theologians, the direct author of his own existence; but he would possess the human equivalent of that divine power if the material conditions that enable him to exist were exclusively the work of his mind directing the effort of his muscles. This would be true liberty.[54]

This religion of the will postulates the union of theory and practice. Its realization is imagined in a sphere of a surmised ideal, in which the perfection of the (theoretical) model is a condition of its practicability, and this in turn furnishes the proof of the model's perfection.[55] Earlier, Alain had written: "We see that under this aspect the distance between theory and practice is abolished. Or better: we must abolish it; put differently, only the most perfect model proves to be truly practical. This nourishes the soul of religions."[56]

In Weil we find an epistemological explanation for why it is imperative to aim at a perfection that, though it lies at an unattainable distance, nevertheless functions as the measure of any concrete and therefore imperfect approximation to it: "Perfect liberty is what we must try to represent clearly to ourselves, not in the hope of attaining it, but in the hope of attaining a less imperfect liberty than is our present condition;

53. Bridoux, *Alain,* 71.
54. *OL,* 117 (*OLE,* 87).
55. See *OL,* 113 (*OLE,* 84).
56. Bridoux, *Alain,* 71.

for the better can be conceived only by reference to the perfect. One can only steer towards an ideal."[57]

Anyone who tries to improve the human condition, even reformism as the preference of the "lesser evil," must develop a concept, related to reality, of an optimum situation that represents the ultimate potential of human improvement,

> for as long as the worst and the best have not been defined in terms of a clearly and concretely conceived ideal, and then the precise margin of possibilities determined, we do not know which is the lesser evil, and consequently we are compelled to accept under this name anything effectively imposed by those who dispose of force, since any existing evil whatever is always less than the possible evils which uncalculating action invariably runs the risk of bringing about.[58]

Such a supporting clarification in the critique of the "lesser evil" seems necessary, if only because in the context of the rivalry between communism and socialism, the term was declared a nonword in Communist newspeak. Reformist meliorism, which appears as the sole meaningful course of action after the hollowness of revolutionary agitation is revealed, is secured by an epistemological argument. No calculation is possible without a yardstick, and the attempt to conceive of an optimal condition of social organization resembles the revelation of a paradigm that can serve as an approach to and tool of social criticism. "The ideal is just as unattainable as the dream, but differs from the dream in that it concerns reality; it enables one, as a mathematical limit, to grade situations, whether real or realizable, in an order of value from least to greatest."[59]

A hierarchy of value requires the recognition of limits. It is an abridged form of the Aristotelian idea of a hierarchy of goods, which implies and presupposes a highest good. The ideological abridgment involved in the train of thought consists, for one, in a demand for perfect clarity in a complex overall pattern of social organization and, for another, in the search for concrete realization of human potential in the ideal, which therefore is not properly called idea. The vocabulary

57. *OL*, 111 (*OLE*, 84).
58. *OL*, 89 (*OLE* 61).
59. *OL*, 113 (*OLE*, 84).

that has not entirely passed out of vogue, surviving in such expressions as "concrete utopia," was part of the jargon even then, to such an extent that it could without further ado betray the user to the Gestapo.[60] According to Alain, what was important in the art of governing oneself was "to reserve the good name 'thoughts' [pensées] for that which carries the sign of the soul: thus our methodical knowledge are thoughts; our chosen, approved, cultivated tendencies [affections] are thoughts; our decisions and vows are thoughts."[61]

The worthy name of pensées is proper only for what Kant would call judgment. Man finds his way to himself, arrives at liberty through contact with nature. The pensée is realized in this contact with the world. "Mind" and "world" do not have separate existences. Ideas are inseparable from the world, are only insofar as they are concretely applied. "[M]an is free only before the object. . . . That man is lucky who hits upon the harsh, resisting, uncaring world."[62]

Weil picks up this topos: "All virtue results from the shock produced by the human intelligence being brought up against a matter both unforgiving and free of falsity." Man—or, more precisely, an active core, a will—stands in an antinomic relation to a nature, which is both necessity and structured universe. "[T]here is no self-mastery without discipline, and there is no other source of discipline for man than the effort demanded in overcoming external obstacles."[63]

It is only confrontation with real—that is, necessary—obstacles that provides man with the occasion and the opportunity for self-conquest—that is, liberty.[64] Liberty turns out to be a willing acquiescence to the structure of necessity clearly and honestly perceived: "Living man can on no account cease to be hemmed in on all sides by an absolutely inflexible necessity; but since he is a thinking creature, he can choose between either blindly submitting to the spur with which necessity pricks him on from outside, or else adapting himself to the inner representation of it that he forms in his own mind; and it is in this that the contrast between servitude and liberty lies."[65]

60. On this point, see Koestler, in Crossman, ed., God That Failed, 39.
61. Bridoux, Alain, 73.
62. Ibid., 68–69.
63. OL, 117, 114 (OLE, 87, 84).
64. OL, 114 (OLE, 84).
65. OL, 115 (OLE, 86).

The means by which man frees himself is not through contact with phenomena as they are available to the unmediated view, but through perception of the intelligible structure of the universe. Geometrical naturalism, which Weil adopted from her teacher, is a further element in her Cartesian view. Alain wrote: "Geometry is the key to nature. Without it we cannot perceive the world in which we live and on which we depend."[66]

For both Alain and his student, following Nicolas de Malebranche, nature is the model of an *idée qui règle l'image* (regulating idea that governs perception). For example, a cube cannot be understood *as* a cube purely on the basis of viewing it from one of its possible aspects. Alain adapted the Platonic metaphor of the cave to his own purposes:

> The shadows in the cave are the phenomena on the wall of our senses. The objects themselves are the true shapes, like that of the cube, which no eye has seen. They are ideas . . . these reflections are the intelligible interrelations that give meaning to the appearances, whose appearance, however, fails to yield the secret. This way of the liberated prisoner is the circuitous route of mathematics . . . leading to that certain logic, which is empty of the senses and rich in understanding.[67]

The external world, formalized into a concept, can be perceived by an *esprit* that has become discernment or judgment. The world is conceived, captured, in a process in which both aspects of reality, the subjective and the objective, take form. Through Alain, wrote M.-M. Davy, Weil realized that "the universe of things is a fact (an effect) of thought."[68] The purification process, occurring in the three phases of imagination, understanding, and reason, is described by Alain as follows:

> The human mind at first is formed in such a way that it always ex-presses the changes and transformations of the body and combines for the time being with emotional stirrings *[motion des humeurs]*: imagination. In second place, the human mind also expresses the nature of things to the extent that it is able to rid itself of the bodily passions: understanding. . . . We must nevertheless understand—and this is the third point—that this purification does not occur

66. Bridoux, *Alain,* 21, n. 1.
67. Ibid., 81.
68. Davy, *Introduction,* 36.

of itself . . . but . . . that the entire force of will is at work in perception: judgment.[69]

The roundabout route of mathematics furnished Weil with her model for ethical action as well:

> As for complete liberty, one can find an abstract model of it in a properly solved problem in arithmetic or geometry; for in a problem all the elements of the solution are given, and man can look for assistance only to his own judgment, alone capable of establishing between these elements the relationship which by itself constitutes the solution sought.[70]

For Alain, man finds a way back to himself by comprehending the world in the manner of synthetic a priori judgment. In order for the judgment that the addition of five and seven results in twelve to be viewed as synthetic, the addition must be considered a process in time. As a methodical process in time, the way that leads man to himself as an integral intellectually lucid and moral entity is work. Thus Alain noted: "Through work he reveals himself to himself."[71]

69. Bridoux, *Alain*, 81.
70. *OL*, 116 (*OLE*, 86).
71. Bridoux, *Alain*, 99.

EIGHT

Work

The concept of work is the linchpin of Simone Weil's thought. It allows her to combine the glorification of labor with Kantian causality, and it permits her to establish an epistemology that is also a doctrine of self-mastery, an ethic. Weil polemicizes against Max Planck and Albert Einstein in order to preserve the concept of work contained in classical physics. That concept is necessary to underpin such statements as "Geometry, perhaps like all thought, is the child of courage and work."[1]

The law of work—that is, the necessity of establishing causally structured series of intermediate means and ends—corresponds to the position Kant develops in the *Critique of Judgment,* according to which the practical function of reason in work is equivalent to the practical function of reason pure and simple. Work and world, according to Weil, obey the same law; that is, in work man reproduces the order of the world, or perhaps indeed brings it about for himself.[2] "The only law that obtains in such a world is juxtaposition: Only in the test represented by work I am given—and always together—time and extension: time as the condition, extension as the object of my action."[3]

Work means an adjustment to something that escapes our direct grasp, and as a formalizing detour it is distinct from arbitrary and

1. Closing sentence of "De la perception ou l'aventure de Protée" ("Concerning Perception, or the Adventure of Proteus"), *Libres Propos* (1929), quoted in P, 1:146 (PE, 62).
2. See the closing paragraphs of *L'enracinement* (*The Need for Roots*).
3. "Du temps," quoted in P, 1:146.

"imaginary" actions. "Work, as opposed to reflection, persuasion, and magic, is a series of actions that have no direct relation to either the original emotion or the goal pursued, or the former with the latter."[4]

Work compels the immediate wishes or stirrings of the empirical self to be still, thus developing the impersonal intelligence of the *je*. "Thus for a man who takes shelter in a cave and wishes to stop up the entrance with a large rock, the rule is first of all that the movements that permit him to do this have no relation to the spontaneous movements that, for example, cause him to fear ferocious beasts, and are even their direct opposite."[5]

In that work reveals and fixes space and time as the fundamental conditions of our existence, it is "the only thing that makes us grasp the idea of necessity." Insofar as the realization of self-mastery is a process in time, it is work. "Since time represents this division between what I am and what I want to be, work is the only way from me to myself."[6] Thus work is the thing that forms the bond of identity, combining the empirical and the noumenal self.[7] Work is the concrete form of the courage that brings about liberty—that is, self-mastery and clear-sighted submission to necessity. "Labour corresponds with the heroic moment, the moment when man separates himself from matter and his own body; he considers himself as something apart from himself with which he must do what he wants."[8] Work is the fundamental pattern of rational action worthy of man, since the willed impetus to lay bare man's hegemonic inner core, his guiding reason, must practice on the "real" hurdles of outer necessity.

Only work reins in the passions, preventing madness: "We have only to bear in mind the weakness of human nature to understand that an existence from which the very notion of work had pretty well disappeared would be delivered over to the play of the passions and perhaps to madness."[9]

Whatever is not work or not like work, according to Weil, is the

4. "Protée," 240 (quoted in PE, 61).
5. Ibid.
6. Cabaud, *Die Logik der Liebe,* 56 (*Fellowship in Love,* 56); "Du Temps," quoted in Cabaud, *L'expérience vécue,* 32.
7. See Vetö, *Religious Metaphysics,* 389–90.
8. Student notebook from Le Puy, quoted in Cabaud, *L'expérience vécue,* 57 (*Fellowship in Love,* 56).
9. *OL,* 114 (*OLE,* 84).

result of pure whim. Even those activities that appear to enjoy the greatest degree of freedom—science, sports, art—are valuable only to the degree that they imitate or even exaggerate the strict rigor and accuracy of work.[10] Pétrement reports that in the Weil household, when Simone was growing up, not a single toy was to be found. The terrible earnestness with which play is taught by work can have consequences for the tone of political life, as Weil herself appears to suspect in one passage. She explains the difference between the English political parties, which she accepts, and the French political parties, which she rejects, as the "element of play, of games," that marks the English parties. She notes that such an element can appear only in institutions with aristocratic origins, and that in institutions with plebeian roots, such as the French parties, everything must be serious.[11] A political tradition such as the English one develops over time; it cannot be exported at will. After Weil cites these contingent reasons for the absence in France of the elements of play found in the English manner, she goes on to develop her ideas of France's institutional order along the lines of the seriousness of work as if it were anchored in the unchangeable structure of being.

Weil's philosophy of work is Stoic in the sense that the revolt against necessity is made to appear foolish rather than heroic. Work is not a mode of Promethean rebellion. The free man determines his own fate, not unlike the helmsman of a small boat who keeps to his course through clever and discerning movements of the rudder and the sail, precisely by taking the waves and winds into consideration, and not because he subdues them.[12] The metaphor of the little boat combines in one graphic image the formalizing use of juxtaposition, a use that involves

10. *OL*, 114 (*OLE*, 85). See also *OL*, 137 (*OLE*, 104).
11. *EL*, 126.
12. *OL*, 133 (*OLE*, 101). See also *OL*, 124: "Conrad: union between the true warrior (a boss, clearly . . .) and his ship, such that every order must come about by inspiration, without hesitation or incertitude. This requires a very different quality of attention *(régime de l'attention)* than reflection and subordinate labor *(travail asservi)*. . . . . Questions: (1) Is there ever a similar union between a worker and his machine? (Difficult to know.)
(2) What are the conditions of possibility of such unions:
    (a) In the structure of the machine.
    (b) In the technical education of the worker.
    (c) In the nature of the job at hand.
Such union is clearly the condition of complete happiness. It alone makes work the equivalent of art."

the art applied by directive reason, by man's *gouverne,* here represented by a rudder, a *gouvernail.* This art is both physical and mental work—or, put differently, the model of work that does not alienate. The fisherman's simple way of life and his love of the sea as the emblem of *amor fati* are further evocative associations. The work of the boatman is very much like that of a free man.[13] The similarity ends at the fact that for any boatman routine and improvisation play an essential part. "[T]he only mode of production absolutely free would be that in which methodical thought was in operation throughout the course of the work."[14]

This unattainable extreme of human liberty requires that the work itself be methodical—that is, that the method exist in the worker's mind and is not brought in from outside. In the scientifically managed factory, the work is organized along lines determined by a method, but it is not methodical work.[15] Man's highest intellectual virtue, attentiveness, is not stimulated; on the contrary, it withers.

> [A]ttention, always forced to concentrate itself on the actual mo-
> ment of execution, cannot embrace at the same time the series of
> relationships on which execution as a whole depends. Hence, what
> is carried out is not a conception but an abstract diagram indicating
> a sequence of movements, and as little penetrable by the mind, at
> the moment of execution, as is some formula resulting from mere
> routine or some magic rite.[16]

Clear-sighted work, understood as active human attention, allows no routine, no habituation, nor any authority or compulsion. The consequences of such a stringent theory of *travail lucide* render learning itself impossible. As Vetö correctly notes, "one might point out that this whole theory, the identification of freedom and rationality with this human variant of continuous creation in a way implies the condemnation of the fact of learning, of experience and its accumulation, and might ultimately lead to the destruction of a human being. What a curious example of the suicidal war which the rational wages against the empirical."[17]

13. *OL,* 133 (*OLE,* 101).
14. *OL,* 126 (*OLE,* 95).
15. *OL,* 122 (*OLE,* 91–92).
16. *OL,* 122–23 (*OLE,* 92).
17. Vetö, *Religious Metaphysics,* 395.

The clear-sightedness of methodical work means foresight in time and grasping of space, and therefore that balance between the *esprit* and its object that defines liberty. In reality, as far as Weil is concerned, we can strive only for an approximation to such an ideal.[18] "True liberty is not defined by a relationship between desire and its satisfaction, but by a relationship between thought and action; the absolutely free man would be he whose every action proceeded from a preliminary judgment concerning the end which he set himself and the sequence of means suitable for attaining this end."[19]

The paradigm of the optimal free society that serves Weil as the measure of the concrete approximations and as an instrument of social criticism provides for a form of material life in which every effort is accompanied and guided by clear thinking, while the effort itself is a concrete confrontation with objective reality.[20]

Work as a confrontation with corresponding obstacles establishes the unity of human reason by giving rise to it.[21] In the opposite extreme of slavery, reason is blocked and stunted because of the dominance of man's passionate nature, grounded in his physicality as an individual and resulting from social denaturation. "A man would be completely a slave if all his movements proceeded from a source other than his mind, namely, either the irrational reactions of the body, or else the mind of other people."[22]

Thus, over and above its other products, work establishes human community by revealing the link of the single reason common to all men. A group of construction workers is held up by a difficulty. Each of them reflects on ways to overcome it, and they continue by unanimously applying the appropriate method, independent of the formal rank of the man who proposed it. In contrast to the sad sight of a team of assembly-line workers, acting under the orders of a foreman, such a moment offers the image of a free community.[23] Thus liberty, equality, and fraternity are realized in free work, performed communally. "Such a society alone would be a society of men free, equal and brothers."[24]

18. *OL,* 127, 122–23 (*OLE,* 95, 92).
19. *OL,* 115 (*OLE,* 85).
20. See *OL,* 130–31, 139 (*OLE,* 98, 105–6).
21. See *OL,* 139 (*OLE,* 106).
22. *OL,* 116 (*OLE,* 86).
23. See *OL,* 133 (*OLE,* 101).
24. *OL,* 132 (*OLE,* 99–100). See also *OL,* 139 (*OLE,* 106): "that manly and brotherly feeling which forms the bond between workmates."

For this reason work must be set at the core of life: "[T]he most fully human civilization would be that which has manual labour as its pivot, that in which manual labour constituted the supreme value."[25]

Along with technological and organizational conditions of possibility, this model, inspired by Rousseau and Proudhon, postulates social conditions organized on the model of work relations as they occur in small workers' communities *(collectives travailleuses),* whose structure can be clearly comprehended by everyone.[26] The humanistic aspects of such a social order take precedence over questions of productivity. But Weil believed that a simultaneous increase in both productivity and clarity is entirely possible, perhaps even causally connected. Nevertheless, such a causality would be sui generis, since, as she quotes: "[S]eek ye first the kingdom of God . . . and all these things shall be added unto you."[27]

Weil spoke of the slavery she described as an extreme case, which serves to measure actual conditions just as much as does the model of optimal liberty. In reality, however, the object of her critique was the contemporary situation, which was not, in her opinion, very far removed from this extreme: "It is impossible to imagine anything more contrary to this ideal than the form which modern civilization has assumed in our day, at the end of a development lasting several centuries. Never has the individual been so completely delivered up to a blind collectivity, and never have men been less capable, not only of subordinating their actions to their thoughts, but even of thinking."[28]

Abolishing social oppression, or at least weakening it to bring it closer to a conceivable optimal situation, is, for Weil, an urgent task. Such a direction she prefers to call the "revolutionary ideal." But this effort must not be based on self-deception; instead, it must be entered on in the full awareness of man's actual living conditions and taking into account the limits that make up the minimal amount of rules necessary for every society.[29] What prospects for success can we hope for, given the present situation? Practically none at all. Real reform would require methodical collaboration between the weak and the strong, with a view toward the progressive decentralization of social

25. *OL,* 137 (*OLE,* 104).
26. *OL,* 139 (*OLE,* 106). See also *OL,* 130–31 (*OLE,* 99).
27. *OL,* 129 (*OLE,* 105, quoting Matthew 6).
28. *OL,* 142 (*OLE,* 108).
29. *OL,* 79 (*OLE,* 55).

life.[30] The aim of probing such prospects motivated Weil in 1936 to join the discussions of the *Nouveaux Cahiers* group, a loose round of debates initiated by reform-minded industrialists; they invited a number of *jeunes patrons,* people from various professional and political circles, to regular meetings.[31] The driving force behind the *Nouveaux Cahiers* was Auguste Deteuf, an industrialist whom Weil met through Boris Souvarine; she soon developed genuine feelings of friendship for Deteuf. As Pétrement made clear, contradicting earlier biographers, this friendship had no influence whatever on Weil's thinking.[32]

Deteuf's supposed influence naturally earned the harshest censure of many critics.[33] It is true that the hopelessness of revolutionary agitation moved her to explore ways of cooperative reform.[34] Nevertheless, she remained deeply skeptical of all possibilities of reform, since in her view they were fundamentally at variance with the nature of things.[35] Of Deteuf, who made it possible for her to experiment with work in his factory, she said that his goodness would not extend to his workers. For "The employer *[le patron]* has the power to think only of himself but no power to be good."[36] What remains is action on the part of the oppressed: wherever the oppressed have united, Weil wrote, so as to be able to exert some real influence, the associations—parties or trade unions—and their organizations have replicated the vices of the regime they attack. Among these she listed bureaucratic oligarchization; the valuing of means as such ("the reversal of the relationship between means and ends"); and the separation of planning, theory, and intellectual work on the one hand and execution, practice, and physical labor on the other—a separation that goes hand in hand with stultification and mendacity. It is the basic conflict, which Weil had already experienced so painfully in the face of the German crisis: "Powerful means are oppressive, non-powerful means remain ineffective."[37]

30. *OL,* 156–57 (*OLE,* 120).
31. P, 2:169–70, 180–81 (PE, 318–19, 323).
32. P, 2:180 (PE, 323), as opposed to the view expressed by Cabaud.
33. See, for example, Dujardin, *Idéologie et politique,* 147–48.
34. Her collaboration with M. Bernard, the director of a small factory, in putting out a "house organ" belongs in this category. See *CO,* 169–218.
35. *OL,* 157 (*OLE,* 120).
36. P, 2:18–19 (PE, 224); *Leçons,* 151 (*Lessons,* 148).
37. *OL,* 156 (*OLE,* 120). Her pessimistic assessment of long-range prospects did not keep Weil from brimming with enthusiasm for the strikes of 1936; she saw them as a spontaneous confirmation of the dignity of the workers. See *CO,* 169–70.

A theory that combines the development of reason with technical and social events raises the problem of false consciousness. How can someone who himself is not free, or not yet free—and who therefore cannot see clearly—conceive of and meaningfully aspire to the model of a free society? As the classical passage notes regarding this problem: "Who would call upon you if he knew you not? For in his ignorance he may be calling upon the wrong rather than the right thing. Or is it one who invokes you in order to know you?"[38] In defiance of Weil's fundamental egalitarianism, what emerges is the concept of an elite that can serve as the avant-garde of social change because in large measure it anticipates the state of consciousness that only ideal social conditions allow and promote. Weil, however, does not take the term to mean any self-appointed group of professional revolutionaries: "The only hope of socialism resides in those who have already brought about in themselves, as far as is possible in the society of today, that union between manual and intellectual labour which characterizes the society we are aiming at."[39]

At the outset the picture of such an elite is indebted solely to Weil's *ouvriérisme*. "The working class still contains, scattered here and there, to a large extent outside organized labor, an elite of workers, inspired by that force of mind and spirit that is found only among the proletariat, ready, if need be, to devote themselves wholeheartedly, with the resolution and conscientiousness that a good workman puts into his work, to the building of a rational society."[40] In the course of her emancipation from the "classics" of socialism, and recalling Alain, Weil would grant increasing importance to the diametrical opposite of necessity.

Weil needed an Archimedean point of leverage, not connected to the rigid framework of material and social conditions. She found such a point in will, in the goodwill of honest individuals. According to her, "The enlightened goodwill of men acting in an individual capacity is the only possible principle of social progress."[41] Beyond the bounds suggested by Alain's philosophy, spurred by her experience in the factory, Weil exalted goodwill as working at a level above the self-

38. See Augustine, *Confessions*, I.i.
39. *OL*, 37 (*OLE*, 23).
40. Ibid.
41. *OL*, 84 (*OLE*, 60).

confirmation of the subject and thus found grounds to justify it. By regarding herself as a *pièce loupée de la créature* (a botched piece of creation), she would come closer and closer to the solution of that other *aliqua portio creaturae* (negligible part of [God's] creation). This progression would also bring about a transformation from *volonté* to *attente:* "How shall they call upon him in whom they have not believed? And how shall they believe without a preacher? And those who seek the Lord shall praise him. For who seeks shall find and who finds shall praise Him."[42]

Only locating the Archimedean point of leverage in the other world could reconcile the fundamental contradiction in Weil's concept of clarity: "The keystone supports a whole building from above. Archimedes said: 'Give me a point of leverage and I will lift the world.' The silent presence of the supernatural here below is that point of leverage."[43]

Before this breakthrough the polarity of human existence, the *aporia,* the starting point for the search for the criteria of an existence worthy of humanity, appears in the form of a conflict between the universally ascertainable enslavement of man and man's inner certainty, felt to be equally undeniable, of having been "born for liberty." The Rousseauian tone is not accidental: "It would seem that man is born a slave, and that servitude is his natural condition. And yet nothing on earth can stop man from feeling himself born for liberty. Never, whatever may happen, can he accept servitude; for he is a thinking creature."[44]

Thought alone is free of the determination of necessity. But, as we saw, thought develops in contact with necessity, when the blinders of the imagination, erected by passionate nature and repression, are removed. Nevertheless, *pensée* appears capable of comprehending the mechanisms of repression even before it is "freed," as if it could develop even under compulsion—a compulsion Weil was surely intent on proving to be a kind of secondary necessity, though in the same breath denouncing it as compulsion.[45] Even if the venture of liberation is unlikely to succeed, Weil's form of courage meant that an examination of the conditions for its realization or prevention was required and therefore *possible.*[46]

42. Augustine, *Confessions,* I.i, quoting Rom. 10:14 and Ps. 21:27.
43. *OL,* 230 (*OLE,* 175).
44. *OL,* 113 (*OLE,* 83).
45. Compare *Ep,* 358–59 (*NR,* 291).
46. See *OL,* 80 (*OLE,* 56).

She well was aware of this contradiction; but, true to the philosophical method of courage, she refused to resolve it prematurely merely for the sake of systematic coherence. And so she wrote clearly about the theoretical presuppositions for revolutionizing or reforming society: "Broadly speaking, blind men such as we are in these days have only the choice between surrender and adventure."[47]

Her stance shortly before she went to work in the factory can properly be described as clear-sighted pessimism, *le pessimisme lucide.*

> The powerful forces that we have to fight are preparing to crush us; and it is true that they can prevent us from existing fully, that is to say from stamping the world with the seal of our will. But there is one sphere in which they are powerless. They cannot stop us from working towards a clear comprehension of the object of our efforts, so that, if we cannot accomplish that which we will, we may at least have willed it, and not just have blindly wished for it. . . . Nothing in the world can prevent us from thinking clearly . . .
>
> [T]he greatest calamity that could befall us would be to perish incapable both of winning and of understanding.[48]

And she rated the chances of success very low. Given the "present situation," what choice was left to those who persisted in respecting human dignity in themselves and others? "Nothing, except endeavor to introduce a little play into the cogs of the machine that is grinding us down; seize every opportunity of awakening a little thought wherever they are able; encourage whatever is capable, in the sphere of politics, economics or technique, of leaving the individual here and there a certain freedom of movement amid the trammels cast around him by the social organization."[49]

The reasons for her decision to do factory work included her desire to explore the possibility of creating such free spaces in place, *au contact de l'objet.*

47. *OL,* 85–86 (*OLE,* 61).
48. *OL,* 37 (*OLE,* 23–24).
49. *OL,* 158 (*OLE,* 121).

NINE

Dialectic and Antinomy

The idea of work as contact with nature and as an intersubjective link—
that is, as the activity that turns an individual into a subject—furnished
Simone Weil with the theoretical basis for her concern with Marx.

Weil's reading of Marx starts from the statement that Marx had a
correct idea of the polarities of human existence. She expressed the
belief that he experienced this tension as a split of the self and that it
"made him suffer really, one might say in his flesh." But, she argued,
Marx attempted to resolve the tension on a level that was too low
and therefore was doing so by force.[1] This force, which was not least
directed against his own freedom of thought, lay, according to Weil, at
the heart of the errors and inconsistencies of Marxist doctrine. In her
later phase Weil would doubt whether it is even possible to call Marxism
a doctrine.[2] For her this judgment is related to the question of whether it
is even worthwhile to revise Marxism, given its disappointing analysis of
actual social and political reality. "One cannot revise something which
does not exist, and there has never been such a thing as Marxism, but
only a series of incompatible assertions, some of them well founded,
some not."[3]

The search for truth and rules of behavior in the form of a genuine doctrine is, as we shall see, particularly remarkable in a dis-

1. *OL*, 226, 215 (*OLE*, 172, 164); see also 151.
2. "Y-a-t-il une doctrine Marxiste?" *OL*, 223 ff. ("Is There a Marxist Doctrine?"
OLE, 169 ff.).
3. *OL*, 201 (*OLE*, 153).

ciple of the enemy of all systems, Alain. The conclusions of the Marxist system—among them primarily the prognoses of inevitable revolutions—contradict, according to Weil, the underlying analytic method. This is not surprising, since, she noted, Marx worked out his conclusions before he had a method.[4] The discrepancy between method and the retroactively postulated "result," rationalized after the fact, grows out of Marx's abbreviated exegesis of the existential contradiction, which Weil presumed to be a fundamental experience of Marx as well as of herself. "The entire works of Marx are permeated with a spirit incompatible with the vulgar materialism of Engels and Lenin. He never regards man as being a mere part of nature, but always as being at the same time, owing to the fact that he exercises a free activity, an antagonistic term *vis-à-vis* nature."[5]

Marx's generic approval of *Anti-Dühring* is not proof to the contrary, she noted in a paper published in November 1933.[6] Later, when her "awe" of the great man had diminished, Weil would no longer make quite such an effort to excuse Marx for lending his own authority to Engels's position.[7] "Crude materialism" consists in circumventing the question of the relationship between thinking and world by simply abolishing one of the terms—thinking—by illegitimately subsuming it to matter, "[a]s if the thoughts of a madman were not, by the same token, 'products of nature'!" Such a procedure, in Weil's view, is the methodical equivalent of idealistic reduction, which eliminates the other term. At this point we must remember that Weil considered the terms *nature, object, matter,* and *natural law* to be interchangeable and epitomized by the concept of *gravity.* The abolition of either the object or the subject of knowledge robs the experience of any significance. "If you want, not to construct a theory, but to ascertain the condition in which man is actually placed, you will not ask yourself how it happens that the world is known, but how, in fact, man knows the world."[8]

Weil attempted to read such a problem of contact with reality into the concept of practice enunciated in the *Theses to Feuerbach,* in spite of the "obscurity" of the formulations. She found knowledge, or even

4. *OL*, 195, 201 (*OLE*, 147, 152–53).
5. *OL*, 48–49 (*OLE*, 32).
6. *OL*, 48 (*OLE*, 32).
7. See *OL*, 226 (*OLE*, 171).
8. *OL*, 47–48 (*OLE*, 31–32).

actual thinking, impossible either as abstract speculation or as a simple epiphenomenon of the external world—that is, an external world understood as *everything* that is not part of pure *esprit*. Reality manifests itself in contact with the world, in the act by which the thinking person seizes the world.[9] Contact with reality is conscious work. In her later writing Weil would no longer, as she did originally, read such an understanding into Marx's total work; she would do no more than grant him a youthful impulse in that direction. With this, however, he loses his outstanding role as the pioneer of a genuine doctrine, a philosophy of work, and must be content with a place alongside other "great minds." "We find, in Marx's early writings, lines concerning labour that have a lyrical accent; we also find some in Proudhon and . . . in Goethe, in Verhaeren."[10]

In his youth, Weil wrote, Marx went about elaborating a philosophy of work, in a spirit reminiscent of Proudhon: "A philosophy of labor is not materialist. It arranges all the problems connected with man around an act which, constituting a direct and genuine grip on matter, contains man's relation to the opposing term. The opposing term is matter. Man is not reduced to it; he is placed in opposition to it."[11] To be true, a philosophy of work would, according to the statements above, itself have to be work. According to Weil, Marx did not succeed in performing this work.

In Weil's view, the revolutionary ideal, which Marx had entertained in his youth, grew out of his "noble sentiments" and a thirst for justice that cannot be separated from the core of the active subject. It represents one pole of dualistic humanity. Materialism, in turn, is the instrument of Marx's exegesis of the opposing pole.

> Unfortunately, loth, as all strong characters are, to allow two separate men to go on living in him—the revolutionary and the scientist; averse also to that sort of hypocrisy which adherence to an ideal unaccompanied by action implies; insufficiently scrupulous, moreover, in regard to his own thought, he insisted on making his method into an instrument for predicting a future in conformity

9. *OL,* 48 (*OLE,* 32).
10. *OL,* 202 (*OLE,* 154).
11. *OL,* 223 (*OLE,* 169).

with his desires. To achieve this, he was obliged to give a twist both
to the method and to the ideal, to deform the one and the other.[12]

Marx's "strong character" is analogous to Weil's courage. It commands the unity of action and thought, of sober observation and
orientation toward the ideal. But it does not deserve the name of
courage, presumably because it is not accompanied by the most rigorous
intellectual probity. In that case courage would consist of enduring
with a clear mind the existential contradiction and, where no link
between ideal and material reality is evident, keeping alive the contrast
of the contradictory results of discursive reason instead of attempting
to reconcile them artificially.[13] Marx and most of his followers had not
intended to lie, wrote Weil. Intellectual dishonesty that deforms both
ideal and method to the same degree is primarily self-deception. Self-
deception is rooted in the emotional strength of Marx's thirst for justice:
"Marx was incapable of any real effort of scientific thought, because that
did not interest him. All this materialist was interested in was justice.
He was obsessed by it."[14]

In order to be able to live with his obsessive idea, Marx required the
expectation that the kingdom of integral justice was just around the
corner, and as for so many, for him, too, desire was the best of proofs.[15]
Thus the striving for justice exists not in the tension between thought
and action—that is, in the area where liberty is realized, in Weil's view—
but in the dream realm of the link between wish and fulfillment.[16] In
one passage—though a later one—Marx is granted another reason for
self-deception beside that of the thirst for justice. "[H]e began to take
himself seriously. He was seized with a kind of messianic illusion which
made him believe that he had been chosen to play a decisive role for
the salvation of mankind."[17]

The ego takes itself seriously, expands, believes in its mission to save
humanity, broadens the realm of the imaginary, and thus leads to the
concealment of reality, errors, and distortions. According to Weil, this

12. *OL*, 195 (*OLE*, 148).
13. *OL*, 228 (*OLE*, 173).
14. *OL*, 248 (*OLE*, 190).
15. *OL*, 226 (*OLE*, 172).
16. See *OL*, 115 (*OLE*, 85).
17. *OL*, 224 (*OLE*, 169–70).

was why Marx was not sincerely able to complete his exegesis of the pole opposed to the human core. Instead he fell prey to wishful thinking, to speculative corroboration of a psychological certainty experienced as a need. His method turned into inexorable materialistic determinism, in which there is no room for liberty. But since at the same time Marx clearly felt the human wish for justice to be undeniable, he had to proclaim this same social matter that prevents men not only from obtaining justice and liberty but even from conceiving of them as being the provider of this liberty.[18] For, according to Weil, that is the inevitable absurdity of any materialism: "If the materialist could set aside all concern for the good, he would be perfectly consistent. But he cannot. The very being of man is nothing else but a perpetual straining after an unknown good. And the materialist is a man. That is why he cannot prevent himself from ultimately regarding matter as a machine for manufacturing the good."[19]

To what extent Weil is correct in holding Marx in part responsible for the doctrine's hardening into determinism, as it is found in Engels, Karl Kautzky, and Georgi Plekhanov, may well be debatable. Even if she does Marx an injustice, by interpreting his failure to disassociate himself from Engels's coarsening versions as evidence that he approved of them, her attitude is easily understood as a reaction to French Marxism in her day. Whether understood as an original adaptation of Marx's work or as a welcome affirmation of homegrown themes, Marxism in France functioned as the socialist variant of the dominant evolutionism. The psychological mechanism Weil was intent on revealing in Marx himself corresponds to the actual growth of revolutionary consciousness in France. The power of resistance of the established order after 1789 and the severe setbacks of 1848–1849 of necessity aroused doubts about the independent "power of ideas" and put a damper on revolutionary enthusiasm itself. Thus after 1850 there was a clear emergence of the tendency, precisely paralleling the psychological pattern described by Weil, to view the realization of revolutionary hopes as rooted in the historical process itself. With this, an approach to the socially dominant progressivist ideology took place, even if the postulated ultimate aim

18. *OL*, 226, 248 (*OLE*, 171, 190).
19. *OL*, 227–28 (*OLE*, 173).

of a humanity ever moving onward and upward was different from Comte's positivist age or the *civilisation* of Emile Durkheim.[20]

The Russian Revolution, which in defiance of all prognostications occurred in an underdeveloped country, bared the theoretical weaknesses of the determinist schema and at the same time, as the work of a determined minority, gave new impetus to the voluntaristic elements deeply rooted in France. Weil's basic antievolutionism felt supported by this trend in the revolutionary environment. The social variation of progressivism proved, however, to be more tenacious than its bourgeois-positivist matrix; unlike the latter, which was discredited by the international economic crisis, progressivism enjoyed the prestige of massive advances in technology in the Soviet Union. And thus, wrote Weil, all her misgivings about the opportunism of Soviet politics, the human cost of the forced industrialization, and the Stalinist terror, which could no longer be overlooked even in the West, were always met by the "orthodox" side only with the "poetry of the five-year plan."[21]

Like so many aspects of her thinking, Weil's view of history also derives from Alain. Alain was an outspoken opponent of the belief in progress, whether bourgeois-positivist or socialist in its coloration: "What characterizes today's socialists is that they have a historical frame of mind *[qu'ils sont historiens]:* 'One society followed by another society, one machine followed by another machine, one justice followed by another justice.' The *radicaux,* by contrast, believe in a timeless justice, which wherever we may find ourselves, we must plant and tend."[22]

It is not true that good painters must follow upon mediocre ones or that Beethoven must be surpassed by subsequent composers. Linear progress can be shown to operate only in technology, not even in science, since every single scientist has to replicate all of science in his own work.[23]

The opposition of *esprit* and *force* remains constant for all time; only the concretely realized relationship is different in each instance. This variant determines whether large or small barricades are required: "Politics has barely changed and will barely change. This is because

20. See Lichtheim, *Marxism,* 152 ff.
21. *EHP,* 200.
22. *Politique,* 19.
23. Ibid., 20.

man's structure remains unchanged." "[T]he thinking individual against sleeping society."[24]

Even the embodiments of the antithetical principals *le peuple* and *les importants* are permanent types throughout their multifarious historical incarnations. Movement in nature is the basis of the laws of mechanics, which themselves are unchangeable. Movements in society proceed in an analogous manner:

> Sociology is not history. The science of societies is concerned less with what once was than with what *is* at all times. The dependency of the average life on needs and necessity would—in light of conditions that always remain binding on people—have to make the thread of politics visible. . . . From this we would, in the manner of Comte, gain the sketch of a social statics. All weak minds begin with dynamics. It is to collapse into history.[25]

Statics determines dynamics. Progressivism appears as mystification or as compensatory fantasy for minds that are not themselves strong enough to bear the reality of statics. "There is deceit in the idea of progress."[26]

Alain has no doubt whatever that technical changes of the means of production are more capable of bringing about change in human conduct than all the sermons in the world. After all, in his view, *esprit* articulates itself in contact with the external conditions of existence. However, duality must be maintained. "To wish that technical progress itself condition all changes in the moral sphere would be to ruin the Marxist idea."[27]

The inevitable objection that, like Alain, Weil is unable to distinguish between the development of the forces of production and those—in the broadest sense—of the technical preconditions of production, between "means of production" and "technology," has been raised by Marxist critics.[28] In fact, neither teacher nor pupil is working with a portmanteau category that, handled with dialectical dexterity, can

24. Ibid., 233, 21.
25. Ibid., 267.
26. Ibid., 37; see also 309: "I do not believe that the state of science and invention helps much to overcome injustice."
27. Ibid., 236.
28. See Dujardin, *Idéologie et politique*, 116; Trotsky, *La vérité*, no. 175, October 13, 1933.

always be applied to salvage the system. But both Alain and Weil oppose more than a crude historical determinism rightly or wrongly attributed to Marx; rather, they seek to replace a dialectical process modeled on the sequence of thesis–antithesis–synthesis with the permanence of an antinomy: the Proudhonist balance.[29]

Weil's critique of Marx begins with observing that he shifts the object of the process of liberation (which process is work) from the individual to the species. Independence of the will is another victim of such a displacement. According to Weil, the reason for the ideological deviation of the drive for justice and knowledge that she ascribes to Marx is that he can thus entrust the liberation to a historical development, an evolution of the forces of production. With this Marx postulates a material convergence of the good and of necessity, occurring in time, in the form of necessity's producing the good. This is, of course, already the pattern in Hegel; whether the mechanism of historical advance is left "standing on its head" or turned around to march on its materialistic feet as Marx believed he had done with regard to his idealist teachers, philosophy of history runs its course. That is why Hegel wrote in *Phenomenology of Mind:* "Knowledge as it exists originally, or the immediate mind, is mindless, senseless consciousness. To become actual knowledge, or to engender the element of science that is its pure concept, it must work through along a long road." And further, with deliberate stress on the concept of work: "The movement of producing the form of knowledge is work, which it [the mind] performs as actual history."[30]

29. See P. J. Proudhon, *Théorie de la propriété,* chap. 1: "The contrasting [*antinomiques*] terms do not cancel each other any more than electric poles annul each other. . . . The problem is to find not fusion, which would be death, but balance—an ever unstable balance, variable according to the development of societies itself."

30. Hegel, *Phänomenologie des Geistes,* 203, final chapter. See also P. Krause, "Die Lehre von der Arbeit im deutschen Idealismus, in ihrer Bedeutung für das Recht" (Ph.D. diss., Saarbrücken, 1965).

TEN

Social Physics

According to Simone Weil's interpretation, Marx's materialist method is based on expressing the one pole of existential duality opposed to the active subject. Weil sees Marx's greatest achievement in the fact that he pointed not only to the necessity but also to the possibility of a social science by calling attention to the existence of a "social matter."[1] Weil is further interested in introducing the concept of a psychological matter, and she believes that beginnings toward such an end are contained in the discipline of psychology.[2] But, in Weil's view, we must thank Marx for the "stroke of genius" of holding out the promise of a social physics: "Marx was the first and, unless I am mistaken, the only one—for his researches were not followed up—to have the twin idea of taking society as the fundamental human fact and of studying therein, as the physicist does in matter, the relationships of force."[3]

In more cautious and later formulations, Weil wrote of the "analogy" of social and physical forces. But, as we have already seen, in Weil—as in Alain—this correspondence tends to merge into a functional equivalence, if not simple identity. The social dynamic is subject to laws, Weil wrote, that cannot be as easily recognized as the laws of physics but that in principle form a law of necessity as intelligible as those that prevail in the physical universe.[4] It is only the natural necessity

---

1. *OL*, 233 (*OLE*, 179); see also *OL*, 215 (*OLE*, 164).
2. *OL*, 233 (*OLE*, 177).
3. *OL*, 225–26 (*OLE*, 171).
4. *OL*, 236 (*OLE*, 178).

and concreteness that allow Weil to see society as a possible object of science, since, as she noted in a later text, necessity is understood through thought alone. "Only necessity is an object of knowledge. Nothing else can be grasped by thought. . . . Necessity is the thing with which human thought has contact."[5] In order to establish the subject–object relation essential to such an understanding of science, Weil needed the category of psychic matter.

In the course of time, and with increasing emancipation from the "great minds," Weil's social analysis gradually shifted its emphasis from economically determined power relations to the mechanics of the formation of collective opinion as the decisive factor of oppression. No longer insisting on Marx as a pioneer, she saw his originality as limited to the analysis of his own time and believed that its beginnings could be discerned in earlier writers.[6]

Besides Marx, Weil would come to consider Thucydides and Machiavelli in particular as laudable because they had been analysts of this realm dominated by natural necessity.[7] The need for a purely realistic assessment of power, as one aspect of the dualistic universe, also explains how a woman obsessed with moral duty could admire a figure such as the Cardinal de Retz. On the other hand, she seems never to have read Hobbes. That a critic should be able to impute a Hobbesian theory of man to her is not because she engaged in direct borrowing; it is rather because there is substantial agreement between the two concerning the nature of reality—that is, that one-half of the whole that Weil understood in dichotomous terms.[8] Weil includes in the term *matter* the existence of social and psychic matter understood in opposition to "spirit." And this is the basis of her concept of materialism, whose cleansing power, whose ability to sweep aside imaginary abstract values, she always welcomes.

> Marx's truly great idea is that in human society as well as in nature nothing takes place otherwise than through material transforma-

5. *CS,* 94 (*FLN,* 143). See Alain, in Bridoux, *Alain,* 102: "Pure necessity, and introduce nothing of your desires, be it of a faraway star or of your close companion. Thus will you know the possible and the impossible, thus will you be able to grasp [reality]."

6. *OL,* 211, 212, 215 (*OLE,* 160, 161, 165).

7. See, for example *OL,* 216, 218, 235–36 (*OLE,* 165, 167, 180).

8. See Pierce, "Sociology, Utopia and Faith," 100.

tions. "Men make their own history, but within certain fixed conditions." To desire is nothing; we have got to know the material conditions which determine our possibilities of action; and in the social sphere these conditions are defined by the way in which man obeys material necessities in supplying his own needs, in other words, by the method of production.[9]

The method introduced by Marx made it possible to look on oppression not as the simple abuse of power but as the organ of a social function. But in Weil's view this method remained virginal and barren because Marx gave in to his emotional need to ascertain his vision of the future by engaging in speculation. As a result, his materialism became ensnared in his speculation on history.[10] On the level of argumentation Weil sees the principal error of Marx's social physics in the implausible prognosis that in the end the weak will have force on their side and will wield power even while remaining weak. But this belief forgets that force remains a relation, a relation of dominance. "Marx's revolutionary materialism consists in positing, on the one hand, that force alone governs social relations to the exclusion of anything else, and, on the other hand, that one day the weak, while remaining the weak, will nevertheless be the stronger. He believed in miracles without believing in the supernatural."[11]

If Marx's method, materialism, was to work, it had to achieve the same kind of progress that Darwin's effort represented in regard to Jean-Baptiste Lamarck's theory.[12] Marx's explanation of social oppression is analogous to Lamarck's biology, according to which function gives rise to emergence or adaptation of a particular organ.[13] According to Weil, Marx and Engels had been right to see a correlation between the organ—that is, repressive domination—and function—that is, the development of productive resources.[14] But along with many other murky elements of Marx's explicatory schema, his claim that social oppression is like a function in the struggle against the forces of nature cannot be called a proper interpretation; at most it is an inadequate

9. *OL,* 67 (*OLE,* 45); see also a later version, *OL,* 197 (*OLE,* 149).
10. See *OL,* 226 (*OLE,* 171).
11. *OL,* 208 (*OLE,* 158–59).
12. *OL,* 82 (*OLE,* 58); see also *OL,* 243 (*OLE,* 185).
13. *OL,* 87.
14. *OL,* 81 (*OLE,* 57).

explanation, similar to Lamarck's elucidations. We may not, wrote Weil, start from a determinism understood so crudely but must begin with the concept of conditions of existence, with Darwin's decisive innovation that turned biology into a science. Although it is surprising that there are animals on earth, it is not really surprising that their organs are adapted to the requirements of their existence. "There is no chance whatever that anyone will ever discover in some remote corner of the world a species whose exclusive diet is bananas, but which is prevented by an unfortunate physical malformation from eating them."[15]

Function must be understood not as the cause but as the result of the organ. The various accidental forms arising from such a relative indeterminacy may prove to be viable or not, and thus limits are set to chance without the need to appeal to a mysterious guiding tendency.[16]

Social *science,* Weil wrote, like biology, deals with structures that have been constructed by no one in particular. "The causes of social evolution must no longer be sought elsewhere than in the daily efforts of men considered as individuals." In the area of social organisms, the sum of individual efforts corresponds to the biological impulse to mutation. In each separate case they depend on temperament, education, all kinds of habits, natural or inculcated needs, and "above all, broadly speaking, human nature, a term which, although difficult to define, is probably not devoid of meaning."[17]

The enormous individual diversity, like biological selection, would allow every conceivable monster if every society were not bound by conditions of existence, and to disregard these leads to the society's destruction or subjugation. The idea of a natural selection of individual efforts that prove viable within the context of living conditions explains the social form without any need to surrender the core of free will in man to an invisible hand that would determine historical changes. For Weil this construction continued to be valid even in later years. Although subsequently she replaced will with a received spiritual spark, she left untouched existential solitude and the individual variety of the search for truth. All that happens is that the "natural" mutating force of the individual proves to be inadequate when confronted with the

15. *OL,* 243 (*OLE,* 186).
16. *OL,* 82–83 (*OLE,* 58).
17. *OL,* 83 (*OLE,* 59).

compulsions of existence. When Darwinian mutation fails to yield a satisfactory explanation, one reaches for fulguration.[18] "Lightning, the vertical shaft of fire that darts from heaven to earth, is the flash of love passing between God and his creation, which is why 'hurler of thunderbolts' is the name above all others applied to Zeus."[19]

To put it in Aristotelian terms, Weil's society comes into being for the sake of sheer survival, but its continuing existence is not legitimated by the fact that it is organized with a view to the good life. The best one can hope for is to mitigate the worst consequences for the individual of the organization set up with a view to survival. Shifting the goal of social reform from "liberation" to "taking root" will bring about a certain change in the later phase of Weil's thought. But as we shall see, this new view is not entirely free of ambiguities. Here, in any case, it is a matter of searching for the conditions of an optimal society that permits the greatest measure of human—more precisely, individual—liberty, though it does not promote it. Weil could hope for nothing more, since in the attempt to develop a social physics as an instrument of reform, society appears as the *object* of the isolated individual. Man's natural sociability is offered up on the altar of *amor fati*.

18. To the best of my knowledge, Konrad Lorenz introduced this term into biology.
19. *E*, 244 (*NR*, 289).

ELEVEN

Critique of Marxism

Weil's critique of Marx has three main facets: one that is technical, one that deals with theories of man, and one that touches on the goal of human self-realization itself. We have already seen that liberty, which has been proclaimed the "ideal," means not emancipation from work, but the possibility of free work, whereby liberty means unimpeded, unvarnished contact with necessity. If emancipation means no more than liberation from slavery, then it is unclear to Weil by what means life beyond compulsion is to be governed. A reduced, instrumental reason can perform such control only in the form of work, actualizing itself in the act of comprehending—that is, actively grasping—the world. The spirit, freed from compulsion, would, in Weil's view, go mad if it did not discipline itself by working through contact with necessity governed by laws.[1] The free labor of socialist man postulated by Marx must appear to her in this sense too free-floating because that realm of liberty comes into being beyond a necessity that must be overcome, rather than in touch with a necessity that is the only real—that is, also the only legitimate—object of human love and knowledge.

Mountain landscapes, the struggles of the boatman who seeks to master the waves, strenuous sports that taxed her awkward and weak constitution—all these were sources of enjoyment to Weil. Hunting, fishing, and dining, on the other hand, seemed to hold no charms for her.

1. *OL*, 114 (*OLE*, 84).

Her basic rejection of an ideal distorted by cheating—the *"coup de pouce"*—naturally governed the other aspects of Weil's critique of Marx. The postulated convergence of the telos of a determinist historical evolution with the object of human hope is, for Weil, an ontological absurdity—a scandal. Beyond this, however, she examines the intrinsic weakness of an argument that cannot rigorously demonstrate the causative factors of a prognosticated future as such. This is where the technical aspect of Weil's critique begins. However brilliant the concrete analyses that present man's progress toward the ultimate area of liberty, driven by the development of the productive forces, they nevertheless fail to throw light on the mechanism of oppression itself. According to Marx and Engels, oppression arises when, with improved productive forces, the division of labor has advanced to the point where a distinct personnel exercises each of the functions of exchange, government, and military command. Once it is established, oppression stimulates the further development of the productive forces. These then affect the forms of oppression; these forms undergo changes according to the requirements of the development of the productive forces; eventually they turn into absolute impediments to further development and must disappear.[2] "An effective change-over of power occurs, followed, after a certain interval marked by more or less violent manifestations, by the corresponding political, legal, and ideological changes. When the manifestations are violent, this is called a revolution."[3] In Weil's opinion, such an outline is based on premises that are logically arbitrary and can be experimentally proved wrong.

It is not obvious why a society, given certain technical conditions of production, must of necessity be structured so as to maximize production. There is no definition of such a "maximum." Yet waste can be observed in every society.[4] To claim that society always tends to improve production is to transfer the liberal economist's view from the individual to society. If we must empirically grant far-reaching validity to this view, we cannot ignore the societies and entire eras in which people "thought only of living as their forefathers had lived before them."[5]

2. *OL*, 81 (*OLE*, 57–58).
3. *OL*, 241 (*OLE*, 184).
4. *OL*, 244 (*OLE*, 186); see also *OL*, 65, 82 (*OLE*, 44, 60).
5. *OL*, 244 (*OLE*, 187).

Although Weil thinks of *homo oeconomicus* as a common human type, historically given, it is not, in her view, a type that is binding on everyone. To project its deficiency onto society by no means legitimates its universalization. But even were we to assume such a tendency intrinsic to society, nothing justifies the assumption of an unlimited potential for the development of productive forces.[6] In other words, why must the social tendency to maximize production always effect improvements as it reflects on the specific conditions of production? The reverse—exhaustion—is just as likely. "It is the story of the hen with the golden eggs. Aesop knew far more about that subject than Marx."[7] To expect unlimited growth in productivity, as everyone, capitalists and revolutionaries alike, does, wrote Weil, means giving in to one of the main vices of our time: extrapolation.[8]

When Weil credited Marx with approving of growth not, in a stance of which he himself boasted, for its own sake but as the embodiment of a promised emancipation, she did not allow the intention to stand for the justification of a blinding obsession with growth. Her judgment was focused *a fortiori* on those believers in growth whose motives are less humanitarian. We must consider that these thoughts developed long before the ecological sensitizing gradually making its way today. It was not so much statistics concerning the earth's copper and oil deposits that determined Weil's ideas in this area but her respect for a fundamental concept of rational thought. It is the concept of limits, which we will find again in another context.[9]

If, in the later text from which the quotation referring to Aesop is taken, Weil restricted herself to the wisdom of the classical fable, she was eager, shortly before starting work in the factory, to figure out the conditions for technical progress—or more precisely, the technical conditions of increased production. These seemed to her to fall into two categories: (1) the development of new sources of energy; and (2) the rationalization of labor. It is far from certain that, as existing energy deposits are exhausted, ever new and adequate energy sources can be tapped. Questions arise especially in regard to sources that

6. *OL*, 65 (*OLE*, 44).
7. *OL*, 244 (*OLE*, 187).
8. *OL*, 69, 208 (*OLE*, 47, 158).
9. See *OL*, 104: "chicken that lays the golden eggs, principle of limit in things, objective resources" (*OLE*, 76).

can be developed with less expenditure and less human labor than the older forms of energy extraction. As far as the basic scarcity of energy sources is concerned, Weil's discussion seems extremely timely. But she combined it with a problem of another order. The discovery and utilization of ever newer sources of energy depends on technical inventions. But applicable scientific findings cannot be viewed as the necessary result of systematic research. They are largely dependent on accidents that turn out to be fruitful.[10] "Now, as soon as chance enters in, the idea of continuous progress is no longer applicable."[11]

Weil may have underestimated the possibilities of organized research and, for humanistic reasons unrelated to the questions of efficiency that are our topic here, may have rejected them. But she indicated an absolute margin, whose validity is not diminished by the fact that it cannot be drawn with empirical precision. Progress that neither steers toward an optimum situation nor can be thought of as unending is not real progress. With this, Weil brought her critique into the area where progressivism claims its highest plausibility, the area of technical progress.

In truth, Weil started from the idea that certain economically indispensable activities—such as mining—must always remain labor-intensive; in view of the enormous increase in capital-intensive methods, the assumption appears most questionable, even if such a development is accompanied at present by the relocation of labor-intensive industry from the advanced industrial nations to the so-called underdeveloped countries.

In contrast to the question of finite energy sources and the limited possibilities for putting them to use, Weil sees a value in "progress" in the rationalization of labor according to the principle of increasing productivity in terms of the efforts by which these sources are combined.[12] The rationalization of labor has a spatial and a temporal dimension. The division of labor—whose economic advantages in speeding up tasks and making work possible that exceeds the strength of the individual or a small group are sufficiently illustrated by the classical example of Adam Smith's pin factory—partakes of both dimensions.

10. *OL,* 69–71 (*OLE,* 47–48).
11. *OL,* 71 (*OLE,* 48).
12. *OL,* 71 (*OLE,* 49).

Spatial concentration, in Weil's opinion, has arrived at its margin of profitability; given rising transportation and general costs, its effect is declining. With a view to the condition of French industry in 1934, this assessment is absurd. It is motivated entirely by the desire to present decentralization—which is considered desirable for humanistic reasons—as advisable for utilitarian reasons as well. Its value, in turn, lies solely in the reference to limits.[13] Quite different, on the other hand, after her experiences of factory work are her concrete proposals for arranging workplaces in the factory so as to save time. These plans give less consideration to increasing production than to sparing the worker.[14]

When Weil spoke of the contemporary coordination of labor as the "most important factor of technical progress," she no longer cared about the critical scrutiny merely of the technical basis for increasing production as the instrument of human liberation. We can see here that an argument nourished by the humanistic substance of her thinking was already contributing to her examination. For machinism, which is narrowly presented as the concrete expression of the organization of labor at the time, was for Weil the sign of human enslavement. Nor could she view machinism heuristically in its strictly instrumental function. She was capable of such a position only in the marginal perspective, in the imagined condition, where "inanimate labour" has replaced living labor in everything, where "all the jobs to be done would be done already." As we have already seen, Weil considered this a chimerical outlook—not only because it is unattainable but also because it would drive mankind mad.[15] "If it were possible to conceive of conditions of existence absolutely devoid of any unforeseen contingency, then the American myth of the robot would have a meaning, and the complete abolition of human labour through a systematic organization of the world would be feasible. It is not so, and these are only fictions."[16]

The reference to the contingent nature of human existence quite properly shows the concept of a totally planned and automated world to be an illusion. But Weil's concentration on labor prevents her from

13. *OL*, 71–72 (*OLE*, 49–50).
14. See Marcelle Monseau, "L'humanisme de Simone Weil dans la condition ouvrière."
15. *OL*, 73 (*OLE*, 50–51); see also *OL*, 114 (*OLE*, 84).
16. *OL*, 75 (*OLE*, 52).

adequately interpreting her intuition, since it is precisely in the area of
the production of external goods and their rational planning that both
calculation and execution can be transferred to machines. *Thinking*—
and here Weil is absolutely right—is something only human beings
can do.[17]

Finally, the anthropological aspect of Weil's critique of Marxism
implies, along with the quite different stress on the independence of the
pensée, that there exists in man an original libidinous drive closely related
to autonomy, a will to power that is more than a mere epiphenomenon
of economic structural conditions. Weil interpreted this drive as also
necessarily bent on expansion, and as such the proper object of a
doctrine of power as psychic and social physics. The outcome of the
Marxist attempt to make the *libido dominandi* dependent solely on the
economy results, in Weil's view, in inadequate interpretations of the
phenomenon of war: "Trotsky wrote that the 1914–18 war was in reality
a revolt of the productive forces against the limitations of the capitalist
system. One may ponder for a long time over such a pronouncement,
wondering what it means, until one is forced to admit that it has no
meaning."[18]

The only kind of war that Marx acknowledged was social war, the
class struggle. He even turned it into the sole principle of development
in history. At the same time the development of production is also
claimed to be the sole principle of historical development, so that we
would have to suppose them attributable to each other. How this can
be is never made clear. "Certainly the oppressed who revolt or the
inferiors who want to become superiors never entertain the thought
of increasing society's productive capacity. The only connection one
can imagine is that men's permanent protest against the social hierarchy
maintains society in the requisite state of fluidity for productive forces
to shape it at will." In this case, however, the class struggle appears as a
negative condition, not an active principle, no more than a mysterious
spirit ensuring that everything moves in the direction of maximized
productivity, what is sometimes called, in the plural, "the productive
forces." "They take this mythology with the utmost seriousness."[19]

17. For the classification of goods, see Aristotle, Nichomachaean Ethics, A, 1094a ff.
18. *OL,* 247 (*OLE,* 189).
19. *OL,* 246–47 (*OLE,* 188–89).

If the development of productive forces is in opposition to social institutions, reasoned Weil, it is by no means necessary that the former will emerge victorious.[20] Conversely it remains equally unclear why oppression—that is, the concrete machinery of repression—as long as it is useful in the sense of promoting productivity cannot be vanquished by a "political" power play.[21] "That is the height of arbitrary reasoning."[22]

20. *OL,* 65, 244 (*OLE,* 44, 187).
21. *OL,* 82 (*OLE,* 58).
22. *OL,* 244–45 (*OLE,* 187).

TWELVE

Attempt at a Functional Repression Theory

In accordance with Alain's theory of the primacy of social statics over so-cial dynamics, Simone Weil accepted the historical materialistic method of Marx insofar as it could be reinterpreted as a mechanistic materialism. Such a method permitted Marx, Weil noted, to establish a new basis for the analysis of oppression. Until that time oppression had been regarded simply as usurpation, which was occasionally opposed by naive armed rebellions. Even when such a revolt was successful, oppression was soon reestablished in a different form. Marx saw instead that the elimination of oppression presupposes removing its causes—that is, the objective or material conditions. "He consequently elaborated a completely new conception of oppression, no longer considered as the usurpation of a privilege, but as the organ of a social function."[1] It is not people or institutions that are the source of oppression but "the very mechanism of social relations." "Actually, Marx gives a first-rate account of the mechanism of capitalist oppression; but so good is it that one finds it hard to visualize how this mechanism could cease to function."[2]

Marx showed, wrote Weil, how wage dependency represents oppres-sion, how the proletariat is deprived of everything except the chance to perform menial labor and a thirst for justice.[3] The stimulus of compe-

1. *OL,* 80–81 (*OLE,* 57).
2. *OL,* 197, 60 (*OLE,* 149, 40); see also *OL,* 185 (*OLE,* 140).
3. *OL,* 211–12 (*OLE,* 161).

tition in capitalism turns the true aim of capitalism into the expansion of the business. The relationship between production and consumption is reversed, and the latter is seen as a necessary evil, to be minimized wherever possible. Man as consumer or producer becomes the simple means, the thing of things; living labor is enslaved to inanimate labor.[4] It would be easy to cover pages and pages with formulas revealing the modalities of the "reversal of the relationship between subject and object."

In the form of a sometimes awkward confrontation with Marxism, Weil set out to sketch a functional theory of oppression. "He [Marx] discovered a formula impossible to surpass when he said that the essence of capitalism lies in the subordination of subject to object, of man to thing. The analysis which he made of it from this point of view is of an incomparable vigour and depth; today still, today especially, it is an infinitely valuable theme for meditation."[5]

In Weil's opinion it is a sign that even the socialists are affected by the repressive nature of the regime that they always place the strongest emphasis on the exploitative aspect of oppression. It is typical of the spirit of the times, she wrote, that the greatest attention is focused on the bookkeeping side, the extortion of surplus value.[6] In this area it is rhetorically easiest to persuade the worker who has the feeling that he is working for the boss *(pour le patron)* that eliminating the competition by collectivizing the means of production is the way to alleviate the evil. But competitive relations characterize not only capitalist enterprises but also any work and production communities, including national collectives, or states. Unless the revolution breaks out everywhere at the same time—an eventuality Marx himself knew to be impossible—states, exactly like industries, will exploit their workers in order to be able to forge weapons to use against their rivals.[7] The political background of these statements is the slogan advanced by Soviet propaganda of the building of socialism in one country.

According to Marx, Weil noted, the present state of technology would permit men sufficient leisure to develop their faculties, if only the capitalist forms of the economy would disappear, and every ad-

4. *OL,* 197, 199 (*OLE,* 149, 151).
5. *OL,* 245 (*OLE,* 164–65).
6. *OL,* 61 (*OLE,* 40); see also variations in *OL,* 219, 268, 181.
7. *OL,* 60–61 (*OLE,* 40); see also *OL,* 200 (*OLE,* 132).

ditional step in technical progress would bring humanity that much closer to paradise. Such an outlook must come to terms with serious impediments. Without going into detail, Weil alludes to the fact that capitalization, in every society, under any kind of government, can result from surplus value alone. The formulations do not allow us to be entirely certain whether, in Weil's opinion, this is true only in societies that are in competition with others or whether it is true as well for a hypothetical optimum condition. In any case, Weil believed that it is illusory to expect simple reapportionment of profit to bring about the preconditions of that leisure, since the reinvested portion of profit would have to be subtracted from the part to be redistributed under any form of government. Propagating such a "solution" is demagoguery. Second, along with the savings from work, which could at least be expected to result from the restructuring of the property system, the additional expenditure in work, which the restructuring and reorientation of the economy would require, would have to be included in all calculations. Further, it would be necessary to make certain that the causes of waste that were abolished along with capitalism were not replaced by others, such as those resulting from excessive concentration.[8] Experience shows, Weil noted, that there is a great deal of waste in every society. To carry out such calculations precisely is certainly not easy, but it seems hardly likely that they would justify revolutionary optimism.[9]

No complicated calculations are required, Weil assures her readers, to determine that the abolition of private property would not in itself relieve the servitude involved in mining or factory work. Incomparably more significant than the expropriation of the products of labor, it seems to Weil, is the power of the industrial system itself.[10] Beside the "method" of Marx, Weil saw his analysis of machinism, which translates work as the act of contact with reality into its opposite, as the "indestructible part" of his work, which has its rightful place in "any healthy doctrine." As early as 1932—that is, two years before "Réflexions sur les causes de la liberté"—Weil wrote:

> Capitalism is defined by the apparent fact that the worker is subjected to the capitalist; in reality, by the fact that the worker

8. *OL*, 64 ff. (*OLE*, 43 ff.).
9. *OL*, 244 (*OLE*, 186).
10. *OL*, 68, 61 (*OLE*, 46–47, 41).

is subjected to a material capital made up of tools and raw materials, which the capitalist simply represents. The capitalist regime
consists in the fact that the relationship between the worker and
the means of work has been reversed; the worker, instead of
dominating them, is dominated by them.[11]

A lively report from the same period, written after Weil had visited a
coal mine, anticipates most of the topics of her critique of machinism,
which she would take up again and again. In spite of its length, the
passage deserves to be quoted in full, if only because of its vivid style:

> At present the drama is no longer played out between the coal
> and the man but between the coal and the compressed air. It is
> the compressed air that, at the accelerated tempo that is its proper
> tempo, drives the point of the pickax into the wall of coal, and
> stops, and then drives again. Forced to intervene in this struggle
> between gigantic forces, man is crushed. Clinging to the pickax or
> drill, his entire body being shaken, like the machine, by the rapid
> vibrations of compressed air, he confines himself to keeping the
> machine applied at each instant to the wall of coal, in the required
> position. Before this he adapted the form and functioning of the
> tool to the form and natural duration of his movements; the pick
> was for him akin to a supplementary limb that was an extension
> of his body and amplified the movement of his arms. At present,
> he forms a single body with the machine and is added to it like a
> supplementary gear, vibrating in time with its incessant shaking.
> This machine is not modeled on human nature but rather on
> the nature of coal and compressed air, and its movements follow
> a rhythm profoundly alien to the rhythm of life's movements,
> violently bending the human body to its service.[12]

Human muscular strength is reduced to almost nothing when the
forces of nature are channeled by machines. Proficiency (habilité) is
shifted from man to machine.[13] The machines, in turn, are monop-
olized by the lords of industry. These do not need to be owners or
shareholders; more crucially, they are managers, a category found in
any form of ownership relations. Natural forces, ability, and knowledge

11. *L'Effort,* March 19, 1932, quoted in P, 1:259 (PE, 122).
12. *L'Effort,* March 19, 1932, quoted in P, 1:258 (PE, 121–22).
13. *OL,* 197, 211, 212 (*OLE,* 149, 161, 162).

are crystallized in the machine and oppose man. "[I]t still remains a question of entrusting to matter what seemed to be the role of human effort."[14]

The principle, once it has been grasped, can be expanded at will. Development leads from the simple prevention of a movement by a resisting object to the—literally—mechanical preservation of relationships between movements, frozen in the matter formed by the process—"relationships which up to then had on each occasion to be established by the mind."[15]

The machine results in a considerable loss: crystallization destroys the tension of the perception, inherent in the simultaneous actualization of thought and reality. The machine is accused of preventing a process of reflective (re)construction of human order because it reifies by absorbing the "roundabout way of the spirit." Similarly, Weil denounces habits and institutions because they transmute the methodical mediation of the working mind into mechanical processes. By so doing they defeat the rational construction of the self as active contact with reality.

According to Weil, privileges, as she believed Marx had demonstrated, do not issue from pure usurpations; rather, they arise from the "objective conditions" of social existence. They occur in every society that is not entirely primitive—that is, in all societies with division of labor. Priests and shamans, soldiers, scientists, coordinators of every description, set themselves apart from the bulk of the population. "[T]hese privileged beings, although they depend, in order to live, on the work of others, hold in their hands the fate of the very people on whom they depend, and equality is destroyed."[16]

But for Weil there is no unspoiled original condition before man's denaturing. Between man's active core and the mathematical structure of necessity, the needs and passions of the empirical self adapt. These elements are reflected in the society. But society is not only a reflection of the human psyche; it also proves for each of its members a further impediment to the contact between the two modes of reality understood as separated in the manner of Descartes. In primitive relationships of production man reacts under the influence of the direct stimulus of his

14. *OL,* 73 (*OLE,* 51).
15. *OL,* 74 (*OLE,* 51).
16. *OL,* 89 (*OLE,* 64).

basic needs. The immediate satisfaction of needs, appearing random, leaves no room for planning, method, and labor. The immediate effect of natural compulsion on basic human physical needs leaves no room for the primary intellectual activity, attentiveness. That is why, on this level of production, necessity appears as magical willfulness and not as an intelligible structure. "At this stage, each man is necessarily free with respect to other men, because he is in direct contact with the conditions of his own existence, and because nothing human interposes itself between them and him; but, on the other hand, and to the same extent, he is narrowly subjected to nature's dominion, and he shows this clearly enough by deifying her."[17]

Weil saw no primal communist idyll in the primitive stage of human organization. Nor, however, did she see that rites serve to do more than to explain away phenomena in the "prescientific" stage of development, that they already are expressions of representative truth, which are also constitutive for primitive societies. An opening to the truth symbolically represented in society occurred for Weil only in her later phase, when not everything that is not work was immediately declared to be mystification. However, this opening would be achieved at a cost: Weil would postulate the existence of a submerged pre-Hellenic Mediterranean institutionalized primal religion, whose restitution resembles the *restitutio ad integrum* of human consciousness.[18]

Work—what else—is said to have been at the center of this primal religion. The saying that history is written by the victors and that the documents and monuments of the vanquished are generally destroyed is meant to legitimate historiographic arbitrariness. As with all such ideological constructs, Weil's primal religion replies to ideological fictions by noting that we have scarce evidence of them. Thus contemporary civilization, compared to the invented primal religion, is not only depraved but practically proves its depravity by destroying the evidence of the primal religion. Such circular reasoning becomes necessary when, as the result of an incomplete experience of transcendence, consciousness cannot do without historically immanent forms of perfection.

The magical alienation of naive primitivity is, according to Weil, dismantled by technical progress to the precise degree that it is replaced

17. *OL,* 87 (*OLE,* 62); see also *OL,* 111 (*OLE,* 81).
18. See *AD,* 229 ff.; see also *Les intuitions pré-chrétiennes.*

by the new alienation through crystallization of the reality-constituting relations in structures of production and domination. What technical progress brings in the way of human dignity with the one hand it snatches away with the other. "In this manner man escapes to a certain degree the arbitrariness of a blind nature only by submitting to the no less blind arbitrariness of the power struggle. Humanity therefore turned out to be a toy in the hands of the forces of nature under the new form lent them by technical progress, in precisely the same degree as in primitive times."[19]

Weil arrived at the conclusion that the higher the level of technical efficiency, the more the drawbacks outweigh the advantages. Contemporary society, she continued, is not far from the limits of "useful progress," if it has not already gone beyond it.[20] We must consider that these ideas were shaped in the midst of an international economic crisis—a crisis whose political and cultural side effects made it appear a crisis of Western civilization.

In manual work, according to Weil, the repetitive mechanical activities are outweighed by the overwhelming impression of diversity. That is why technical inventions, which made industry possible, must be preceded by the division of labor in industry. The *modi* of technologically determined social being and consciousness become paired and remain directed to one another as they evolve. A third phase of development brings about automation, capable of executing a combination of varied operations.[21]

The chasm separating physical and mental work deprives the worker's mind of all value.[22] "Thus the worker's complete subordination to the firm and to those who run it is founded on the factory organization and not on the system of property."[23] Weil further based her argument on Marx, though eclectically, when she continued to view specialization as the identifying trait not of industrial organization alone but of the whole culture. Modern science, even if it does not deal with technology or industrial management, is for Weil

19. See *EL*, 157.
20. *OL*, 76–77 (*OLE*, 53).
21. *OL*, 74 (*OLE*, 51–52).
22. *OL*, 197, 212, 244 (*OLE*, 149, 162, 187). See also the longest quotation from Marx in Weil, *OL*, 62 (*OLE*, 41).
23. *OL*, 62 (*OLE*, 41).

monopolistic by nature and cannot be reconstructed by laymen, who are presented with ready-made dogma. Marx further realized, Weil wrote, that state oppression occurs through organs of government that are permanent, that are distinct from the population, and that recruit by co-optation.[24] This separation is also an expression of what Weil considered a fundamental distinction between controlling and executive functions. "The whole of our civilization is founded on specialization, which implies the enslavement of those who execute through those who co-ordinate."[25]

Weil's attempt to arrive at a functional explanation of social relations ends in a theory of the convergence of industrial societies. The goal toward which the developed industrial nations jointly steer seems calamitous. The state—composed of bureaucracy, police, and army—is, according to Weil, itself a sort of machine, which must be oppressive by its very nature.[26] The fusion of the economic and political governing bureaucracy—already a reality in Russia, heralded by clear signs in other countries—creates a situation where both the bourgeoisie and the proletariat are placed under a new technocratic class. "At one blow, the traditional dichotomy 'bourgeoisie-proletariat' was replaced, in the thinking of critically minded Marxists, by a new and disconcerting one: the antagonism of rulers and ruled in a totally planned and bureaucratized society which was also a hierarchical one."[27]

Because Weil sought the significant area of liberty not beyond the work process but within it, she considered all societies driven by the pragmatic reasoning of management to be equally totalitarian. This definition includes the Soviet Union under Stalin, National Socialist Germany, and the United States during the New Deal! Such minor gradations as are acknowledged are determined merely by the extent

24. *OL,* 62, 197, 211 (*OLE,* 41–42, 150, 161).
25. *OL,* 62–63 (*OLE,* 42).
26. *OL,* 211–12 (*OLE,* 161).
27. Lichtheim, *Marxism,* 183. Lichtheim refers to the work by Bruno Rizzi, *La bureaucratisation du monde* (1934; translated by Adam Westoby as *The Bureaucratization of the World* [New York: Free Press, 1985]), which is claimed to have resolved the internal disintegration of the Trotskyite movement. Its affinity with Weil's thinking during this period is obvious. The formula by which the imminent "bureaucratic era" is seen in these circles was, in Lichtheim's words, " 'Knowledge equals power,' where 'knowledge' stood for 'intellectual knowledge' and power for 'power over operatives' " (*Marxism,* 189).

to which the various planning hierarchies have already been integrated and the degree to which the economy is centralized.

If, wrote Weil, we believe with Marx that a hierarchic, repressive society does not come about by accidental usurpation but is functionally determined, we must be puzzled by any expectation that liberty can flourish in such a society. How should those who are chained to the technological circumstances of the means of production and remain cogs in the social machinery become the "ruling class"? How are the techniques of war, policing, and administration to cease being the monopoly of permanently distinct castes if they continue to remain specialized professions?[28] Surely we must feel skeptical when we see that the specialized-monopolistic structure can already be found in the working-class movement as well?[29] Building on his own premises, Marx could have foreseen the establishment of the totalitarian state. Instead, he was determined to see the harbinger of justice in the inadequate social mechanism.[30]

The views of the anti-Stalinist intellectuals of the left, which Weil expressed here, are summarized by George Lichtheim:

> Totalitarianism was a special variant of bureaucratic omniscience and omnicompetence. In principle every bureaucracy was totalitarian, and a labor bureaucracy most of all, since it rested upon a class condemned to passivity by the production process itself. . . . All the organisations created by the working class—from simple trade unions to the Communist party—had in due course transformed themselves into autonomous mechanisms sustaining a system of exploitation, and they had done so in Western democracies no less than in the USSR.[31]

It is precisely the exemplariness, posited by Marx and adopted by Weil, of the bourgeois revolution to explain social change that compels us to see in the revolution nothing more than the consolidation of rule in a new class, which controls the socioeconomic functions to a very great degree.

28. OL, 199 (OLE, 150–51).
29. OL, 63 (OLE, 42).
30. OL, 212 (OLE, 161–62).
31. Marxism, 189.

An overt revolution can be realized only when the real revolution has already been invisibly accomplished.[32] "When a social class noisily seizes power, it is because it already silently possessed that power, at any rate to a very large extent; otherwise it would not have the strength necessary to seize it. It is an obvious fact, from the moment one regards society as being governed by relationships of force."[33]

"Visible" revolutions can sweep away privileges that no longer fulfill any social function, but they cannot bring about a considerable re-structuring of the functions themselves and of the forces that pertain to them. It is easy to imagine that the parasites, stockholders, men who sit on boards of trustees, and retailers forfeit their positions and that this change will occur with thunder and lightning. This image sheds no light on how those people who are the victims of the mining or factory machinery will be freed from their enslavement. Not they but others would gain the advantages of the revolution.[34] The nature of power as a relationship determines that the underclass cannot at the same time be the ruling class. To speak of a ruling working class is absurd, since the possession of power changes the class nature of those who hold power; eight hours on the assembly line remain eight hours on the assembly line. "Far from capitalist society having developed within itself the ma-terial conditions for a régime of liberty and equality, the establishment of such a régime presupposes a preliminary transformation in the realm of production and that of culture."[35]

Starting from functional premises, Weil's analysis of the ruling struc-ture cannot discover any new function for the proletariat—by which it would, of course, cease being the proletariat—that might promise an emancipatory revolution. Raymond Aron presents the problem in plain language: "The proletariat represents neither new productive forces nor new production relations within the structure of capitalism. That is why comparing the rise of the proletariat with the rise of the bourgeoisie is a sociological error."[36]

By contrast, for Weil a new domination announces itself no longer in the name of capital but in the name of technical "know-how." To

32. OL, 184 (OLE, 138–39).
33. OL, 242 (OLE 184–85).
34. OL, 185 (OLE, 139).
35. OL, 63 (OLE, 42).
36. Les grandes doctrines de sociologie historique, 149.

prognosticate an emancipating revolutionary development on the basis of industrial capitalism was, in Weil's opinion, possible for Marx because he identified, not men, but the productive powers, not only as the stimulus but also as the actual subject of history. "The essential task of revolution consists in the emancipation not of men but of productive forces."[37] Weil's discussion leads to the statement that once human actions have been objectified as productive forces, concretization cannot be undone by their becoming "emancipated" as forces. Overcoming the handicaps of the development of productive forces does not lead to the humanization of society. The coincidence of the two tasks—emancipation of the productive forces and emancipation of humanity—in the current stage of development was, in Weil's opinion, the basic assumption that allowed Marx to reconcile his "idealistic aspirations" and his "materialistic conception of history." A dynamic immanent in matter, which by itself strives for the good, would, however, be too good to be true. "It is seldom . . . that comforting beliefs are at the same time rational."[38]

To postulate the fulfillment of human strivings as a function of progress in production means assigning to matter a quality that, according to Weil, is the essence of mind—an unceasing aspiration toward the good.[39] By subsuming the task of emancipating humanity under the emancipation of the forces of production, Marx not only reduced it to a technical chore in the literal sense but also kept it from appearing as a problem to be solved; instead he presented it as the result of a materially conditioned automatism. To dissolve the tension between man and his (material) living conditions by a technical convergence occurring in time resembles, according to Weil, a religious attitude. "[T]o believe that our will coincides with a mysterious will which is at work in the universe and helps us to conquer is to think religiously, to believe in Providence."[40]

Weil would later speak of a "low form of religion," but even after her "conversion" she would firmly reject any idea of Providence as an intervention of the first cause in the area of the secondary causes, that is,

37. *OL*, 68 (*OLE*, 42).
38. *OL*, 63–64 (*OLE*, 42–43).
39. *OL*, 65 (*OLE*, 44); see also *OL*, 245 (*OLE*, 188).
40. *OL*, 66 (*OLE*, 44).

any history–immanent sense or finality, arguing that it was idolatry.[41] She would equate Providence with the natural laws binding the universe, in keeping with her *amor fati*.

Such a self-delusion, which identifies the fulfillment of human aspiration with the course of things "in the last analysis," requires that people are viewed as mere instruments of this Providence and therefore can be oppressed with a clear conscience. Weil still allows Marx to be motivated by a generous will to liberty and equality but cannot find a word of praise for those who strive to establish a provisional tyranny.[42] Among these is none other than Trotsky, who before her journey to Germany appeared to Weil as the model of courage, a genius at combining deed and reflection.

41. *Ep*, 351 (*NR*, 279).
42. *OL*, 64 (*OLE*, 43).

THIRTEEN

In Touch with Reality

From December 1934 until nearly the end of August 1935 Simone Weil worked in heavy industry in the Paris region. She had sought active contact with the reality of industrial work for a long time—a reality she was inclined to equate with genuine social reality pure and simple. Just as her whole life was an effort to combine knowledge and compassion, the experience of factory work was both research and spiritual exercise. The difficulty of factory work was made even worse for her by her fragility and physical clumsiness. These would have made it impossible for her to share her fellow workers' feelings to any meaningful degree if they had not been compensated for by her gift for astute observation. This, together with her highly developed faculty to generalize from her own person, turned her factory journal into "the only book in the huge literature on the labor question which deals with the problem without prejudice and sentimentality."[1]

The experience of factory work changed Weil profoundly, but this change took place not on the level of her ideas but on a deeper psychic level. It is as if her basic impulse—an erotic orientation toward the good, no longer impeded in its development by an ideated barricade but held back now by a real obstacle—was dammed up behind this barrier, only to overflow it. We are dealing with an intensification similar to

1. Hannah Arendt, *The Human Condition,* 131, n. On the actual observations and suggestions for improvements that legitimize Arendt's evaluation, see Monseau, "L'humanisme."

what happened when Weil's consciousness was affected by social reality only in the immediacy of the German crisis—which, France still being comparatively spared, had held for the moment only purely speculative interest. In Germany, Weil saw a speculative scheme become real as the lived experience of others; in the factory she experienced it in her own person. Viewed from outside, the factory appeared to Weil as "a place where one makes a hard and painful, but nevertheless joyful, contact with real life."[2]

During her first days in the factory she wrote to one of her students that she felt as if she had escaped from a world of abstractions in order to go among "real men": "among real men—some good and some bad, but with a real goodness or badness." But what she actually experienced was a "gloomy place . . . where people only obey orders, and have all their humanity broken down, and become degraded lower than the machines."[3]

In her seventh week she noted in her journal that she was too exhausted to remember the real reasons for spending time in the factory, that she felt the strongest temptation not to think anymore in order not to suffer. Only on Saturday afternoons and Sundays she felt reminded that she was a thinking being. Wretchedness itself made it impossible to think about wretchedness.[4] Within a few weeks, she wrote to Albertine Thévenon, the daily experience of brutal constraint radically destroyed her sense of personal dignity and self-respect. And what surprised her most: brutal constraint provoked in her not rebellious reaction but docility.[5] Even later Weil would remember that during her time in the factory she felt rebellious only on Sundays. "Revolt is impossible, except for momentary flashes (I mean even as a feeling). First of all, against what? You are alone with your work, you could not revolt except against it—but to work in an irritated state of mind would be to work badly, and therefore to starve. . . . We even lose consciousness of the situation; we just submit. Any reawakening of thought is then painful."[6]

2. *CO,* 19 (*SL,* 20).
3. *COp,* 33, 25 (*SL,* 11, 20).
4. *COp,* 68 (*FW,* 171).
5. *COp,* 27 (*SL,* 21–22).
6. *COp,* 68 (*FW,* 171).

The speculative schema that compresses into experience is the problem of false consciousness. More than a year before she went to work in the factory Weil wrote:

> All oppressive societies give birth to a false conception of the relationship between man and nature, from the mere fact that it is only the downtrodden who are in direct contact with nature, that is to say those who are excluded from theoretical culture, deprived of the right of and opportunity for self-expression; and conversely,
> · the false conception so formed tends to prolong the duration of the oppression, in so far as it causes this separation between thought and work to seem legitimate.[7]

Now she learned that, in "contact with the object," her theoretical culture was just as unsuited to turning silent obedience into articulate revolt. She encountered nothing of the joy in contact with the object that, according to her expectation, should have arisen through the hardness of the work, either in herself or in her fellow workers. As she put it later, the experience killed her youth and robbed her forever of a certain lightheartedness.[8] The experience of factory work changed "my whole view of things, even my very feeling about life. I shall know joy again in the future, but there is a certain lightness of heart which, it seems to me, will never again be possible."[9]

Actual contact with work in industry deprived Weil of the certainty that "nothing can stop" us from "being clear-sighted." The will to liberty, justifying itself, cannot hold its own against a structure of error and oppression, appearing to be determined of necessity. In her "Testament" she wrote, "[N]othing in the world can stop man from feeling born to liberty. Never, no matter what happens, can he reconcile himself to servitude: because he thinks."[10] Her experiences of life in the factory, however, led her to conclude that "oppression, beyond a certain degree of intensity, does not engender revolt but, on the contrary, an almost irresistible tendency to the most complete submission."[11]

7. *OL,* 46 (*OLE,* 30).
8. *AD,* 74–75 (*WG,* 100); *CO,* 22 (*SL,* 23).
9. *COp,* 19 (*SL,* 15).
10. *OL,* 38.
11. *CO,* 107 (*SL,* 35).

On the brink of despair, Weil resolved to continue the experience of contact with suffering until she had herself back in hand. This, too, is an imperative of courage. "Slowly and painfully, in and through slavery, I reconquered the sense of my human dignity—a sense which relied, this time, upon nothing outside myself and was accompanied always by the knowledge that I possessed no right to anything, and that any moment free from humiliation and suffering should be accepted as a favour, as merely a lucky chance."[12]

Truth was revealed in the privation of all external props for the ego, in the nakedness of the soul, which in suffering had cast off all illusory, consoling disguises, *sub specie mortis*. "Truth shows itself only naked, and nakedness is death, that is the dissolution from all ties that serve humanity for a reason to live."[13] Wretchedness, *malheur*, is physical pain, affliction of the soul, and social degradation all at the same time: all three, in Weil's experience, are elements in the lives of factory workers.[14]

Contact with reality remains work or worklike, but no longer as an activity that has a liberating effect mingled with intellectual joy; now it is pure submission to necessity. The experience of work with the characteristic of irreducible enslavement is only the most generalized consequence of the limits of the human condition, the barriers of the "natural" abilities of the empirical "hateful self"; only so, impeded in their libidinous expansion, do they permit the expectant opening of the soul: "The *irreducible* nature of suffering, which makes it impossible for us not to have a horror of it at the moment when we are undergoing it, is ultimately designed to arrest the will, just as an absurdity arrests the intelligence, or absence, non-existence, arrests love. So that man, having come to the end of his human faculties, may stretch out his arms, stop, look up, and wait."[15]

This experience led Weil to suspect that action and knowledge can never adequately be posed in the form of a mathematical problem to be solved. She learned that the errors and vices of a rationalistic culture cannot be overcome by proceeding with more thorough rationalism.[16]

12. *COp*, 27 (*SL*, 22).
13. *SG*, 85.
14. *AD*, 81 ff. (*WG*, 117 ff.).
15. *C*, 2:413 (*N*, 2:415).
16. See Michael Oakeshot, *Rationalism in Politics*, 5 ff.

The experience of insurmountable limits to embodying the good in immanence did not, however, slake Weil's thirst for the absolute. What it did do was break the rationalistic frame. Weil made use of the old image of the baby chick breaking through the shell of the world egg. The poles of the existential contradiction of man were no longer slavery and drive to liberty but power (force) and justice.

> The essential contradiction in the human condition is that man is subject to force, and craves for justice. He is subject to necessity, and craves for the good. It is not his body alone that is thus subject, but all his thoughts as well; and yet man's very being consists in straining towards the good. That is why we all believe that there is a unity between necessity and the good.[17]

For Weil this union takes place beyond existence, in that existence, equated with autonomy, is abolished; strictly speaking, then, it occurs not beyond existence but in its stead.

The *"attention"* of the intelligence determined by the will is transformed into an *"attente,"* an expectant openness. But this change does not restore the fullness of reason; instead, through the calculating rationalistic *ratio,* a sensorium of transcendence is established in place of the will. It is a "smallest" part of the soul, but it is not an extension of the other parts of the soul; it stands in opposition to them. The dualistic nature of Weil's thinking leads to a binary structure of the soul, in which the "mediocre" part is the object before the highest part. Thus, following the model of mechanical physics, not only a social but also a soul mechanics is outlined: the rational peak seeks to transform the rest of the psyche into an equivalent of the *res extensa.* Weil uses Plato's heuristic myth, distorted by radicalizing reifications. We find that when the highest part governs, the soul does not attain harmony; instead, we see domination by a principle opposed to the passions, a principle that seeks to radically suppress the passions as best it can. The kinship with Manichaeism is evident. Reason of this nature cannot be the basis of identity as composed, rather than forced, coherence. It is not a matter of passion being the principle of individuation; rather, passion represents the existential mode of the self, the should–not–be that defines the individual's subjectivity. As such, the should–not–

17. *OL,* 209 (*OLE,* 159).

be proves to be creatureliness itself. Work no longer has a liberating effect but redeems as an imitation of death, the ascetics of self-control, redeeming as a constant reminder that human existence is of necessity finite. The details of the "spirituality of work" and the anthropology and theology of wretchedness *(malheur)* have been presented so often that we need not dwell on the doxographic details.

Weil's political thought contains an ambiguity. On the one hand, because of the transhistoricity of criteria, the reconciliation of a political order with the otherworldly perfection must be conceived in categories of participation. On the other hand, all that is political is part of a twilight zone; according to Weil, its complete disappearance—its "de-creation" *(décréation)*—will allow contact between divine love and deified necessity. The intellectual fascination always exerted on her by the inescapable determinism of matter is now strengthened by adoration of the Creator and is revealed as a premonition of this revelation.[18]

There is no way to resolve the discrepancy between the purity of the ascetic postulate and the compassion that must act in the area of *metaxy*. Thus, in a late text, Weil expressed the hope that God will forgive compassion.[19] The problem arises because—if we are to adopt Weil's Platonic schema of explication—the "necessary cause" of Timaeus has been erroneously equated with the causality of phenomena, and Platonic *metaxy* is reduced to human autonomy. The opening to transcendence causes, in Weil, a spiritualization of work but not the discovery of a *humanum* beyond work.

When it turned out that reason, actualized in work as spontaneous practical problem solving, was identical among all subjects, this identity served as an intersubjective link, creating community. Behind the intersubjectivity, work, transformed into acceptance, merely indicates a real ground in which all reason can take root. This ground is kept from being reified by the fact that it is settled beyond existence. Insofar as people share in this ground, they need no longer be understood as subjects but as rational human beings. Weil, however, articulated such a consequence only inadequately, since her dualistic theory of man, which does not provide for a rationally structured soul, admits only a *restitutio ad integrum* resulting from the silence of the passions. When the

18. Vetö, *Métaphysique religieuse,* 21.
19. Quoted in Davy, *Introduction,* 44.

libidinous and social intermediate areas are removed, the "eternal part" of man and his physical basis, mind and matter, confront each other in merciless clarity. "And the Spirit of God moved upon the face of the waters." The integrity of the spirit is restored along the gnostic model: "[T]he god of the Beyond to whom the Gnostic speculator wants to return must be identical, not with the creator-god but with the god of the creative tension 'before there was a cosmos.' "[20]

For Weil, the conscious submission of the autonomous self to necessity, brought about in loving understanding—a docility signifying the disintegration of autonomy—was the equivalent of the Platonic turn from the shadows of the cave to the true light; characteristically, she called it *decréation*. Weil projected this spiritual drama onto the cosmos. The de-creation of man is an imitation of God's creative love: creation becomes renunciation, God relinquishes being everything, there is a *diminutio* of his omnipotence. Weil engaged in frequently highly poetic discourses on how the Creator, by being the Creator, diminishes himself; these could easily have come from the heresiarch Markion himself.[21] Creation—that is, God's loving self-diminishment—is equated with the Fall. This questionable theologoumenon is explicated as follows: "Genesis separates creation and original sin because of the necessities inherent in an account composed in human language. But by being created the creature preferred itself to God. Otherwise, would there have been a creation? God created because he was good, but the creature let itself be created because it was evil. It redeems itself *[elle se rachete]* by persuading God, by the power of prayer, to destroy it."[22]

For Weil, the creation is not the creation of the physical world. It begins only after the heavens and the earth have been created. Weil's God creates not ex nihilo but out of himself. The natural-law universe seems to be the attribute of God qua necessity. Creation and the Fall belong together because creation—that which is not God—means the birth of autonomy. "The order from God was an ordeal proving that Adam had a will of his own. . . . It is clear that there never was a period of time in which he was in a state of innocence."[23]

20. Eric Voegelin, *Order and History,* vol. 4, *The Ecumenic Age,* 20.
21. See, for example, *CS,* 70–71; *AD,* 150; *Les intuitions pré-chrétiennes,* 84; *C,* 2:166.
22. *CS,* 70–71 (*FLN,* 123).
23. *C,* 2:166 (*N,* 1:268).

Autonomy "crucifies" and dismembers God; its abolition leads him back to himself. By "de-creating" himself, man removes the separating screen (écran) that his autonomy places between God and God. Thus man becomes the vehicle for God's union with himself, by rescinding his creation. The creature's sinfulness is equated with its creatureliness. An asceticism that seeks to master sin understood in this way must be a contemptus mundi. "When the formerly unknown god of the Beyond reveals himself as the goal of the eschatological movement in the soul, the existence of the cosmos becomes an ever more disturbing mystery. Why should a cosmos exist at all, if man can do no better than live in it as if he were not of it, in order to make his escape from the prison through death?"[24]

In Weil's thinking, the rejection of a world composed of nothing more than human autonomy on the one hand and ineluctable social dynamics on the other and the attempt to abolish such a world are given a spiritually heightened Lucretian assurance by the lawfulness of nature. Weil continued to find the most common form of this "de-creating" assurance in work as it preeminently represents the imitatio mortis. "Death has been transformed into fatigue."[25]

Work remains the essential link between men, and the camaraderie of free workers continues to be the model of the good society. In spite of "being rooted," subjectivism has been salvaged in the necessarily lonely language of salvation; this does not permit any friendship for the sake of the good, and therefore cannot provide a yardstick for the various bonds that hold a political society together. An ascetic will to purification does allow Weil to turn to a ground of truth in the other world; but its severity does not permit the distinction between historical and ontological givens. For Weil, the political sphere does not constitute itself above necessity but, like autonomy itself, is dedicated to revealing necessity, removing compulsion and error. The rigorous consequences of Weil's thinking make the political sphere responsible for abolishing itself. Such an objective, however, collides with the meliorism of the political action she postulates. In the spectrum of the humanisms that define the intellectual climate of contemporary France, Weil's work proves to be a shift from the labor humanism of

24. Voegelin, Order and History, 4:19.
25. C, 1:178.

her youth to a unique religious humanism marked by clear traces of its origins.[26]

Of course Weil's thinking in religious terms did not spring full-blown from her year of factory work. It reflects a series of events, following the experience of factory work, that led to her "conversion." In a small Portuguese fishing village, where she went with her parents, she witnessed a ceremony or procession involving boats; it awakened her awareness that Christianity was the "religion of slaves." The osmosis of the Franciscan spirit and the atmosphere of the Church of Santa Maria degli Angeli in Assisi seem to have moved her deeply. Finally, she counted her presence at the Gregorian liturgy during Holy Week in 1938 in the Abbey of Solesmes as among her most significant contacts with Christianity.[27] Shortly afterward, while reading the poem "Love" by George Herbert, an English metaphysical poet, she had an experience of ecstasy that she described by saying, "Christ himself came down and took possession of me."[28]

The process of mentally interpreting her religious experiences and their metaphysical implications is captured in her notebooks written between 1938 and her death in 1943. We will not try here to trace either the ecstatic experience itself or the systematic aspects of her metaphysics, since several studies have been dedicated to the specific topic. We will rather cite a poem that reflects Weil's spiritual *démarche* most simply and concisely.

> *La Porte*
> Ouvrez-nous donc la porte et nous verrons les vergers,
> Nous boirons leur eau froide où la lune a mis sa trace.
> La longe route brûle ennemie aux étrangers.
> Nous errons sans savoir et ne trouvons nulle place.
>
> Nous voulons voir des fleurs. Ici la soif est sur nous.
> Attendant et souffrant, nous voici devant la porte.
> S'il le faut nous romprons cette porte avec nos coups.
> Nous pressons et poussons, mais la barrière est forte.

26. See Thomas Molnar, *Kampf und Untergang der Intellektuellen,* 316, 383, 395 (*Decline of the Intellectual,* 250, 303, 313).

27. This abbey has been the center of an important liturgical movement since 1850. See Curtius, *Die französische Kultur,* 81.

28. *AD,* 45 (*WG,* 69).

Il faut languir, attendre et regarder vainement.
Nous regardons la porte; elle est close, inébranlable.
Nous y fixons nos yeux; nous pleurons sous le tourment;
Nous la voyons toujours; le poids du temps nous accable.

La porte est devant nous; que nous sert-il de vouloir?
Il vaut mieux s'en aller abandonnant l'espérance.
Nous n'entrerons jamais. Nous sommes las de la voir.
La porte en s'ouvrant laissa passer tant de silence.

Que ni les vergers ne sont parus ni nulle fleur;
Seul l'espace immense où sont le vide et la lumière
Fut soudain présent de part en part, combla le coeur,
Et lava les yeux presque aveugles sous la poussière.[29]

The Door
Open then the door for us and we shall see the orchards,
We shall drink their cold water marked by the moon.
The long path burns, an enemy to strangers.
We roam about unknowing, and we find no place.

We want to see flowers. Here thirst is upon us.
Waiting and suffering here we are before the door.
If need be we shall break down the door by dint of blows.
We shove and we push but the gate is too strong.

We must pine and wait and gaze in vain.
We gaze at the door; it is closed, unmovable.
We train our eyes, we weep under the torment.
We always see it, the weight of time overwhelms us.

The door is before us; what good is to want?
Better to leave, abandoning hope.
We shall never enter. We are weary of seeing it.
The door, opening, let through so much silence.

And neither the orchards nor any flower appeared;
Only the vast space of emptiness and light
Was present suddenly from end to end and filled the heart,
And washed our eyes that had been almost blinded by the dust.

29. *PSO,* 35–36.

FOURTEEN

The Politics of Spirit against the Powers

Just as Simone Weil's philosophy and anthropology were influenced by Alain, her political thought in the narrow sense of that term also bears the clear marks of her teacher's views. Raymond Aron saw Alain as the man who put his philosophical stamp on the *esprit contre* of the period between the two world wars; Aron mentions this spirit as one of the principal causes of the collapse of France. The title of Aron's book, *L'homme contre les tyrans,* is a critical reference to *Le citoyen contre les pouvoirs,* the title given to a collection of Alain's *propos* as well as the phrase summing up Alain's doctrine for the general public. Aron wrote: "Nothing is more characteristic of the period between the wars than this will to think in terms opposed to the social order. Alain's historical importance may lie in the fact that he developed the philosophy of this *pensée contre.*"[1]

But it is not as if the *pensée contre,* which during the 1930s was unquestionably taken to an extreme, was a new phenomenon. Rather, it is an innate trait, an essential element of the Third Republic. Radicalism was considered the very soul of the Third Republic, both its core and a microcosmic repetition of the underlying republican consensus.[2] This radicalism was, as we have seen, a social consensus directed against two objectives. Even ideologically it manifested itself as a defensive

---

1. Aron, *L'homme,* 111.
2. G. Lagneau, "Radicalism, Radicalisme: Essai d'identification des idéologies radicales," 147; Albertini, *Freiheit,* 57.

position. "The first thought of a republican congress should be the idea of unity *against* the common enemy. This is what has imposed itself on democracy against the conspiracies and attempts at insurrection." Thus read the first two sentences of the first proclamation, edited by Camille Palletan of the Radical Party, founded in 1901.[3] Alain never appeared in public as a party ideologue, and certainly never thought of himself as one, even if he sympathized with the Radical Socialists all his life. Furthermore, he stood out by the way he lived his life, an attitude correctly called stoicism, and by his personal selflessness and independence from a largely compromised group of contemporary political figures.[4]

He is, more accurately, the spokesman for an entire republican order, with Radicalism at its core, not for a particular party. The earliest collection of his *propos* dealing with political matters is entitled *Eléments d'une doctrine radicale*. Even in the period between the wars those who were most expert on French politics considered Alain's doctrine to be the best articulation of an intellectual stance that determined the political style of the regime as a whole; this assessment has retained its validity to the present day.[5]

Alain did not create this mentality; he merely personified it in an exemplary fashion and propagated it. He is the most eloquent representative of a human type that formed the backbone of the Republic: the "grumbling citizen" *(citoyen grognard)* who proudly insists on his rights as a *citoyen*—the equal of every other citizen, regardless of social function—and therefore harbors a deep distrust of anyone inclined to give himself the airs of a "gentleman." Participation in power means betrayal of the *peuple,* crossing over to the other side of the barricades, the side of *pouvoir.* But any hint of prestige, any cosmopolitan

3. The proclamation was dated June 25, 1901; quoted in Kayser, "Radicalisme," 79. On the Radical Party, see Claude Nicolet, *Le radicalisme;* Francis de Tarr, *The French Radical Party;* J. Kayser, *Les grandes batailles du radicalisme;* John Anthony Scott, *Republican Ideas and the Liberal Tradition in France.*

4. On "stoicism" see Albertini, *Freiheit,* 61. On the corruption and loss of prestige of the parliamentarians, see Robert K. Gooch, "The Antiparliamentary Movement in France."

5. See the positions taken by Siegfried, *Tableau;* Thibaudet, *République des professeurs;* Bertrand de Jouvenel, *Über Souveränität;* and Arnold Bergsträsser, *Staat und Wirtschaft in Frankreich.* For the postwar period, see, along with Albertini, *Freiheit,* for example, Maurice Duverger, *Institutions politiques et droit constitutionnel,* 681.

mannerisms, is suspect in this *république des petites gens;* it is a sign of treason against equality, since any kind of privilege is considered *eo ipso* illegitimate. Institutionalized suspicious civic pride *is* the Republic. "A strange regime," André Siegfried called it, "which emerged almost of one piece out of an act of protest, out of an attitude of distrust."[6]

If Aron is correct in declaring that Alain is a corrupter of the young, his assessment can apply just as easily to the Republic itself. In that Weil's political thought appears to be a variation on Alain's doctrine, it is presented for what it is: both a symptom of and a response to the crisis of the liberal system in France.

Guided by a republican–individualistic will to self-preservation, the radical may nevertheless acknowledge "no enemy on the left." Radicalism is "left" in the sense that it stands in constant opposition not only to the church but also to the state, even when the prime minister comes from its ranks, as he generally does. This dissenting stance does not by any means impede the radical person in his fundamental support of the institutions of the Third Republic. *Toujours à gauche mais pas plus loin!* (always on the left but no further). The *esprit contre* is the most common expression of a doctrinaire generalization of the effort to overcome concrete evils—in this case the evils of absolutism. At the same time, and to the degree that these revisions are successfully accomplished, the *esprit contre* is the attempt to consolidate these achievements by trying to protect them from further revolutionization, by seeking to preserve those elements of the generally condemned order that are essential to the purpose. But those who are eager to legitimate themselves by the revolutionary impulse, those who feed on the prestige of 1789, cannot stand still without being overtaken on the left. This situation results in a politics of outbidding each other on the left. This maneuver fades away into a relatively harmless verbalism so long as "replacement majorities" affect moves to the right calculated to "save the Budget."

But once the institutionalization of suspicion is seen by some "progressives" as endangered and by others as obsolete, as was increasingly the case during the 1930s, questions arise about the Republic itself. Its basic principles turn against the *esprit contre,* which becomes a vicious circle. The fact that the Republic, which has been abandoned by the republicans, is not therefore spared by its traditional enemies makes the situation all the more acute.

6. *Tableau,* 220.

Slow industrial development and the firmness of social connections combined to enable the radical balance in France to survive for so long. At the same time this nation met the challenge of facing the prospect of industrialization with a constitution that was legitimate only to a limited degree and was almost impossible to put into action.

Weil shared the attitude of the majority of her fellow students at the Lycée and the Ecole Normale: she was inclined to take the "war" between Citizen Alain and the "powers that be" "very seriously and perhaps to overestimate the extent of the hostility."[7] Like her fellow students, she tended to adopt the political aspects of Alain's doctrine in particular in a somewhat exaggerated fashion. The age difference if nothing else saw to it that Weil was not steeped in traditional radicalism in the same unquestioning manner as was her teacher. The political scene was a different one, in part because the chief demand of radicalism—laicism—had been met and in part as a result of social development and growing sensitivity to the consequences of the so-called second industrial revolution. These changes altered the tone of the outrage that stimulated critical speculation: "A certain passion is always required to make us take up the pen," wrote Alain.[8]

True, but surely a *politique de l'entendement,* such as Alain called for, must suffer from it. The radical disposition serves Alain as firm support, the fixed point from which the free flight of ideas takes off, only to find its way back with a sure homing instinct. "I like the thought that ideas have wings. But I also want them to find their way back to the dovecote. Freedom, it seems to me, needs a fixed point. In short, without some sort of bias *[parti pris]* we cannot help but drift from one system to another, we travel among ideas, we are idea tourists."[9]

Doctrinal opinions dot the landscape like intellectual scenery. The idea tourist spends time in each spot in turn, without gaining anything. The succession of opinions does not do away with passion. The thinker who is rooted, who can connect the sights he has seen abroad to his native structures, has a better chance. But where are his roots? In bias, in *parti pris.* But if there must be bias, why this particular one? Why purify original "naive" radicalism by a "tour" through socialism, anarchism, monarchism, rather than settling in one of the

7. P, 1:103.
8. Alain, *Politique,* 1.
9. Ibid., 43.

other intellectual landscapes and making it the starting point for a journey through radicalism? The question does not arise for Alain: "I was born a radical. My father was one, as was my grandfather on my mother's side—and not merely in their views but also (as a socialist would put it) by their class; for both were petits bourgeois and fairly poor. I have always harbored very strong feelings against tyrants and an egalitarian passion. . . . Instinct held me by the roots."[10]

The struggle against government tyranny, against proportional representation, against state secrets, advocacy of radical equality, of a form of obedience that nevertheless withholds respect—all arise from unequivocal presentiments and enthusiasms, "from the certainty of a hunting dog's instincts [*l'instinct d'un chien de chasse*]." Alain adds, "These impulses are not proof, but they prod us to search for proof."[11]

If one had not been born and raised a radical, if one were a dog whose instincts had been bred differently, would one still be entitled to search for proof of one's instincts? The problem remains even if the *parti pris* is defended with subtle arguments and is presented to us in the guise of *volonté* and raised to the level of "philosophy."[12] Nevertheless, the form in which Alain's political preferences was substantiated showed his students a path to genuine *prohairesis*—though they did not steadfastly pursue it all the way. "In the sphere of immanence [*les choses d'ici-bas*] faith [*croyance*] produces deceptions. Only in relation to divine things and in the moment when a soul turns its longing and its alertness to God does faith have the ability to produce realities, and it does so as the product of desire. The conviction [*croyance*] that creates reality is called faith [*foi*]."[13]

Alain's politics envision, as do his anthropology and his cosmology, two opposing poles of reality, one necessary and one good; they are respectively represented by power and spiritual force. Between them exists an area of what is ethically and intellectually reprehensible; its presence puts the lyre of good order out of tune. This intermediate area, in turn, consists of two elements: the first pertains to the human individual as such. It reflects the effect of power on man's emotional nature as well as the corresponding illegitimate demands on the spiritual

10. Ibid., 43, 44.
11. Ibid., 44.
12. See Aron, *L'homme*, 111.
13. Quoted in Schumann, *La mort*, 90.

force by low elements of the soul. The second is a social element. Within this component, the disorder caused by power and the corresponding idolatry are heightened by the natural dynamic of social mechanisms.

Alain's cosmological and psychological dualism appears as a speculative elaboration of the basic stance of the meditative citizen, the duality of compliance and resistance whose precarious balance, according to Alain, makes up civic virtue: "The two virtues of the citizen are resistance and obedience. By his obedience he guarantees order. By his resistance he guarantees liberty."[14]

For Alain, society is a natural phenomenon. He may have meant this metaphorically, but the metaphor is strictly applied. As a natural phenomenon, the "social element" is subject to natural laws, and in the last resort these are strictly analogous to the laws of mechanics or to mechanical laws.[15] That means that society is viewed as a network of *force* relations, as a coefficient of powers, all of which can be traced back to the physical concept of force—or an analogous concept, identical to the physical. It becomes evident that such a physicalism equates power and force, and this, too, is the basis for the universally binding character of Weil's concept of work. She, too, saw social power—generally equated with oppression—as a natural phenomenon. "However, it is still the same pressure exerted by nature that continues to make itself felt [that is, on the level of production, which is no longer primitive], although more indirectly; for oppression is exercised by force *[force]*, and in the long run all force originates in nature."[16]

Here Weil found a place for the Baconian-Hobbesian *scientia propter potentiam*. Transferring the mechanical notion of power to social reality presumes limiting the explanation of human action to the operation of natural laws in the libidinous expansion of the self. "For several centuries now, ever since the Renaissance, men of thought and men of action have laboured methodically to give the human mind mastery over the forces of nature; and their success has surpassed all expectations. But during the last century it came to be realized that society itself is a force of nature, as blind as the others, as dangerous for man if he does not succeed in mastering it."[17]

14. *Politique,* 27.
15. Ibid., 29, 30, 35.
16. *OL,* 88 (*OLE,* 63).
17. *OL,* 33 (*OLE,* 19–20).

Galileo's introduction of the concept of force was, according to Weil, the basis of the enormous engineering feats that have taken place since the Renaissance. She noted, however, that social science was still waiting for its Galileo before being in a position to realize the rationalist dream of the social engineer. "And we, who claim to set about equipping the social side of life, will have not even the crudest knowledge of it as long as we have not formed a clear notion of social force. Society cannot have its engineers as long as it has not first had its Galileo."[18]

Only the analogy of the two spheres, nature and society, and thus the postulate of the concept of power as the starting point for social science, is taken as established. This was what Alain had felt earlier. He specifically applied Bacon's phrase about controlling nature to society. "Every constitution takes these things into account . . . there is no vote on the law of gravity. We merely invent levers, spools, tackle blocks—in short, artifices to conquer gravity by obeying it."[19]

It is necessary to adapt to the external order of force before it can be modified. Inequality is a datum that necessarily results from the effect of powers *(l'action inévitable des puissances)*.[20] Weil came to the conclusion that the anarchists' attempt to abolish power and therefore inequality must remain a utopian dream, since they fail to take into account the essential existential conditions of society. The conservatives' attempt, in turn, to stabilize power by establishing a balance between the rulers and the ruled is, according to Weil, equally unrealistic because it is not possible to moor a stable balance of power in such shifting sands as human beings.[21] As she puts it in a later essay: "You cannot base a certitude upon man."[22]

For both Weil and Alain, every person in power is a tyrant by nature. Of necessity, the possession of power leads to the misuse of power. "[I]t is not the manner in which use is made of some particular force, but its very nature, which determines whether it is oppressive or not."[23]

Alain assures his readers, "All power is absolute. . . . There are not two ways to rule. . . . There is a single face of a tyrant, and everyone

18. *OL,* 187 (*OLE,* 141).
19. *Politique,* 36.
20. Ibid., 38.
21. *OL,* 92 (*OLE,* 66–67).
22. *OL,* 227 (*OLE,* 172).
23. *OL,* 88 (*OLE,* 63).

knows full well how to be a tyrant just as soon as he has the chance."[24] And Weil quotes from Thucydides: "It is always necessary for everyone to command wherever he has the power to do so."[25]

No distinction is made between tyrannical rule and other forms. Conversely, Hobbes defines tyranny as merely a term thrown around by opponents of a particular rule that reflects on the position of those who use it while saying nothing about the nature of the rule itself.

> And because the name of Tyranny, signifieth nothing more, nor less, than the name of Soveraignty, be it in one, or many men, saving that they that use the former word, are understood to be angry with them they call Tyrants; I think the toleration of a professed hatred of Tyranny is a Toleration of hatred to Commonwealth in generall, and another evil seed, not differing much from the former. For to the Justification of the Cause of a Conqueror the Reproach of the Cause of the Conquered is for the most part necessary: but neither of them for the Obligation of the Conquered.[26]

In contrast to Hobbes, for Alain and Weil the parallel between rule and tyranny results neither in the reduction of tyranny into a propagandistically deprecating nomenclature nor in the normativity of the actual established rule. On the contrary, and for Weil to a perhaps greater degree than for Alain, actuality is seen as an obstacle to, even the opposite of, normativity. In this sense Hobbes's judgment that "professed Hatred of Tyranny" was the same as "hatred of Commonwealth in generall" correctly applies to Alain and Weil, as well as to the fundamental antistatism they articulated and carried to an extreme. "For Alain, who in this regard incorporated public opinion, the government is less an expression of the nation as an organism of its own, which always tends to view itself as the end in itself, fundamentally reactionary, and those who share in it as corrupt."[27]

In this view democratic politics is nothing like regulated participation in the decision-making process, a championing of positions that, though antagonistic, are seen as legitimate. It stands for fundamental opposition.

24. *Politique,* 193; see also 157, 188.
25. *EL,* 45; see also *OL,* 218.
26. Thomas Hobbes, *Leviathan,* ed. A. D. Lindsay, 388.
27. Siegfried, *Tableau,* 77–78.

The concept of a loyal opposition—characteristic for English politics and essential for any well-ordered democracy—is impossible; the form of submission that withholds respect, Alain's civic virtue, is its exact opposite.

Whatever is not perfect is bad. To identify all rule with tyranny is identical with that dualistic rigidity whose formulations Alain and Weil at times take from the Stoics: "There are no little faults [fautes]." "All faults are worth the same. There is only one fault: incapacity to feed upon light; for in the absence of this capacity, all faults are possible and none is avoidable."[28] Such rigor is likely to result in a situation in which it takes a very long time before the difference between a Hitler and a Poincaré can be understood.

As we saw in the context of her confrontation with Marxism, Weil recognized a source of oppression located in man's autonomy, in an original will to power that is not determined by the conditions of production. This thirst for power is a cause of repression that reaches beyond the structural enslavement of man, presumed to be the result of overcoming the existential necessity of production. "Obedience and command [le commandement] are also phenomena for which the conditions of production do not provide a sufficient explanation."[29]

Deciding that the drive to power is not an epiphenomenon of the means of production would surely have cost Alain less effort than it did his student. But for Weil, too, in the final analysis the autonomous will to power was the most alarming social fact: "Inequality could be easily mitigated by the resistance of the weak and the feeling of justice of the strong; it would not lead to a still harsher form of necessity than that of natural needs themselves, were it not for the intervention of a further factor, namely the struggle for power."[30]

Limits are set for every expansion of power. Weil again derived this conclusion from the fundamentally compelling character of the concept of limit for all earthly—that is, phenomenal—things. The limit is a necessary corollary of the operation of laws. "In general, one can only regard the world in which we live as subject to laws if one admits that every phenomenon in it is limited."[31]

28. Bridoux, *Alain*, 71; *C*, 2:125 (*N*, 1:223).
29. *OL*, 188 (*OLE*, 142).
30. *OL*, 90 (*OLE*, 65).
31. *OL*, 103 (*OLE*, 75).

With reference to power, several times in her writings she gave the name of *Nemesis* to this limit.[32] Because power never remains in the same hands, the only constant being the striving for power, the goal of infinite expansion proves to be essentially unattainable. "I would colonize the stars," was Cecil Rhodes's absurd cry. Furthermore, as the relationship between unlimited aspiration and limited possibility, the objective proves to be hollow, unreal. But the pursuit of unreal goals is madness.[33] In contrast to the power of discretion over inert matter, rule over human beings must eliminate the autonomy of the subjects, its radical consequence being the death of the subject. Since power is a relationship—it is always power over someone weaker—at its extreme limit, killing, it abolishes itself by abolishing one of the poles of the relationship. In this respect, too, the exercise of power leads to madness. It is worth noting that Weil, and in similar passages Alain as well, trapped in their physicalism, were not out to discover a criterion for differentiating between power and force. If killing radically turns the victim into an object—that is, a corpse—then every exercise of power is analogously a relationship that deals in material objects. Weil derived such a doctrine from the *Iliad* by declaring its true hero to be might *(force)*.[34]

Those who suffer always live under the more or less disguised threat of death,[35] since the power to kill another human being is enough to half-kill him, turn him into a thing. The suppliant Priam is nothing but a thing to angry Achilles.[36] But if the imploring king can regain his humanity, those who must make their way into slavery are, in a certain sense, dead for the rest of their days. "Free for nothing that originates in themselves."[37] The exercise of power is like alienation conditioned by the means of production in that it reverses man's elementary relationship with nature by making the subject par excellence into an object. For Weil—who remains true to the Hegelian tradition on this point—the master is as alienated as the servant. This is so because, first, he does not,

---

32. *OL*, 104 (*OLE*, 76); *C*, 1:104.
33. *OL*, 92 (*OLE*, 67).
34. *SG*, 22 (*IC*, 24). "Perverse interpretation of the Iliad," as George Steiner correctly notes in *Language and Silence*, 8.
35. *OL*, 112 (*OLE*, 83); see also *OL*, 170 (*OLE*, 128).
36. *SG*, 13, 15 (*IC*, 26, 28).
37. *SG*, 16.

in Weil's terse sense, perform work and, second, because he is trapped in the vicious circle of the necessity to preserve and expand power.[38] The absurdity—that is, the ontological contradiction—of rule tarnishes knowledge, which is covered with the imaginary, with madness.

The tyrant is, according to Alain, so enraptured by his own tyranny that he is unable to have a thought worthy of being called an idea.[39] In this sense he is inevitably stupid: "Even if he has all the talents of a genius he is stupid, he can't help being stupid, he owes it to his own majesty to be stupid."[40] To be right, to be in the right, cannot be reconciled with the exercise of power. Actual power is not even necessary: any kind of distinction suffices to bring about aberrant dimming of awareness and must be combatted and ridiculed from the outset. Here, too, Alain is articulating a stance that is prevalent in the Third Republic, a "democratic dread of betrayal, whose first evidence is snobbery."[41]

The independence of the political sphere from the economy in the Third Republic that Albert Thibaudet and Robert de Jouvenel talk about creates, to the extent that it actually exists, not an arena for public debate but the site for an ideal confirmation of equality, even if this were to mean mediocrity.

> It is not refined to be anticlerical.
> That is why it is essential to be anticlerical. We must not feel any respect for the Académie Française. We must not become members of the Institut [de France]. We must not seek either the votes nor the praise of this elite, which makes every effort to govern us. And it is not enough to give up seeking them; we must arrange matters in such a way that we do not deserve them.[42]

The radical republic is prepared to come to terms with the concrete reality, perhaps even with the inevitable existence, of a *classe dirigeante,* as long as that class does not boast of that accomplishment. Alain chose to teach in the *universités populaires* (extension courses for working-class audiences) "less in order to teach the people than to establish a firm

38. See, however, *CO,* 124: "Master and servant. Today servants *absolutely* servants, without Hegelian reversal. It is because of the mastery of the forces of nature."
39. See *Politique,* 205.
40. Ibid., 188.
41. Siegfried, *Tableau,* 214.
42. *Politique,* 78.

friendship with them, against the castles, against the academies and the important people *[les Importants]*, whom I dislike. An important person who has been toppled and debased is the most beautiful spectacle as far as I'm concerned."[43]

The strength of the radicals in the Third Republic lies precisely in the fact that they instinctively and fundamentally took the side of the "little man" against the "greats," the "office holders"—or perhaps more correctly, the "officious people." "The entire economic program of radicalism consists of raising an adjective to an eminence where it is mystically surrounded by admirers. The adjective is *small*."[44] Radicalism means to take the part of the *little* man, of the *small* farmer, of the *small* merchant, of the *small* saver, and so on, to the point, when amnesties come into play, of the *small* swindler.

The "important people" embody power. They exercise power and thus fall prey to the madness of the tyrant. They are opposed by "the people," who are at least potentially the embodiment of the *esprit*. "What seems to me most obvious in whatever political situation is that the people is worth more than its rulers."[45]

The advantage the slave has over his master is that, precisely because he is the object of power and does not exercise it himself, he can more easily understand that it does no one any good. The slave arrives at "Aesopian" wisdom because he is forced to practice patience and silence, and man, wrote Alain, can think only in solitude and quiet in the face of things.[46] "Man learns *[s'instruit]* from the harshness of the ruler and, better still, from contact with matter *[la chose]*, which make no concessions. I feel sorry for those who find dinner ready for them on their plate."[47]

Importants and *petites gens,* tyrants and subordinates, masters and slaves: it is important to note that Alain is not referring to the historical classes even when he speaks about the bourgeoisie and the proletariat. As her Marxist critics have correctly pointed out, Weil also employed historically universal types, even though she paid a great deal more

43. Ibid., 1.
44. Thibaudet, *République des professeurs*, 25.
45. *Politique*, 21.
46. Ibid., 115, 204, 207.
47. Ibid., 203.

attention to the specifics of what she considered contemporary slavery than did Alain.

The transhistoricity of the type is only reinforced when Weil assigns a liberating function, going beyond the "Aesopian" wisdom of Alain, to the status of slavery, which she equates with *malheur*. At the same time the particular historically specific manifestation of suffering gains increased significance:

> Happy are they who have felt in their own body the wretchedness/misery/suffering *[le malheur]* of the world in their lifetime. They have the chance and the task to recognize the *malheur* of the world in its true nature and to observe it as it really is. It is the task of salvation itself. Two thousand years ago, in the Roman Empire, slavery was the *malheur,* its final limit being crucifixion. Unhappy those, however, who, though this task is given them, do not fulfill it.[48]

Membership in one or another group depends less on a sociological criterion as traditionally understood and only tangentially on an ethical criterion.

> Some functions are carried out according to protocol, some are not. There are two distinct patterns that split every society into two classes. In each society these take the type of the proletarian and the type of the bourgeois. The proletarian is someone who affects the external order so as to take its products from it—for example, a miner, a carpenter, or a smith. The bourgeois, on the other hand, is someone who acts upon the human order to draw a profit from it—for example a priest, a minister, a professor, a banker, or a tradesman.[49]

Ceremonies are nothing but mystifications, camouflage mechanisms, which, according to this theory, seem to conceal more from those who carry them out than from those for whom they are performed. However, in her late phase Weil interpreted religious ceremonies quite differently. In an extremely positive sense they became "bridges" to the ground beyond, as symbolizations of the ineffable. "For the rest, the

48. *PSO,* 76.
49. Alain, quoted in Lagneau, "Radicalism," 152.

social and human participation in these sacraments, to the extent that they are ceremonies and symbols, remains an excellent and beneficial matter as a stage for all these whose way is marked on this track."[50]

Whoever does not affect nature directly but acts on the *ordre humain* is alienated and alienates others. Alain touched on the question of the servant's alienation, however, only in random asides: "There is no thinking except in the mind of a free man, a man who has promised nothing, who withdraws, who lives in solitude, who does not care whether he pleases or displeases. The executive is not free, nor is the boss. Both are occupied with this crazy undertaking."[51]

The only thing that can evade the delusory mechanism of power is the sphere of the mind.[52] But thought is fundamentally individual: "The number *2* thought of by one man cannot be added to the number *2* thought of by another man so as to make up the number *4*."[53] It is not possible to unite various human minds into a collective mind; collectives do not think; and, according to Weil, it is nonsense to speak of collective thinking or a collective psyche.[54] Alain wrote, "Man thinks in solitude and silence against things. From the moment when men begin to think in unison, everything becomes mediocre." And Weil assures us: "[T]he individual surpasses the collectivity to the same extent as something surpasses nothing, for thought only takes shape in a mind that is alone face to face with itself."[55]

The actualization of the spirit before things or before itself comes to the same thing. Alain's thinking, which was the starting point for Weil's thinking, is unambiguously solipsistic. *Cogitatio* is always of *cogitata* until faced by the "obstacle" of necessity. Even in her final period she wrote: "How should human thought ever have any other object but thought?"[56]

Weil's epistemological dualism means that one's fellowman can never be encountered directly, in the second person, but only by means of a third instance, which is not a person, but reality as the network of natural

50. *AD*, 40.
51. *Politique*, 305.
52. *OL*, 130 (*OLE*, 98).
53. *OL*, 111 (*OLE*, 82).
54. *OL*, 111, 129 (*OLE*, 82, 97).
55. *Politique*, 115; *OL*, 130 (*OLE*, 98).
56. *Ep*, 329 (*NR*, 262).

necessity, a reality that is supposed to be made available by work—a term that has a disconcertingly broad range of meaning. Accordingly, any "we" must appear to Weil as a lie and a phantom, if it is conceived as a meeting of "I" and "thou," rather than as the coming about of one "I" alongside another "I" before a common "it" mediated by work.

In Alain, and for the time being in Weil, the unstoppable expansion of power finds its limits, quite in the spirit of liberalism, in the finitude of individual existence. To that extent Trotsky's criticism is quite justified. Alain taught: "The thinking individual against sleeping society—that is the eternal story." Here lie the roots of Weil's insistence on the spontaneity of revolutionary action, the profound conviction with which she quoted: "The emancipation of the workers will be carried out by the workers themselves, or it will not take place at all."[57]

The vital task of putting controls on the repressive social mechanism would mean to submit it to the human spirit, "which means the individual": "In the subordination of society to the individual lies the definition of true democracy and that of socialism as well."[58]

Even if the arbitrary decisionism of the radicals—or, in Weil's case, bias in favor of work—is replaced for her by the workings of grace, the fundamental rejection of any collectivity remains. Weil would interpret Christ's phrase, "wherever two or three come together in my name," as a numerical maximum.[59] Even the *corpus mysticum* is sacrificed to the pneumatic purity of the *unio mystica* required by radical dualism: "our true dignity is not to be parts of a body, even though it be a mystical one, even though it be that of Christ."[60]

Only the individual is capable of the *politique d'entendement*. The collective reinforces only the madness of tyranny and with it despotism. Alain noted, "Leviathan is stupid. He elicits the most enticing sentiments, and therefore the greatest evils of this world. The coming together of people repels humanity." Group discipline or a search for the warmth of the nest, a striving for union, kills the free, essentially individual critical spirit. "To avoid that which separates us, to choose what draws us together—that is not thinking. Or rather, it is thinking

57. *Politique*, 21; *OL*, 36 (*OLE*, 22); see also *OL*, 181 (*OLE*, 137).
58. *OL*, 34 (*OLE*, 20).
59. *AD*, 58 (*WG*, 80).
60. *AD*, 59 (*WG*, 80).

about becoming united and remaining united—and about nothing else."[61] Precisely because there is strength in union, union is suspect.

> Union confers strength. Yes, but whose strength are we talking about? The popular Leviathan will carry everything along if a single idea lives in every head. And then? I see the permanent fruits of union. One strong power; dogmas; dissidents persecuted, excommunicated, driven into exile, killed. Union as a powerful being that likes itself and nothing else. . . . The power of imagination is intoxicated with this harmony.[62]

Union is suspect. Suspicion is the resistance of the residue of reasonable humanity that finite individuality represents against the totalitarian-democratic demand of a leveling republic. This suspicion is realistically stimulated by the excessive use of the slogan of the *union sacrée* and its very forceful emotional effect during the First World War. Alain himself served in the armed forces during the war, and Weil could still clearly perceive its aftereffects. The concern, given the *Leviathan populaire,* arises in the face of the fact, documented during the war, that *pari passu* with democratization of the nation the demands for loyalty from the population had increased.[63] What matters is to resist the temptation of a consoling—that is, a reality-concealing—melting into a totalitarian phony union.[64] "To withhold oneself from the holy union [union sacrée]" is what Alain demands,[65] and Weil would refuse to join the church after her "conversion" because of similar considerations. Instead, she would feel specifically called to remain on its threshold. "Social enthusiasms have such power today, they raise people so effectively to the supreme degree of heroism in suffering and death, that I think it is as well that a few sheep should remain outside the fold in order to bear witness that the love of Christ is essentially something different."[66]

The *union sacrée* not only destroys individuality, it also usurps a quality that can never pertain to the factual: holiness. The temporal powers

61. *Politique,* 155, 305.
62. Ibid., 305.
63. See Lichtheim, *Europa,* 60.
64. See Erik Erikson, *Insight and Responsibility,* "Identity and Uprootedness in Our Time," 81 ff.
65. *Politique,* 195.
66. *AD,* 60 (*WG,* 81).

usurp spiritual authority. Luther's differentiation between the tolerable administrative force of princes, which is restricted to their subjects' bodies and possessions, and an intolerable one, which also controls the spiritual sphere, is altered in such a way that *any* power, at least tendentiously, raises a claim to theocracy.[67]

> Thus at bottom the spirit of the powers is theoretical, and persecution is the worst sin. Every tyrant would like to compel obedience. However, he would like to see it offered without force, and nevertheless he wants to punish those who refuse to render it. He does not stop at actions. He wants to be loved for his power. That is the madness of tyrants.[68]

The tyrant, in his madness, wants to control not only the actions but also the thoughts of men. For Alain and Weil power is therefore essentially totalitarian because, corresponding to the perverse modern concept of praxis, action as such is excluded from the meaningful, legitimizing sacral sphere. "Participation, even from a distance, in the play of forces which control the movement of history is not possible without contaminating oneself."[69]

That which is "social," the combination of the blind, libidinous expansion of power and opinion, is transgression par excellence. For Weil, that which is social finds support neither in the democratic option of Alain's *parti pris* nor—in her later phase—in the seed of grace taking root. Rather, it is bent on removing these obstacles to its course—that is, impeding their development. That which is social is—so Weil stated literally in several passages—the actual realm of the princes of the world, identical with the beast in the Apocalypse characteristically identified with the Great Beast in Plato.[70] Christ's temptation by the devil, who offers him the riches of the world, is the iconographic type of Weil's

67. See Martin Luther, *Von weltlicher Obrigkeit: Wie weit man ihr Gehorsam schuldig sei.*
68. *Politique,* 31.
69. *OL,* 192 (*OLE,* 146). For Weil's truly irritating depiction of National Socialism as a pale imitation of "totalitarianism" in the Roman empire, which emerges in countless passages, see especially "Reflexions sur les origines de l'Hitlérisme," in *EHP,* 11 ff. It took an enormous fixation on the dangers of power in general, as quasi autonomous, of its agents as independent of its representatives, and of centralized administration in particular to be able to write in 1940: "One cannot outdo the Romans in the art of perfidiousness" (*EHP,* 24).
70. See, for example, *OL,* 236 (*OLE,* 180).

psychomachy. "The central, fundamental conception in Plato—which is also a Christian conception—is that all men are absolutely incapable of having on the subject of good and evil opinions other than those dictated by the reflexes of the beast, except for predestined souls whom a supernatural grace draws towards God."[71]

The "great beast," a frequently misused Platonic metaphor, is used here, among its other purposes, to combat a concept of society that at the time was fashionable in France: the formulations of Emile Durkheim. Conscience or consciousness *(conscience)* is precisely the thing that, for Alain and his student, can never be collective. To see a functional equivalent of religion in a *conscience collective* means to confer divinity on the collective libidinous foolishness of creating an idol. Nevertheless, Weil took the image drawn by Durkheim to be an accurate description of abominable "society": "No matter how foolish Durkheim's thesis that combines the religious with the social, it nevertheless encapsulates a truth—namely, that the social sense is the spitting image of the religious sense. They resemble each other like a fake diamond resembles a real one to such an extent that those who do not possess the supernatural talent of distinguishing between the two cannot help but be deceived."[72]

A solution of "true opinion" as suggested by Plato's *Statesman* is possible neither for Alain nor for Weil, since by definition opinions cannot be true. The process of clarification by means of which Plato arrives at this "second (second-best) journey" cannot be reenacted by these thinkers, caught as they are in post-Kantian categories.

If every government is seen as tyrannical, mendacious, and usurpatory, nonconformity turns into a fundamental civic virtue, independent of the actual content of the dominant orthodoxy. "If we adapt truth to a rigid system of opinions, as the Catholic concept of orthodoxy does—the Inquisition being a direct consequence—we will drive ourselves into the darkness. It is so completely independent of whatever system we choose."[73]

Weil took the fundamentally correct insight that truth cannot be grasped in doctrines about truth, but she went further, and deduced

71. *OL,* 236 *(OLE,* 180); see also *OL,* 216 *(OLE,* 165).
72. *AD,* 50; see also *EL,* 103.
73. *EL,* 58–59.

a right—more than that, a duty—to heresy. She is a heretic in the technical sense of the term, since she had no intention of submitting herself to the yoke of faith but selected a number of propositions from the Catholic canon by appealing to the sources of knowledge.[74] In contrast to her master, Alain, however, she at least suspected this source to be located in a place beyond this world, and she was not content with willful self-positing of the individual subject. The nature of such a procedure, which, compared to genuine orthodoxy, really is doctrinaire, becomes clear in Weil's attempt to comprehend her experience of truth after all *as* a doctrine.[75] Her mysticism, too, turns out to be a variation of rationalist gnosticism when she writes, "The science of the soul and social science are alike impossible, if the idea of the supernatural is not rigorously defined and introduced into science on the basis of a scientific conception, so as to be handled with the utmost precision in all matters relating to science."[76]

The rationalist search for a primer—which here manifests itself in Weil as well—always threatens to reduce the substance to a set of directions for use. Thus, for example, it is easy to confuse the description of the *technique* of mystical contemplation in Saint John of the Cross with instructions for perceiving the ineffable. Although, once again, there is undoubtedly a doctrine in Alain,[77] we cannot for all that read into his writing any *desire* for a doctrine—more likely the reverse.[78] Instead, it seems that in him, who never established the individual outside itself, the total meaning of heresy consists in the right to heresy. Alain saw the corrective to the stirrings of the "great beast" in the presence of a lively, nonhomogeneous way of thought:

> [A]roused thought is wonderfully split against itself. A heretic does not establish a church; instead, he establishes . . . almost as many churches as there are people. For what heresy establishes is the right to heresy. Every thinking person makes use of this right; that is his point of departure. Thus thinking creates an equality worthy

74. See Saint Augustine, *De utilitate credendi,* XXI.
75. *EL,* 151: "Doctrines are always inadequate, but it is necessary to have one, if only in order to avoid the false ones."
76. *Ep,* 370 (*NR,* 294–95).
77. See P, 1:73 (PE, 63).
78. See *EL,* 151.

of attention: All are thus bosses, and there is no longer a boss. The anarchic spirit is the basis of the revolutionary spirit.[79]

Anarchy, which Alain correctly pointed to as related to his liberalism, is clearly noticeable in the Proudhonian nature of the revolutionary gesture and the proposals for shaping Weil's world of work. It is only the common speculative background of the existential contradiction— instead of, say, a Marxist antithesis ending in historical syntheses—that allowed Weil to overtake her teacher "from the left" and later to replace his voluntarism with a theology of grace without ever having to break continuity with his thinking.

The tyrants' usurpation consists for Alain in the fact that in addition to the factual—we could say physical—they also lay claim to spiritual power—perhaps better: authority. By analogy with Auguste Comte, he demanded that spiritual power remain unsullied by the other kind and be set in opposition to it.[80] And Weil assures us: "Spiritual servitude consists in confusing the necessary with the good; for we do not know what a distance separates the essence of the necessary from that of the good."[81]

The anarchic spirit conjured up by Alain does not urge—or no longer urges—storming the Bastille. It manifests itself much more as a refusal: "[N]o human being is stupid. Everyone, then, thinks in his corner, holding in his hands some book written in solitude. Others, an invisible assembly. These brief moments of refusal would suffice, if we only understood why a human horde can become a fearful beast."[82]

In the revolutionary tradition—and Alain sees himself as its adherent —the struggle against the church's spiritual patronage corresponds in the narrower sense to the political will to emancipation. Anticlericalism is an essential element of radical ideology and a crucial point of divergence in French political opinion. For Alain, the idol of a hierarchic, monarchic, dogmatic, intolerant church—a church that stands on the *pouvoir* side of the barricades—finds its counterpart in the invisible community of rejecting loners. The secular school is their strongest support. "The spiritual power *[pouvoir spirituel]* is transferred. Religion

79. *Politique*, 206–7.
80. Ibid., 70 ff.
81. *OL*, 216 (*OLE*, 165); see also *OL*, 219, 239 (*OLE*, 167, 182).
82. *Politique*, 155.

condemns religion. It is not the school but the church that is god-less. . . . The enemy of Catholicism is fundamentally catholic, a citizen of the world, a brother and friend to the oppressed, opposed to the oppressor."[83]

The scandal of the church consists, for Alain, of the fact that it en-deavors to present particulars as generalizations and attempts to simulate the legitimation of an absolute in conditional matters, most obviously in the simultaneity of the various "God is with us" shouts during the war; as Weil put it, "But as for the churches, they offer us the supreme scandal of clergy and faithful asking God at the same time, with the same rites, the same words, and it must be supposed, an equal amount of faith and purity of heart, to grant a military victory to one or other of two warring camps."[84]

This kind of church is opposed by the universal church of humanity, consisting of those who are in touch with natural law, who therefore are at home in the cosmopolis, the church of Comte: "silent churches, marked by the arts and sciences. A church commingled with the masses, created from those who live together in rational union and through whom the universal spirit is meant to spread and manifest itself. Universal friendship would take shape; the positive church is full of friends who do not know one another."[85]

According to Aristotle it is not possible to speak of friendship between people who do not know each other. Here the opposite is true: it is inevitable that wherever true contact exists, interested and affective moments will creep in, allowing the "social" to arise and blur the purity of "friendship in reason." Friendship for the sake of good is not, as it is in Aristotle, the tip of a hierarchy of possible friendships; it is the only friendship. In the final analysis, to preserve its purity, such a friendship can exist only between strangers! That is how far we can drive fear of reifying institutionalization. Institutionalization, contact with defiled *pouvoir*, according to Alain, corrupted even the spirit of the original church. Weil never tired of mentioning the devastating consequences of the union of the church with the prototype of the libidinous beast under its spiritual landscape, the Roman empire. For

83. Alain, *Propos sur la religion*, 5, 19.
84. *E*, 109 (*NR*, 123); compare Alain, *Propos*, 57, 58.
85. *E*, 109 (*NR*, 123).

Alain, the positivist church is nothing more than the spirit of Christ, once more operative, in its pre-patristic purity: "It is there, where the old church spread its spiritual forces. Religion lives in the form of 'irreligion.' But that is not reason enough to say the church is dead. Knock on its grave. It is empty."[86]

In contrast especially to Weil in her late writings, Alain wore his "Christianity" lightly. For him it was a way of thinking that—granted, very respectfully—he could utilize. If Weil's religious experience functioned on a level quite different from Alain's, her attempts at explication nevertheless remained indebted to her teacher's interpretation of Christianity. And how radical a tone does the Sermon on the Mount take on when spoken from Mont Sainte Geneviève! "The Christian spirit includes contempt for power, respect for all souls as equally deserving of salvation, and finally a preference for poverty and work, from the sense of human weakness in the face of so many temptations."[87]

The silent religion of the arts and sciences has no room for the resurrected Christ. But it does have room for the crucified, powerless just man who is spirit. Christianity is "the cult of the crucified spirit, which implies a conflict between the spirit and the powers, [is] partisanship against the powers."[88]

It was as the result of such schooling that Weil—in the thrall of her factory experiences and in the face of the futility of actively coming even slightly closer to the Proudhonian paradise—would come to see Christianity as the "religion of the slaves," and therefore her own. Driven by aesthetic stimuli, in a moment of ecstasy she became certain of this. From this time on, the cross signified for Weil in the last analysis time and space, the defining conditions of human existence, which are simultaneously the universal a priori of formalized knowledge. Man, drawn by grace, cancels his spatiality and most especially his temporality in death or its rhythmic imitation, work; he abolishes the Creation, thus permitting God to arrive at God. Whether the transparency of the soul transformed *sub specie mortis* is not already enough to permit this *unio mystica* is a question left moot by Weil until the last. The god who finds his way to himself through this purification is crucified by his

86. *Propos,* 15, 19.
87. Alain, *Définitions,* 55.
88. Ibid.

own creation in the form of infinite space and unending time. In the final analysis Weil replaced liberal laissez-faire with the determination of a *laisser faire Dieu*. "[E]very time I think about Christ's crucifixion, I commit the sin of envy."[89]

Weil's theology remains a theology of the cross as well. The rejection of the anticipation of metastasis to glory in this world as being idolatry is transferred to the next world as well. And whom does Alain see as the crucifying Pharisees? *Les Importants*: "If we think about the Pharisee in his 'importance,' we can understand the cross and the fiery stake."[90]

For Weil, the pharisee is someone unable to distinguish between *je* and *moi*.[91]

89. *AD*, 51.
90. Alain, *Propos*, 17–18.
91. *Leçons*, 206–7; see also *Les intuitions pré-chrétiennes*, 164.

FIFTEEN

War and Peace

From Pacifism to Résistance

Simone Weil's pacifism was the result of her analysis of power. In this, as in so much else, she followed her mentor, Alain, who in turn was in debt to Proudhon, the man from whom Tolstoy borrowed the title of his major novel.[1] "War is in itself good, say the conservatives, because it supports the powers and encourages obedience. That is why every conservative mind loves war . . . there is a rage of the elite against peace, the people should think about that."[2]

Weil's theory of power states that the conduct of, or even the preparation for, war would bring about an enormous increase in oppression within one's own country, through the militarization not only of goals but also of the command structures in the economy and in society. "The great mistake in almost all studies of war—a mistake that the socialists in particular have made—is to view war as an episode of foreign policy, and yet it is primarily a domestic matter, and the most cruel of all."[3]

A distrust of "great politics" and the primacy of domestic over foreign policy, in themselves perfectly sensible attitudes, are both characteristically exaggerated by the radical republic.[4] Pacifism is a further

---

1. See Pierre Joseph Proudhon, *La guerre et la paix*.
2. Alain, *Eléments d'une doctrine radicale,* 69. See also 240: "The radical is against war because he understands that war will strengthen the tyrants."
3. *EHP,* 234.
4. See Siegfried, *Tableau,* 112.

exaggeration of radical principles. "[W]eapons that are traded by a sovereign state organization can never bring freedom."[5]

The ethics of responsibility, which has hardened into the "materialistic method" of analysis of functional social determinants, applies to every modus of the exercise of power, but in the highest measure to war: "The materialistic method consists first and foremost of examining every possible human datum. In the process it is less important to be concerned with the aims to be pursued than with the consequences that are of necessity brought about by the interplay of the means used."[6]

The victory of a just cause is not a just victory. For Weil, this truth also removes the legitimation of revolutionary warfare, which she was more inclined to see as the cause of the erroneous interpretation of the inspiration of 1789.[7] The experience of the effect on mass psychology of war under modern conditions had already caused Alain to clearly distance himself from Jacobin patriotism. The criticism of a patriotism based on libidinous delusions of desire is one of the themes that runs through L'enracinement. If the exercise of power invariably and always means delusion, war is the total loss of reality. "War is unreality itself."[8]

The greatest conflicts are always waged for illusory goals, just as the Trojan War was fought over Helen's shadow. The unreality of the objective determines the excess of violence. Weil believed that the key to the contemporary loss of order lay in the struggle over puffed-up abstractions. "If the struggle has no goal [objectif], there is no longer a common yardstick, no balance, no ratio—comparisons are no longer possible . . . the significance of the battle is measured solely by the sacrifices it requires, and . . . the sacrifices already brought constantly call for new ones."[9]

For Weil, as for her political friends at the time, civil war belonged in a different category. During the Spanish Civil War she could not bear the feeling of always wanting victory for one side and yet being far from the front herself. Her courage, that aversion to the gap between will and action, overcame her loathing of violence, and she traveled to Spain in order to fight in the ranks of the syndicalist CNT.[10] Because of

5. *EHP,* 234.
6. Ibid., 233.
7. See ibid., 229 ff., 240 f.
8. *PSO,* 75.
9. *EHP,* 256–57.
10. See letter to Bernanos in ibid., 220–21 (*SWR,* 106).

an accident—she stepped into a large pot of boiling oil—she returned to France after two months without having fired a shot. For her it was the chance to join in the battle "in the ranks as a soldier," to join in a popular uprising, as she had put it in her "Rejection of Politics," to take part in a rebellion in which, she believed, spontaneity and noble motives outweighed fanaticism and cruelty. Actual contact taught her differently. In Spain itself she felt carried along by the dynamics of the war. When she had time to reflect, however, from the distance enforced by her accident, she arrived at the following conclusion: "I no longer felt any inner necessity to participate in a war which, instead of being what it had appeared when it began—a war of famished peasants against landed proprietors and their clerical supporters—had become a war between Russia on the one hand and Germany and Italy on the other."[11]

It was not only the fact that Spain served as the stage for an international conflict camouflaged as a civil war that dampened Weil's enthusiasm. More important, learning that the exigencies of warfare and the intoxication of violence destroy libertarian and humanitarian objectives even where these used to exist had a sobering effect. "The compulsions that become evident in the civil war, and the atmosphere of civil war, turn out to be much stronger than the aspirations that men attempted to turn into reality by way of the civil war."[12]

Military and police coercion, coercion at work, mendacious propaganda, social gradations, despotism and cruelty, all of which the war was intended to abolish, would be reconstituted in full intensity in the fighting republic and under anarchist ministers.[13] The civil war also turned out to be a loss of reality, with harsh consequences. Civil war must, believed Weil, like any international war—with which, furthermore, it would seem inextricably tied henceforth—be avoided if at all possible. "If the bad luck of the time decrees that today a civil war becomes a war like any other and is inevitably connected with war between nations, then we can draw only one conclusion: to avoid civil war as well."[14]

Weil saw an absurdity not only in revolutionary and, a fortiori, exploitative war but also in the struggle against fascism in the form of war. She demanded of Léon Blum—whose noninterventionist policy concerning Spain she approved of at the time, even when she felt

11. *EHP,* 221 (*SWR,* 107).
12. *EHP,* 218.
13. Ibid., 217–18.
14. Ibid., 249.

herself called to fight for the republic—that he expand the principle to apply even to all those cases he had excepted because of existing French treaties. If even the deep sympathy and sentimental loyalty of a popular-front government for "our comrades in Catalonia," in spite of all bitterness, was rightly unable to legitimate the possible provocation of a European war, how much less appropriate, according to Weil, must be such a risky step because of a piece of paper in favor of a "quelconque Tchécoslovaquie" (some Czechoslovakia or other). For Weil, appeasement is a choice between prestige and peace. "No matter if you refer to fatherland, democracy, or revolution, the policy of prestige is war."[15]

Although this would be her way of responding to the Munich agreements, she never deluded herself that they were a victory or a final securing of the peace or anything other than a humiliation for the Western democracies. Neither Czechoslovakia nor Alsace-Lorraine—not to mention Morocco—could serve Weil as a *casus belli*. She advocated unconditional avoidance of war, even at the price of accepting German hegemony, not only in central Europe but over the entire Continent, not excluding France.[16] In her view, the injustice meted out to the Sudeten Germans would be balanced by the injustice a German protectorate would inflict on the Czechs: "Injustice against injustice, since there must be injustice in any case, let us choose the one that least threatens to lead to war."[17]

The pairing of injustices is a lame argument, as becomes even more obvious when the same concessions that excuse anti-Semitism and anti-Communism in both the Czech and French cases are taken to be tolerable: "The Czechs can ban the Communist Party and keep the Jews out of important positions without the slightest loss to their national life."[18]

Weil, who was so eager to place justice at the center of any social order, found it tolerable, given the danger of war, for the life of a nation to be constructed on the foundation of an injustice dictated by a hegemonic foreign power. The theoretician of the expansion of power that follows natural law, which is by nature boundless, genuinely believed

15. Ibid., 252–53, 273 ff., 249.
16. Ibid., 253, 249.
17. Ibid., 274.
18. Ibid., 274; for a similar application to France, see ibid., 286.

that the ideological demands of the National Socialist hegemonic state could be sated by the exclusion of Jews from public service and a ban on the Communist Party. Her animus against the people of her ancestry is particularly intolerable in a heart that was capable of "beating across the whole world." Even if in 1939 Weil knew none of the details about Oranienburg and Dachau—information she never tried to obtain, in contrast to other fairly inaccessible information—her indifference to the persecution of the Jews is staggering in someone who placed human misery at the center of her thinking. The misery of the present century is not the factory but the gas chamber. It, too, as we all know, operated under the slogan "Work Makes Us Free."

Weil believed that the smallest evil lay in capitulation without a fight—the extreme consequence of pacifism—for if surrender were to result in the establishment of totalitarian rule, it would at least prevent the horrors of war. Preparing for a defensive war would also evoke totalitarianism by tightening the governmental structures and yet would do little to eliminate the danger of war. Since she saw the causes of oppression in the machine and the "social machine," she, with Karl Liebknecht, saw the primary enemy as her own country.[19]

Hitler's invasion of Prague seems to have unleashed a process of rethinking. But it developed timidly and was never written down. When war was declared, perhaps because it could no longer be avoided, she believed that France would have to fight loyally at England's side.[20] At the news of the brutal suppression of a student demonstration in Prague by the occupation troops, she thought up a wildcat scheme for dispatching a unit of volunteer paratroopers, of whom she proposed to be one. She tried to get a hearing for her plan in official places. But above all she insisted that it was not enough to be less inhuman and less violent than the enemy; what mattered was to be in a position to confront the prestige of power with the prestige of the opposite virtues.[21] What to her was the burden of the two remaining democratic states in Europe in this respect was colonialism. Weil's actual change of heart, however, did not come until the collapse of France. Here, too, actual contact was required, in this case with the German occupation.

19. Ibid., 238–39.
20. P, 2:220, 2:233 (PE, 347, 353).
21. *EHP*, 313 ff.

The pacifist of long standing now wrote: "It does not take a tank or an airplane to kill another human being. A kitchen knife will do. Deliverance will occur quickly if at the moment when the troops deal the decisive blow, all who have had enough of the Nazi murderers rise up as one."[22]

When France was actually "dropped" by the French, to use Weil's phrase, the painful loss made her understand that in a foreign invasion it is not merely a matter of changing the people who exercise the monopoly of power; in addition, identity-embodying traditions are put at risk, extinction threatens an entire "vital milieu," whose continuity embraces and transcends the individual in that it goes beyond it in both past and future time.[23] The specific forms of any culture cannot be replaced for people who grew up in that culture because truth is accessible to them only in a medium that is appropriate to their specific identity, the particular expression of their sensibility. Like her faith, Weil's patriotism grew as a form of love for a reality experienced in its absence.[24] "Today every Frenchman knows what it was he missed as soon as France fell."[25]

There are contradictions in Weil's works that will have to go unresolved because they reflect the contradictoriness of reality or at least of the possible *modi* of perceiving reality. But there are contrasts that can be attributed to deficiencies in her thinking. Weil's way of thinking was strongly influenced by a particular intellectual tradition. When her intuition went beyond the framework of that tradition, she had no tools available with whose help she might have been able to carry out an adequate exegesis of the appropriate experiences and their implications.

Work in the factory, the experience of the reality of God in his absence, the nation's collapse, and the experience of the reality of the *patrie* in its absence broke through the rationalistic framework. Accordingly, there was a mitigation in the universal claim to a "method" that seeks to solve all the problems of human existence along the lines of a problem in mathematics. When the individual can no longer make sure of himself by means of his calculating reason, but instead experiences himself as dependent on a source outside himself, the

22. Ibid., 315.
23. *Ep*, 62–63.
24. See, for example, *Ep*, 132 (*NR*, 101); *E*, 194 (*NR*, 147); *EL*, 154.
25. *Ep*, 203–4 (*NR*, 159); see also *Ep*, 271 (*NR*, 215).

contingent multiplicity of *modi* and of symbolizations of the contact with reality gains new interest. Weil developed a heightened sense for the legitimate diversity of various traditions; human collectivity, as the embodiment of such traditions, assumes the trait of valuable uniqueness. From this time on in Weil's thought the traditions appear as more than organizations arranged by monopolies and balances of power.[26]

Nevertheless, Weil needed a tool not natural to her intellectual construct in order to interpret the reality of the *patrie*—a reality experienced in its painful loss. The deeply ingrained stance of refusal of habitual conduct did not allow her to interpret and explain the intuitively perceived "partnership with the past" with the aid of such categories as "way of life" and behavioral habits. She tried instead to understand tradition as the hereditary transmission of discursively understandable scraps of truth. This explains her attraction to buried, underground, defeated— that is, poorly documented—tradition.[27] The transhistoricity of the criterion caused Weil to assume an equivalence of all experiences of reality and its explicatory symbolisms, regardless of their level of differentiation. In this attempt she regarded those symbols that did not correspond to her schema never as inadequate but always as wrong, since she considered errors and lies to be synonymous. This is a residue of her confidence in the power of universal but instrumental reason—to the extent that it can develop without hindrance—which makes anything that is not knowledge firmly corroborated by methodology appear to be simply ignorance. To the extent that this assurance was suppressed, it was replaced by the certainty of an inspiration that permitted Weil to combine intellectual arrogance with a gesture of humility. When she spoke of ideas that "had been placed in her" and that through her person—unworthy in her own eyes—could affect others, she relieved herself of responsibility for these ideas in a dual sense of the word. This is the background of her so-called syncretism, which furthermore rests not infrequently on arbitrary borrowings of fragmentary traditions.[28]

Held spellbound by the transhistoricity of the referent of symbolism, she ignored all too easily the conditions of the symbolic forms

26. E, 13 (*Ep,* 15; *NR,* 8).
27. See "The wisdom [*savoir*] of pre-Roman antiquity which has entirely disappeared," about which statements are nevertheless made. *Ep,* 237 (*NR,* 187). On the "underground" tradition in France, see *Ep,* 142 (*NR,* 110).
28. *EL,* 203 (*SWR,* 171); *AD,* 228 ff.

themselves. Thus at times she sought to manufacture "syncretic" connections, *rapprochements verbaux ou nominatifs*, on the basis of her very wide but often superficial reading. "She had such a gift for inventing likenesses without taking into account either places or dates, and of elaborating hypotheses while evading all the data which interfered with them that it was quite disconcerting at times."[29]

The gnostic mode of experiencing a transcendence weighted down with cosmic ballast leads to an intoxication of allegory that turns Adonis, Osiris, and Christ into equally valid incarnations of the Logos; Weil also saw equally valid equivalencies in the Egyptian Book of the Dead, in Babylonian texts, in the Pythagoreans—who will always remain a favorite object of arbitrary speculation, since so little is known about them—in the *Oresteia,* in Occitanian Catharism, in François Villon, in fairy tales from all over the world; these Weil declared to be the *philosophia perennis.*[30] "Obvious as are the fluctuations of morality in accordance with time and place, it is equally obvious also that the morality which proceeds directly from mystic thought is one, identical, unchangeable. This can be verified by turning to Egypt, Greece, India, China, Buddhism, the Moslem tradition, Christianity and the folklore of all countries."[31]

Weil had an extraordinarily strong sense for the coded nature of symbols. To have a psychic and cosmic drama make symbolic sense, she used themes from poetry, mythology, the fine arts, and history. For example, she discussed the problem of power with illustrations from the *Iliad.*[32]

She was not concerned with philological pedantry or even with the presentation of historical *res gestae,* "how it really was." Rather, she cared about heuristic mental constructs. At times she nevertheless fell victim to hypostases of her own intellectual themes. If the ahistorical treatment of religious and artistic symbols, of fairy-tale characters and literary figures, appears problematic, such a position applied to history gives rise to even greater misgivings: she dramatized and stylized historical facts to a high degree, only to present them again as historical facts, authoritatively claiming them to be truth. This current runs through

29. Perrin and Thibon, *Telle que nous l'avons connue,* 64 (*As We Knew Her,* 54).
30. Druids in touch with Pythagorean ideas are discussed in *Ep,* 281 (*NR,* 281).
31. *OL,* 211 (*OLE,* 161).
32. *SG,* 11–42 (*IC,* 24–55).

Weil's entire body of work. If, on the other hand, we are aware of this tendency to poetic license concerning history, her historical elaborations as drama become intelligible. Father Perrin and Gustave Thibon were the first to point out Weil's original way of dealing with symbols. As deliberate, orthodox, practicing Catholics, however, they could not help but overestimate the revelatory nature of the symbolic structure of the Catholic Church, which for them was a living thing, as Weil used it. This was especially so since Weil made every effort, especially in contact with these men, to explicate her thinking—what she experienced as her calling—through the medium of Catholic symbolism.[33] The presentation of parts of her work by these two men initiated a long and eventually fruitless debate concerning Weil's "orthodoxy" and the question of whether her way of life can be understood as an—incomplete—progression from unbelief to Catholic Christianity. In his introduction to the German edition of Perrin and Thibon's book, Karl Pfleger wrote: "Certainly she is not to blame for the fact that she had far too little time for the very long journey from unbelief to the baptismal font."

The shortness of Weil's life, however, was not entirely independent of her will. The statement, which tends to use oversimplification to sharpen interpretation, is based on what is surely meant to be generous but is no less mistaken wishful thinking. A correct reading of the dramatic configurations of Weil's thought makes it clear that for her to join the Church, even if she had lived, was quite impossible. Her stance of remaining "on the threshold" was not a station on her life's way but the manifestation of a permanent attitude. We will not have to deal with the details of this debate, which blocks access to Weil much more than it smooths the way. For our purposes what is important is the fact that Weil was not able to develop a genuine understanding of habitual behavioral virtues. This lack could not help but have an effect on her analyses of institutions. Striking psychological observations in this context are often muddied by the tendency to examine institutions for their principles instead of their usefulness.

---

33. Understandably, and as the title of their book modestly attests, Perrin and Thibon wrote about the Simone Weil they knew.

SIXTEEN

The Crisis of Patriotism

Explaining the collapse of France in 1940 solely as a matter of treason, as the outcome of a deliberate plot fueled by the self-interest of a few individuals or groups, will, like any conspiracy theory, fail to account for events. Social phenomena are never the direct result of deliberate actions.[1] Such explanations were often floated, however, not least by Gaullist propagandists, and they began even as the war was still going on, in London.[2] The psychological lure of a conspiracy theory is immediately apparent: it relieves strained nationalism and opens the door to the idea that in the reconstruction period catharsis can be brought about by punishing a few individuals. But it is precisely the obvious attraction of such an interpretation that suggests ethical and intellectual laziness. Refusing to be satisfied with an interpretation that bases the French debacle of the summer of 1940 on a plot does not mean either accepting a compelling social reason for the collapse or denying the personal responsibility of the active participants. All these considerations do not, of course, apply to the occupying power, who must be judged in another context; they merely concern the French response to the defeat.

Simone Weil saw the collapse not as the result of a conspiracy by self-appointed pseudo-elites but as an act of negligence, an abdication on the part of the entire nation—the culmination of a long process of

1. See Karl Popper, *The Open Society and Its Enemies*, 99.
2. Thomson, *Democracy in France*, 211–12.

decay.[3] The argument that France "deserved" its defeat was used also to justify collaboration. Weil, already active in the Résistance when she was staying in Marseilles, wrote the following while she was working with the Free French in London:

> The French people, in June and July, 1940, were not a people waylaid by a band of ruffians, whose country was suddenly snatched from them. They are a people who opened their hands and allowed their country to fall to the ground. Later on—but after a long interval—they spent themselves in ever more and more desperate efforts to pick it up again; but someone had placed his foot on it.[4]

Three distinct events are usually grouped as the "fall of France": the military defeat, the armistice, and the abolishing of the Republic in favor of the Vichy government. The technical, logistic, strategic, and diplomatic causes of the military catastrophe are not covered in Weil's analysis—a fact that is surely no accident but the consequence of a stoicism that excludes power as an ordering factor. The defeat, which by its nature was not brought about by the vanquished alone, was a grievous event, but in itself it was not a sign of guilt. Rather, in Weil's eyes, the disgrace lay in the decision, joyfully welcomed on all sides, to lay down arms.[5] In a letter to Jean Wahl she wrote:

> There was a collective act of cowardice and treason, namely the armistice; and the whole nation bears responsibility for it, including Paul Reynaud, who ought never to have resigned. I myself was immediately appalled by the armistice, but in spite of that I think that all the French, including myself, are as much to blame for it as Pétain. From what I saw at the time, the nation as a whole welcomed the armistice with relief and so the nation bears an overall and indivisible responsibility for it.[6]

The joy with which the fighting was halted was for Weil a first sign that the majority of the French population believed that it had nothing

3. *EL*, 60.
4. *Ep*, 131 (*NR*, 101); see also *EL*, 60–61.
5. See William Shirer, *The Collapse of the Third Republic*, 860–62.
6. Letter to Jean Wahl, in *Deucalion* 36 (October 1952): 253–57 (*SL*, 158).

to lose. The second was the indifference with which the population received the liquidation of the Republic:

> The macabre comedy that put an end to the Third Republic took place in Vichy in July, and the abolition of the government did not cause even a tinge of regret, pain, or anger in the hearts of the French—except in the tiny circles of those who by profession were connected with the destroyed institutions. There was just as little interest in the succession. There was total indifference. Only later did the Pétain legend take on some life.[7]

Only some time later, stimulated by deprivations and the loss of honor that came along with the occupation, was the unquestioning acceptance of political events replaced by a sense of substantial loss.[8]

Weil pointed out that as the language increasingly took on distorted meanings and ethical concepts in particular became blunted, the words *traitor* and *treason* nonetheless retained their full force. "Amidst the general debasement of all words in the French vocabulary, which have anything to do with moral concepts, the words *traître* and *trahison* have lost none of their forcefulness." The determined strength of the concept of treason works as an indication for Weil of the unextinguished awareness that there is something that can be betrayed—that is, a reference to the presence of a legitimate object from which loyalty can easily be withheld. "For men feel that there is something hideous about a human existence devoid of loyalty."[9] The reality of the object of loyalty, which contributes to justifying identity, is clearly experienced in the vacuum left by its loss, and this experience leads to the revitalization of loyalty.[10]

Unlike the relatively recent sovereign national state, patriotism is an age-old phenomenon. Weil considered it a variant of those effects that emerge at all times and are an indication of the link with something that transcends individual existence temporally in both directions. After the experience of the fall of France, she named this link as one of humanity's basic needs. "To be rooted is perhaps the most important and least recognized need of the human soul. . . . A human being has

---

7. *EL,* 60.
8. *Ep,* 130–31 (*NR,* 101–2).
9. *Ep,* 164 (*NR,* 127).
10. *Ep,* 130–32 (*NR,* 102–3).

roots by virtue of his real, active, and natural participation in the life of a community, which preserves in living shape certain particular treasures of the past and certain particular expectations of the future." Natural participation is something that is automatically brought about by place, condition of birth, profession, and social surroundings.[11]

In that the state is intent to amass all human needs for loyalty and affiliation to itself alone, a finite entity, it destroys the multiplicity of the *milieux vitaux* and leads to the devastation of the forced homogeneity of uprooted individuals. "Owing to the fact that the State had remained, in the midst of a total void, the only reality entitled to demand of Man his loyalty and sacrifice, the notion of homeland *[notion de patrie]* presented itself to the mind as an absolute value."[12] The crisis of patriotism thus appears as the withdrawal of loyalty from a state that claims it absolutely and by this claim turns it in another direction.

But what was dropped in the act of this withdrawal of loyalty was not only the state, which was promptly replaced by an even more repressive regime. France as the natural soil for putting down roots disappeared. The First World War, according to Weil, represented a strain on the population's capacity for loyalty to a state, which is not in itself worth loving, though it has also made itself the only possible object of veneration. With her unique psychological perspicacity, Weil explains this phenomenon with a graphic comparison to a family where one member is an invalid. The others feel resentment for the sick person, whose need for care goes far beyond the affection he inspires, but because it is impossible to express such a feeling, the resentment is suppressed. "A loveless idolatry—what could be more monstrous, more heart-rending?"[13]

According to Weil, as a result of the sense of disgust, carried to an extreme by the First World War, in 1940 the state was denied the loyalty that until then had been offered it as the only remaining focus of loyalty.[14] The crisis of patriotism was for Weil one of many episodes in the drama of the fullness of human love, which, as for Ivan Karamazov, has become meaningless since the "death of God."[15]

11. *Ep,* 61 (*NR,* 43).
12. *Ep,* 168 (*NR,* 130).
13. *Ep,* 165 (*NR,* 128).
14. *Ep,* 164 (*NR,* 127).
15. See Albert Camus, "L'homme révolté," in *Essais,* 424.

Weil sketched a history of the loss of substance of *patrie*, which eventually led to the point where, in 1940, it crashed to the ground, entirely voided of substance. This development is paired with the process of consolidation of the centralist state. There are two aspects to this process: (1) the elimination of intermediate links of political articulation; and (2) the disappearance from the conception of self, from the demands and actions of the constituent powers, of any ordering factors except that of force.

Weil lamented the process of assimilation that not only brought under one rule the various landscapes of which contemporary France was made up but also to a great degree destroyed its cultural uniqueness.

> Although the kings of France are praised for having assimilated the countries they conquered, the truth is that they to a large extent uprooted them. . . . People who have their culture taken away from them either carry on without any at all, or else accept the odds and ends of the culture one condescends to give them. . . . The real marvel is to assimilate populations so that they preserve their culture, though necessarily modified, as a living thing. It is a marvel which very seldom takes place.[16]

The most pitiful example of the uprooting of a regional characteristic was for Weil the conquest of Occitania, soon consolidated by the introduction of the Inquisition.[17] The diversity, which the *ancien régime* still tolerated in spite of everything, was finally eliminated by the Revolution. The awareness of belonging to the sovereign nation provided internal impetus for abandoning regional identity in favor of a national one, which was felt to be identical with the creed of liberty. Foreigners were only people who continued to be the slaves of tyrants. When the proud intoxication wore off and "national sovereignty" was revealed to be a fiction, the centralist, repressive, uprooting state remained in existence.[18] The technical evolution of means of transportation and communication did its part to eradicate the characteristic life of the provinces and place them under the rule of monotony and boredom.[19]

16. *Ep*, 141 (*NR*, 109).
17. *Ep*, 198, 189. Occitania was, for Weil, a spiritual landscape of a model political existence, if only because of the dualism of the Albigensians, persecuted by the Inquisition. Compare "En quoi consiste l'inspiration Occitanienne," in *EHP*, 75–84.
18. *Ep*, 141 ff. (*NR*, 109 ff.).
19. *Ep*, 154 (*NR*, 119).

Each successive regime having destroyed at an ever increasing rate local and regional life, it had finally ceased to exist. France was like a dying man whose members are already cold, and whose heart alone goes on beating. Hardly anywhere was there any real throb of life except in Paris; but even there, as soon as you reached the suburbs, an atmosphere of moral decay began to make itself felt.[20]

Anyone who today knows the still vital diversity of the French landscape sees at once that this is a strongly exaggerated picture.[21] The aversion to technology in general and to administrative technology in particular is certainly exaggerated. According to Weil, they brought nothing that could even begin to make up for what they had swept aside.

It nevertheless remains true that the present state of technology has everywhere led to greater monotony; technology is not only an aesthetic problem—as if that were not reason enough—but an eminently political one to the degree that the readiness to participate depends on a multilevel, associative, historical, aesthetic, and affective bond that, for example, can only work to negate the mania for incorporation, which causes distinct, naturally evolved entities to vanish in favor of "administrative units." No doubt Weil also touched on a truth when she wrote about life in French provincial towns. "In those outwardly peaceful days before the war, the ennui of the little French provincial towns constituted perhaps as real a form of cruelty as that of more visible atrocities."[22]

There can be no question that this was the result of first an absolutist and then a Jacobin and Bonapartist centralism. But the fact that this price bought the almost unparalleled splendor of the capital had no bearing on Weil's ascetic temperament. And perhaps the brilliance of Paris is no consolation for someone who must spend her days in the dreary provinces.[23]

Encouraging regional life would be one of the urgent tasks devolving on postwar France, wrote Weil. But, she argued, this effort must not

20. *Ep*, 157 (*NR*, 122).
21. For a more balanced account of the period between the wars, see Curtius, *Die französische Kultur*, 37 ff.
22. *Ep*, 158 (*NR*, 122). On ennui as a causative factor in the crisis of patriotism among the bourgeoisie, see *Ep*, 198 (*NR*, 155).
23. See the affectionate chapter "Paris" in Curtius, *Die französische Kultur*, 151–73.

lead to separatism, for in the course of time so many ties had grown up that partition could cause only deeper uprooting.[24] A revitalization of the regional areas, an abatement of the absolute claim of the national state, would smooth the way for a link to something larger as well as something smaller than the nation, Weil wrote, anticipating a European community. Only, what a scandal it would be in her view that such a community was to be initiated by way of the European Coal and Steel Community, an industrial concentration! What is true is that supranational bonds and regional life signify a modification of the sovereignty of the national state. At the very least, connections between related subnational cultural groups that happen to find themselves on opposite sides of national frontiers—the Basques, the Catalonians, and the Provençals, the Bretons and the Welsh, the Irish and the like— should be brought about, an exchange Weil seemed to expect to bear significant fruit.[25] Here we sense the degree to which Weil's late discovery of the meaning of indigenous traditions is freighted with romanticism and represents a continuation of her Celtomaniac anti-Romanism.[26] Her Marxist critics in particular have tried to use such beliefs to group her with nationalist reactionary thinkers, just as they delighted in accusing her, the comrade in arms of the Free French, of serving as a political model of the "Vichy type."[27] We must not block access to an idea by stressing an association that does not apply, attractive as it may be. It is therefore important to heed Weil's admonition: "That the Vichy Government should have put forward a regionalist doctrine is neither here nor there. Its only mistake in this connection has been in not applying it. Far from always preaching the exact opposite of its various battle cries, we ought to adopt many of the ideas launched by the propaganda services of the National Revolution, but turn them into realities."[28]

The desire to give real life to Vichy's slogans could characterize a large part of the thinking of the Résistance, which, like important

24. *Ep,* 206 (*NR,* 162).
25. *Ep,* 207–8 (*NR,* 163).
26. On "Celtomania," see Curtius, *Die französische Kultur,* 53.
27. See Dujardin, *Idéologie et politique,* 173. Dujardin also makes the comparison between this model and those of Plato, Sorel, Catholic social doctrine, Helvetius, and so forth. If one is a dialectician, one can compare apples and oranges and pears. See also ibid., 181, 195.
28. *Ep,* 211 (*NR,* 166).

elements of the ideology of the collaborators, went back to the shared—antiliberal—tone of the opposition of the 1930s. Since Dujardin could not list Weil among the prophets and pioneers of the historical transformation, he was determined to give her the stigma of someone in the opposition: he depended on her antiliberalism in order to stamp her a reactionary.[29] Thus he charged her with abandoning, in her later thinking, the republican triad of *liberté, égalité, fraternité* in favor of the "values" of the Vichy slogan. He accused her of wishing to cluster her political ideas around "family" and "fatherland"—an allusion to her thinking about the need for roots. These slogans are cited only for the sake of their emotional associations; after all, who can object to *famille* and *patrie* if they are not clichés, are not set up as absolute abstractions? And Dujardin knew better: he carefully avoided mentioning the first word in the Vichy slogan—work. Work stands at the center of the social connections of political articulation that, next to the geographic cultural values, in Weil's view, were swallowed up by the centralized state. Among the "very complicated, but also very human" net of medieval loyalties, whose variety is what prevents totalitarian closure, she named towns, provinces, countries, and Christendom, but the only social link that engaged Weil's attention was the guilds. The estates, the parliaments, and the seigniories are nowhere mentioned.[30] Even as she bemoaned the abolition of the guilds, she wanted to indicate her distance from contemporary corporatism:

> Much as the French Revolution did, by suppressing the trades corporations, to encourage technical progress, morally speaking it created a corresponding amount of evil, or at any rate finally sealed an evil already partly accomplished. It cannot be too often repeated that nowadays, whenever people refer to such organizations, in no matter what circles, the last thing they have in mind is anything resembling the old trades corporations.[31]

Syndicalism had preserved a strong element of loyalty in working-class solidarity, Weil wrote. Two things impair the bond that evokes loyalty within the trade-union movement, however: the—reformist—primacy of money, the *gros sous,* that turns professional ethics into a rule

29. See Dujardin, *Idéologie et politique,* chap. 8.
30. *Ep,* 135 (*NR,* 104).
31. *Ep,* 159–60 (*NR,* 124).

of commercial honesty by stressing the commodity nature of work, and the—revolutionary—delusion of existential rebellion with apocalyptic expectations.[32] The role of trade unions in tariff negotiations, in strikes when the need for these arises, and in similar functions remains for Weil indispensable within the context of the balance of power, but in her opinion it must be played by organizations other than the representatives of humanistic aspirations.[33]

Weil saw the guild as something that ties people into an awareness of the past and a vision of the future within the context of their work. At the same time it represents an environment for ideas that must operate *outside* the machinery of government while at the same time being able to affect the government. Weil postulated the activity of such groups in postwar France and saw a highly promising attempt in the Catholic workers' youth group JOC (Jeunesse Ouvrière Chrétienne). What Weil was searching for in such *milieux d'idées* was a site where the *volonté générale* could be found, safeguarded from the passions of power, a site that, in her plans, must keep in touch with work. Her recommendations for the actual translation of truth, once it is found, into action—that is, the possibility of influencing the government—remained sketchy in the extreme.[34] Her corporatism is neither organic nor *"mutuelliste"*— even if it was indebted to the latter. Instead, it practices abstinence from power. She did not make the corporatist assumption that the interests that can relevantly be represented are to be found in the professions; instead, she searched for the circumstances that make possible the kind of thinking that is not self-interested and therefore leads to the *volonté générale*. Unlike the framers of the American Constitution, she made no attempt to turn the necessity of representation into a political virtue, one that promises to create harmony between freedom and order. Prey to so many aberrations of modernism, Weil ignored the greatest achievement of the modern age, to work out the problem of a just government in a corrupt society, and her recommendations remained hopelessly conceived as postulates.

According to Weil, the French state devoured everything, until, having nothing to rest on, it collapsed. And how is the damage to be

32. *Ep*, 160–61 (*NR*, 124–25).
33. See *EL*, 157, 170.
34. *Ep*, 212 (*NR*, 166–67).

repaired? Weil speaks of "The duty, which falls to the State, to ensure that the people are provided with a country *[patrie]* to which they really feel they belong."[35] The gorged wolf, moved by divine inspiration, spews out the kids he has swallowed and, as if that were not enough, takes over their education.

The social deracination illustrated by the example of the decline of the trade unions is the counterpart of the deracination of work through dedication to machinery and bureaucracy, which Weil discussed at length and which we need not take up here. We need only point to her hopes for decentralization, which she linked to the gradual substitution of electricity for other forms of energy. In this hope she was by no means alone. Her statements on this topic coincide with those of Joseph Caillaux or George Duhamel, wrote Dujardin. He quoted, "The world, as well as France, must move in the direction of small industry in agriculture and the manual trades, which are made so easy by electricity."[36] However, those things the quotation mentions as a good French example are merely postulates for Weil. But we need not note once again the extent to which Weil underestimated the survival of traditional work methods and social mores in France.

The second aspect of Weil's historical sketch of the decline of the object of patriotism is striking for the clarity with which she grasps the stages in the development of contemporary political concepts that make power absolute.[37] But the lack of historical precision reduces the value of this retrospective. The basic, though imperfect, opening of the historical horizon permits Weil to seize on a differentiation that lately has tended to be suppressed all too frequently and systematically: the qualitative distinction, still present to the fifteenth century, between good political order and disorder—that is, the possibility of distinguishing between a king and a tyrant, a distinction that remains significant apart from the number of rulers, since democracies are also sovereignties and represent, not the government of each person over himself, but the rule of all over each one. The disappearance of this problem from political reflection is described by Bertrand de Jouvenel: "The theoreticians who for a long

35. *Ep*, 213 (*NR*, 167).
36. Dujardin, *Idéologie et politique*, 171, quoting Maurice Crouzet, *Histoire générale des civilisations*, 7:178.
37. "Déracinement et nation," in *Ep*, 129–233 ("Uprootedness and Nationhood," in *NR*, 99–184).

time concerned themselves with the question of how a public power should act now only cared to determine in what way they must be legitimated. Thus it only remains to judge whether the embodiments of public power are in possession of a valid title, but not whether they acted properly."[38]

Searching for the properties of the French state that make the French hate it, Weil, specifically referring to the authority of Montesquieu, pointed out that, after Charles V, France ceased to be a monarchy, declining to the status of a despotism.[39] What is important here are not the very loosely manipulated and oddly documented historical details but the basic distinction between—in the words of Fortescue— a *dominium politicum aut regale* (rule political and royal) and a *dominium regale tantum* (rule merely royal) except that Weil would consider the first to be a formal contradiction. The problem of the emancipation of the Crown from power, which the Jacobin republic failed to solve by abolishing the Crown but attempted instead to explain away with devastating consequences, Weil tried to solve by the reverse device of abolishing power. Her insight that such a kingdom cannot be of this world is compromised by the fact that she takes the other world to be a kind of geometrical figure. The points of departure of her political thinking are promising because she did not make internal systematic coherence into the criterion of truth. Where the absolute could not be found, she made an effort to seek relativities directed toward the absolute. Thus she wrote of Richelieu, who understandably played a key role in her historical survey:

> Here is more or less what he said: We should beware of applying the same rules to the welfare of the State as to that of the soul; for the welfare of souls is attended to in the world above, whereas that of States is only attended to in this world.
>
> This is cruelly exact. A Christian ought to be able to draw therefrom but one conclusion: That whereas to the welfare of the soul, or in other words to God, a total, absolute, and unconditional loyalty is owed; the welfare of the State is a cause to which only a limited and conditional loyalty is owed.[40]

38. Jouvenel, *Über Souveränität*, 16.
39. *Ep*, 135 (*NR*, 104).
40. *Ep*, 149 (*NR*, 115).

"Politique d'abord," said Maurras. But politics with a view to what, asked Weil, and she reminded us that to posit an absolute value in this world is idolatry.[41] She epitomized the loss of substance and legitimacy that absolutism signifies in a brilliant example of her lively style: "L'Etat c'est moi. Ce n'est pas la une pensée de roi."[42]

Although the Revolution put away the worn-out symbol of the king, it left the repressive governmental apparatus and strengthened centralization. Patriotism, grounded in the pride of national sovereignty, illuminated the paradox of referring, not to a continuity, but to a breach. Further, national sovereignty turns out to be an empty phrase. "The operation whereby national sovereignty was substituted for royal sovereignty under the Revolution had only this drawback, the nonexistence of national sovereignty. As in the case of Orlando's mare, that was the only defect to be found."[43]

On the merry-go-round of the alternating modes of loyalty those, too, proved to be "true patriots" who were prepared to serve France under all regimes—that is, to serve the French state. These were precisely those like Talleyrand, who would appear as *archi-traître* to a later generation.[44] Weil then continued to follow events to 1940 in an attempt to explicate the accumulation of disgust. This interpretation is replete with both perspicacity and originality.[45]

The basic experience that motivates this historical excursus, which at times is somewhat eccentric, is that of a national unity that resulted from the destruction of all intermediate links of political articulation and the loss of individuality of the population by radical atomization. The precise degree to which Weil exaggerated the pulverization of French society would require a careful historical analysis, which cannot be provided here. In any case, Weil's judgment goes as follows. "The sudden collapse of France in June, 1940, which surprised every one all over the world, simply showed to what extent the country was uprooted."[46]

41. *Ep*, 150 (*NR*, 116).
42. *Ep*, 151 (*NR*, 117: "*L'Etat, c'est moi* . . . is not a kingly conception").
43. *Ep*, 152 (*NR*, 118).
44. *Ep*, 144 (*NR*, 111).
45. *Ep*, 146 (*NR*, 114).
46. *E*, 49 (*NR*, 48).

Like a tree with rotted roots, the country fell. But the illness did not infect France alone, even if it took different forms elsewhere. "If France offered a spectacle more painful than that of any other European country, it is because modern civilization with all its toxins was in a more advanced stage there than elsewhere, with the exception of Germany. But in Germany, uprootedness had taken on an aggressive form, whereas in France it was characterized by inertia and stupor." England, on the other hand, with its well-preserved and living tradition, she continued, was best able to withstand the first wave of the attack.[47] "Spiritually, the struggle between Germany and France in 1940 was in the main not a struggle between barbarism and civilization or between good and evil, but between the first of these two errors [idolatry] and the second [the loss of feeling for the holy]."[48]

47. E, 49 (NR, 48–49).
48. EL, 18 (SWA, 56).

SEVENTEEN

The Cult of Legitimacy

There is a conflict between the demand for purity of individual think-ing—or, in Simone Weil's later writings, the uncreated portion of the human soul—and the necessity of defiling social action. It is a conflict of which Weil was very much aware. Perhaps she was not entirely consistent in her egalitarianism and in the claim to universal validity of her asceticism, but she was also very insightful when she wrote to Maurice Schumann, "My mental disposition [conformation mentale] is such that I cannot evade suffering and danger. It is lucky that not everyone has this disposition, or any organized action would be impossible, but I can't help myself."[1]

Danger and suffering, which in Weil's schema are the only things that can eradicate the defilement caused by every action (as the opposite of passion, as autonomy),[2] cannot, at least empirically, be expected of everyone. Obviously Weil was quite clear about the limits of the strict consistency of an ethical approach. She strove for nothing more than for "the trained relentlessness in viewing the realities of life, and the ability to face such realities and to measure up to them inwardly."[3]

The fact that such efforts could not make their way out of the mists of epistemological formulations is another problem. Weil was always aware of the temptation of the acosmistic "inner life."[4] Acosmism is

1. *EL,* 199.
2. See *EL,* 47.
3. Max Weber, *Politik als Beruf,* 65 (*Politics as a Vocation,* 53).
4. P, 1:9 (PE, vii).

one of the "lies" through which people try to escape from their duty, obligation, responsibility *(obligation)*.[5]

In addition to this "spurious mysticism, spurious contemplation," idolatry and the denial of responsibility are lies of this kind. Idolatry means positing one or more objects of this world as if they contained the perfection that alone is obligatory. The denial of responsibility—that is, of orienting ourself to the good—is always a lie, since everyone at times pronounces an opinion on good and evil, if only to find fault with someone else.[6] Political action is enrolled in an unbalanced relation, a relation of strict—that is, in one sense, absolute—obligation to a limited, relative object. Here, too, Weil inclined to polarity. "Never in this world can there be any dimensional equality between an obligation and its subject. The obligation is something infinite, the subject of it is not."[7]

Politics, like any obligation, is not therefore any less necessary. "We have to accept the situation provided for us, and which subjects us to absolute obligations in regard to things that are relative, limited, and imperfect."[8] The obligation to conditional things hinges on their relation to the good. Thus obedience to the state is a loyalty displayed, not for its own sake, but for the sake of a higher authority, not unlike children who obey a mediocre governess for the sake of their absent parents.[9]

Loyalty is owed to the constitutional authorities *in loco parentis*. The government institutions appear legitimate—that is, entitled to expect obedience—to the extent that they are able to represent the true foundation of loyalty. The representative respect—corresponding to the principle of orthodox icon worship—takes the place of the obedient contempt of the disgruntled citizen. The transformation is possible because the respect is offered to a representative reality that is not grounded in negation itself, a reality that the negating—that is, the self-confirming—finite individual cannot call up.[10]

5. *Ep*, 201 (*NR*, 158).
6. *Ep*, 202 (*NR*, 158).
7. *Ep*, 201 (*NR*, 157).
8. *Ep*, 202 (*NR*, 158).
9. *Ep*, 227 (*NR*, 178).
10. On this problem, even beyond its political dimensions, see *PSO*, 135 ff., and the discussion in Schumann, *La mort*, 86–101.

Alain's negation begins the attempt at symbolic legitimation of government, in the paradoxical form of a permanent opposition. A nonmaterial contrast to authority can both be an institution and be thought of as free of any defiling participation in authority. "I would never say that the powerful director is mad," Alain wrote about Mussolini in 1930, "but just the reverse, that the intoxication caused by power is just as strong as the result of wine. Wisdom consists in not drinking."[11]

Perhaps Alain could have been reminded of Socrates, whose name he frequently used for his own purposes, who kept a clear head at dawn after the night-long symposium. Wisdom does not mean abstinence but the ability to drink without becoming drunk. For Alain, however, abstinent politics is the only true politics. "What remains to those who look for power under no form whatever? True politics remains a constant effort against militaristic and political despotism, which are one and the same."[12] The will to emancipation, which constantly rebels against the "powers," does not express itself in great, spectacular actions.

> The true power of the voters . . . is determined more by resistance to the powers than by reforming actions. . . . The important thing is to set up a little barricade every day or, if you will, to bring some king before a people's court each day. Let us add that, by daily preventing a new stone from being added to the walls of the Bastille, we spare ourselves the trouble of having to take it down again.[13]

The adjective *small* characterizes everything valued by the radical, even his own revolution. Here too the idea comes from Comte. The Republic institutionalized the revolution of small steps. The daily accumulation of small revolutionary gestures forestalls the horror of the one great revolution. The emblem of the republican order that fights tyrants is universal suffrage:

> From this standpoint the significance of universal suffrage is crystal clear. The very fact that a representative is elected is fatal to the monarchy. This is even more true when the representative is a

11. *Politique,* 186.
12. Ibid., 12.
13. Ibid., 7–8.

> republican, but in fact it makes no difference. Every voter expresses himself against the authorities merely by sticking a ballot in the box. To vote means to be radical. And in a certain sense we can say that every ballot is unquestionably cast for the republic.[14]

For Alain, the true meaning of the act of voting lies in the confirmation against the "authorities," which he invokes not only in fact but most of all symbolically. By comparison, the outcome of an election, the formation of majorities, making concrete political programs possible or preventing them—these all are immaterial. "Everything else—reforms, social organization, new laws—all this is determined very much more by the circumstances and conditions of work than by the will of the peoples. Even an absolutist king would without a doubt have issued the law concerning occupational accidents."[15]

On the one hand, then, according to this view, given the situation, clear limits are set to any opportunities of meeting social problems by way of political participation and influencing control. It is the topos that Weil, in the tradition of outdoing the left, elaborated into a functional repression theory. On the other hand, keeping the state in check is a postulate Alain sets all the more easily as a certain determinism emerges in a society imagined separate from the state. The important thing is to dethrone kings, but even under an absolutist ruler the introduction of workers' compensation insurance would have been inevitable. The occasion for the *Propos* from which the cited passages are taken is characteristic for Alain: his argument is directed against those who oppose the vote for women because it would mean a shift of election results to the right. His reasoning addresses the demand for the women's vote as precisely what it was: a consequent extension of radical-liberal claims as they had become effective in the course of the nineteenth century:

> Elections mean the sovereignty of the people and a challenge to kings. If women are given the right to vote, their ballots would mainly mean: republic. By this act each of them will assume a slightly larger space against the authorities; each of them will be invested with political power; and the republic will rest on more

14. Ibid., 8.
15. Ibid.

solid foundations. To vote for the king and the priest nevertheless means to vote against them.[16]

A political system that is able to reconcile universal suffrage with monarchic representation is unthinkable to the radical mentality. An England that does not show the Manichaean polarity of *peuple-pouvoir* should really not exist. For Weil, a syndicalist and pessimist, republican elections were no more than part of the "illusory" parliamentary game, and for this reason universal suffrage plays only a subordinate role in her reflections. Only in the phase of taking root would the franchise become significant as an essential element of republican legitimacy. In this phase, however, in contrast to her teacher, she was well able to understand monarchic legitimacy, even if, at least in the case of France, she considered it outmoded. The essential part, wrote Alain, was not how authority is derived.[17] Weil went further. Institutional forms could be suited in different degrees to promote the legitimacy of government, even though they do not contain within themselves the substance of legitimation: "A king can be legitimate. The head of a parliamentary government can be legitimate. A king can be illegitimate, as can a parliamentary head, even when the most rigorous procedures have been observed."[18]

The violation of legality can undermine the legitimacy of the regime, as did government by *decret-lois* in the final years of the Third Republic, but this is not a necessary result. The British wartime government, wrote Weil, also deviated from legality, but no prime minister was ever as legitimate as Winston Churchill.[19] "The administration of a head of state is legitimate if above all things it desires to be the legitimate head and if almost the totality of the people view him as the legitimate ruler and sense that he wishes to continue to be so."[20]

Legitimacy therefore requires that both rulers and ruled are subject to a higher permanent law. Legitimacy is the axis of the balance that

16. Ibid., 7–8.
17. Ibid., 9.
18. *EL,* 59.
19. *EL,* 60.
20. *EL,* 59. See also *EL,* 66: "If who governs is motivated by a concern for justice and the public good, if the people have the assurance that it is thus and reasonable grounds to believe that this shall continue, if the chief does not wish to retain power unless the people maintain this certitude, there is legitimate government."

creates order, an equilibrium that emanates from a superordinate order; it is present in our world as an infinite smallness, as a point. In the geometric imagery of Weil the point is both real and nonexistent, since it has no dimensions. It is characteristically nonmaterial and decisive in the balance of material things. "Balance represents the submission of one order to another order transcending it and present in it under the form of something infinitely small. Thus a veritable royalty would represent the perfect polity [cité]."[21]

The philosopher-king can realize justice within society without conjuring up the perils attendant on reifying the institution. The true king is the wise man, whether or not he rules, and thus potentially everyone is the embodiment of that "infinitesimal" psychic element that roots him in the overriding order. It is typical of the overall tone of Weil's thinking that for her the archetype of this wise man is not the silent Socrates of the *Statesman* but the Stoic slave: "Each one in society is that infinitely small something which represents the order transcending the social order and infinitely greater than the latter. Cf. the Stoics: The sage is always king, even though he may be a slave."[22]

Legitimacy is based on the ruler's will not only to justify himself rhetorically but also to be genuinely legitimate, as well as on the subjects' understanding that the rulers have such a will—that is, that they are inclined to justice now and in future. Weil saw positive and negative mechanisms to promote this will and to strengthen the ties with legitimacy.[23] We will have occasion to consider the negatives in our discussion of controlling institutions.

For kings, the positives are education, consecration, and ceremony; for parliamentary governments they are elections. Weil sees the principal significance of the election ritual to lie in its effect not on the consciousness of the voter but on that of the elected candidate. It is only because she came to believe that the, as it were, sacramental effect of election will have an effect on the person who is elected, as consecration will affect the consecrated individual, that she felt free to abandon her earlier theses. At that time she thought of the entire process of political representation as an exercise in dissimulation. "The function [vertu] of

21. *C*, 3:83–84 (*N*, 2:466).
22. *C*, 3:83 (*N* 2:66).
23. *EL*, 66.

elections consists, not in the fact of selection—which results more or less arbitrarily—but in the feeling it imparts to the elected candidate that he has been chosen and is therefore under an obligation."[24]

In time, as we will see, Weil developed a sense for the symbolic representation of truth. But when it came to descriptive representation, this change did not make her abandon either her fundamental antiparliamentarism or her Proudhonist aspirations. The policies of the Third Republic that made it hostile to participation were the source of her disbelief that elections had the potential of bringing about substantial programmatic decisions. In her last phase Weil returned to the very radical habit of the politics of the symbolic gesture. But now she interpreted it according to its real significance—that is, the symbolic legitimation of the regime. And this is no "mere" symbolism; rather, it commits the ruler, who rules in the awareness that he is permitted to rule in the name of the dignity of the subject qua *citoyen*. Although Alain was a high priest of radicalism, he also condemned all ceremonies, considering them mystifications. For Weil in her late phase the problem of mystification remained acute, but it no longer applied to every ceremonial act. "Ceremony: Process by which that which is inauthentically holy, and which is linked to the collective, is expunged by the experience of the authentic—which emerges more strongly in every individual than does the first—horribly easy decline. The church is a collective. Those who believe in Christ because of the Church and not the other way around are idolaters."[25]

It is hard to persuade modern populists of the significance of ceremonial for politics—though they engage in it all the time. It is extremely difficult, in a nation such as the United States in which the head of state (the "Crown") was never separated from the head of pragmatic government (and patronage), to imagine a highest source of honor that is not *eo ipso* compromising. In this context the French liberals practice better than they preach, since they know full well that to be genuinely republican, it is hardly necessary for a republic to be stingy in bestowing honors. All institutions have a symbolic dimension, in that they are not mere objects of the external world, about which we can think, but are realities that must first be thought up, that come into being in

24. Ibid., 67.
25. Ibid., 158.

the act of their symbolic articulation. In this sense they are analogous to language, and Weil herself made the comparison. And again like language, they are not arbitrarily established, nor are they conventional. "Political institutions basically develop a symbolic language. A language is never something arbitrary, a convention; far from it. Something of this nature grows like a plant."[26]

A political order can be said to be legitimate to the extent that it is "symbolic," that is, to the extent that it reflects and directs attention to the order of the "whole"—in the mode of necessity or in the mode of love—and is itself imbued or transparent for that order. Force on the other hand means usurpation by a part in the name of the whole, which makes it both illegitimate and idolatrous.[27]

Because symbols are in fact parts that stand for the whole, they are always in danger of becoming opaque and occluding rather than transmitting meaning. They then become a part of the mechanism of force.

Monarchy, according to Weil, is a worn-out symbol that, in spite of support from someone like Bernanos, can have no place in contemporary France, desirable as it might be in many respects.[28] It seems that Weil saw the Crown as a sign pointing beyond the temporal sphere and thus contributing to the growth of roots. She also felt, however, that for this purpose it must be emancipated from power not only in itself but also in the consciousness of the citizens. The forms of social life must be arranged in such a way that they remind us of the otherworldly ground of legitimacy. In the French case, monarchy is incapable of this task, since in the consciousness of the French people, the negative associations predominate.

> The forms of social life must be arranged in such a way that they constantly remind the population in the symbolic language the citizenry understands—the language that is most consonant with its traditions, its ties—of the sacral character of this loyalty, the

26. Ibid., 59; see also *Ep*, 231 (*NR*, 182): "The State is sacred, not in the way an idol is sacred, but in the way common objects serving a religious purpose, like the altar, the baptismal water, or anything else of the kind, are sacred. Everybody knows they are only material objects; but material objects which are regarded as sacred because they serve a sacred purpose. That is the sort of majesty appropriate for the State."
27. See the subtle discussion of Kühn, *Deuten als Entwerden*, 184.
28. *E*, 137 (*NR*, 169–70).

freely given promise from which it grows, the strict obligations that result from it.

From this perspective, in France the republic, universal suffrage, independent trade unions, all are absolutely essential. But they are far from enough.[29]

But in a republic the ruler is collective, he is "the social," and therefore poses special problems.

29. *EL,* 55.

EIGHTEEN

The Antisocial Contract and Love for the *Cité*

Simone Weil had been taught by Alain: "Small party or large party, small newspaper or large newspaper, league or nation, church or assembly, all these collective entities lose the spirit *[esprit]* in their search for unity."[1] Alain countered the "social," which tends to sacrifice the spirit to unity, with an "antisocial" contract, arising from the "democratic spirit."

> The most obvious thing about the democratic spirit may be that it is antisocial. . . . Society can be seen as a kind of great beast . . . it seems to me that every democratic movement is directed against the reactions of the great beast and tends to balance the natural community—let us say, the social organism—with a kind of contract that is mistakenly called the social contract, since in reality it is antisocial. Thus it is vowed and sworn that we will withstand the instinctive stirrings of the great beast and, as far as possible, make them subject to the rules of justice that will be accepted by individuals.[2]

The characteristic reference to Rousseau's title indicates the interpretation of society as a natural phenomenon, not merely as the result of social denaturing. A counterforce to social forces is sought beyond nature (natural law), in an alliance of the *esprit* of thinking

1. *Politique,* 306.
2. Ibid., 28.

individuals. Weil modifies Alain's qualification of the antisocial spirit as "democratic." "Democratic thought contains a serious error—that is, it confuses assent with a particular form of assent, which is not the only one there is and which, like any form, can easily become empty."[3]

In that for Weil the antisocial spirit no longer rests only in the left-leaning posture of finite individuals, the antisocial contract justifies not only tolerable social conditions but also republican legitimacy, the possibility of an *obéissance consentie,* as the ground in which liberty can grow.[4] Democracy, as well as the law and the person, cannot be absolute goods for Weil because they are part of a middle region, a region that comes very close to the Platonic *metaxy* in its concrete application.[5] Her explicit use of the term *metaxy,* however, is a misnomer, which is characteristic of her modernistically skewed reading of Plato. For her, *metaxy* is the bridge that allows the uniting of man with his true self, the "eternal part" of the soul with God. She included in the concept art, methodical science, and, of course, the prototype of all the others, work. In search of contemplation *in actu,* which she correctly considered the development of human nature, she committed the modern error par excellence: confusing the difference between potential and actual with the difference between theoretical and practical.

Thus, for Weil in her later years, democracy was not a good in itself—not an end but a means. It belonged to the middle region. "Democracy, the power of the majority, are not goods. They are means with regard to the good that are correctly or mistakenly considered effective."[6] The fact that power is exerted by everyone or by the majority does not cleanse it of its demonic nature. Weil was more consistent than Alain in equating all rule with tyranny.[7] "In the same way, there is no guarantee for democracy, or for the protection of the person against the collectivity, without a disposition of public life relating it to the higher good which is impersonal and unrelated to any political form."[8]

The *modi* by which the good is crystallized in society, the legitimizing ties to justice, must be invented, since, according to Weil, there are no

3. *EL,* 52.
4. See ibid.
5. *EL,* 43 (*SWR,* 77).
6. *EL,* 127.
7. See *EL,* 127, as well as *OL,* 208 (*OLE,* 158): "When force changes hands, it still remains a relation of stronger to weaker, a relation of dominance."
8. *EL,* 43 (*SWR,* 77).

models.[9] Because, as we saw, her theory of man does not admit of any genuine friendship—nor, *a fortiori,* any political friendship—as the basis of a legitimate and ordered shared existence, Weil was forced to look for substitute constructions of Aristotelian concord *(homonoia);* she found a kind of revisionist Rousseauism to sketch these within the framework of the antisocial contract. According to Weil, republican legitimacy springs from the *volonté générale.*[10] Her reading of Rousseau, as that of her teacher before her, is eclectic, however. Rousseau saw two ways to solve the problem of freedom:

> a. either that the individual becomes moralized and seeks the happiness of his *"être intelligent"* in the true order that his conscience lovingly enfolds
>
> b. or that man, who has been denatured into the citizen, identifies himself with the community of republicans and, as a participant in this community, wants the *"volonté générale"* that issues the laws that are binding on him as an individual.[11]

Both Alain and his disciple renamed the social contract because they excluded the second choice. They deliberately constituted the "social" as a tyranny of opinion—what should not be—as an adaptation to the stirrings of the great beast. The only solution that remains is finding shared truth and justice by virtue of the individual's moral-virtuous desire in the "silence of the passions."[12] "When a single collective passion seizes an entire country, the whole country is united in crime. When two or four or five or ten collective passions share it, then it is scattered into several gangs of criminals."[13]

Weil went further; she did not merely point out the weakness of an order based on the mechanistic mutual neutralization of various special interests, totally eliminating reason. Whatever is not pure reason is, for Weil, pure passion, error, and crime. Where the Stoic model considers any deviation from pure reason to be criminal to begin with, pluralism of any kind is unthinkable.

9. See *EL,* 44 (*SWR,* 78); 127.
10. *EL,* 127.
11. Iring Fetscher, "Rousseaus Freiheitsvorstellungen," 137.
12. See *EL,* 127 ff.
13. *EL,* 130.

The search for a meaningful—that is, more or less genuine—con-sensus between individuals is possible in principle, according to Weil, because opinions developed independently of each other are congruent in their reasonable parts. They deviate from each other, on the other hand, in their errors, which are rooted in passion, the *principium indi-viduationis*.[14] But even the possibility of consensus dwindles when the clash of collective passions replaces the silence of the passions.

> The [collective] passions do not cancel each other out, as would be the case for a dust cloud of individual passions fused into a mass. Their number is too small, each one's power is too great for there to be a balance. The battle intensifies. They clash with a truly hellish din, which makes it impossible to hear, if only for the length of a second, the voice of justice and truth—which at the best of times are almost imperceptible.[15]

Weil was quite right in her belief that the realization of a dispassionate unanimity, which cannot be friendship, has no precedent in actual societies. In spite of gaining a dimension of rootedness in human existence, the buried *homonoia* is not laid bare by Weil; but—and this holds true to a large degree for Alain before her—the dangers of a reduced substitute like the *volonté générale* are felt acutely: the problem of propaganda, forced homogeneity, transferring *amor sui* to the collective.[16]

For Alain the subjects, in their "Aesopian wisdom," were also the embodiment of the antisocial *esprit*. They were in a position to put a stop to tyranny because they failed in their inner devotion. In the rhetorical culture of the radical republic, the power to praise and especially to criticize, leaving out *les importants,* seems sufficient. This criticism seems to hit the core of tyrannical infatuation: the addiction to recognition.[17]

14. Ibid., 128.
15. Ibid., 130.
16. Ibid., 129: "The true spirit of 1789 consists in thinking not that something is just because the people want it but that under certain conditions the will of the people has a better chance than any other will to be in accordance with justice." Ibid., 130: "When there is collective passion in a country it is likely that any particular will whatsoever is closer to justice and reason than the general will, or what constitutes its caricature."
17. *Politique,* 38.

"And we may not say that it is a small thing; for each tyrant wants to be adored. The more passion he has, the more is this true, and the more we have a hold on him if we understand how not to adore power."[18]

But in Weil's view no one can succeed in summoning up this refusal, because those who experience—that is, incur the reality of—domination are unable for that very reason to articulate the experience; and those who have the capacity of articulation in their turn lack the experience. "Many indispensable truths, which could save men, go unspoken for reasons of this kind; those who could utter them cannot formulate them and those who could formulate them cannot utter them. If politics were taken seriously, finding a remedy for this would be one of its more urgent problems."[19]

Only those who by a kind of miracle of grace are able to endure in suffering without taking refuge in despair or illusion have achieved such a saintly status that they can function as embodiments of the *esprit*.[20] Love of the reality of a world that manifests itself openly only in endured suffering is a delusion, a *folie d'amour*. Only a holy madness is able to eliminate libidinous and social delusions. Weil gave us one of the countless examples of the transition—expressed perhaps most elegantly by Erasmus—from pagan *stultitia* to Pauline *môria*.[21]

To the extent that Weil has a concrete image of the "crystallization of the good in society," it consists of the call for a new saintliness of this sort, one that does not permit so much as the awarding of a medal or other recognition in the world. She envisaged an elite of *môroi* who do their work unrecognized and yet are inspiring:

> In the cultural area the masses are creative only when genuine elites inspire them. Today an elite must let the virtue of poverty in spirit blaze up among the wretched masses; to this end, this elite must first be poor not only in spirit but also in fact. Each day they must feel the pain of the humiliation of wretchedness in their soul and their flesh. There is no need of a Franciscan order. A hood, a monastery represent separation. These people must go among the masses and must touch them with nothing setting them apart.[22]

18. Ibid., 39.
19. *EL*, 28 (*SWA*, 64).
20. See *EL*, 48, 49, 56, 57; *AD*, 72.
21. On this topic, see Lynda G. Christian, "Metamorphoses of Erasmus' Folly."
22. *EL*, 105; see also *AD*, 95–107.

Weil never claimed or believed that she herself had attained this state; she merely felt unequivocally called to it. The strangest thing about it is that this stringently ascetic demand is not accompanied by apocalyptic hope.

Weil's legitimate ruler, like Alain's true politician, abstains from power in un-Socratic ways. Weil discovered that the radical trust in the *peuple* as an incarnation of the *esprit,* also in its exaltation of the "worker," was deceptive, since the truth of wretchedness is unbearable for most people and leads to escape into fantasy. The exceptions are only the few cases where the willing acceptance of wretchedness engenders a kind of saintliness in the person.

The ground of legitimacy, justice, can therefore be found neither in the active nor in the passive pole of the exercise of power. Weil found her way out of this quandary by laying bare a source of order that contemporary consciousness had buried. "Whether one exercises power *[force]* or is its target, contact with power transforms man into a thing. Only whatever escapes its touch deserves the name of the good. But God alone is free of this touch, as are in part those people who have transferred and hidden a part of their soul in love for Him."[23]

The just exercise of power continues to seem a *contradictio in adiecto,* since the just man is by Weil's definition not only powerless but also removed from contact with power.[24] The social order is a necessity that may not be dreamily interpreted away, but that does not make it a good, since "a great abyss separates the good from the necessary," as Weil never tired of quoting Plato. But by "the good" she understood the obligation of religiously heightened noumena and by "necessity," the facticity of phenomena.

Thought—now partnered with love—is, as it was earlier in Alain, fundamentally subversive. The purity of a scale of values "that is not of this world" is occasioned by the fact that the impulse urging toward an upward path must be the enemy of the forces that control society.[25]

As it is in Alain, the *esprit* is still antisocial, but it is no longer revolutionary. According to Weil, revolutionary action has no choice

23. Quoted in Davy, *Introduction,* 100.
24. See ibid., 101.
25. *OL,* 192 (*OLE,* 145).

but to compromise the purity of its objectives, since it must avail itself of power and of lies. Renouncing these methods, however, condemns the revolution to failure. Weil would never believe that the ends justify the means, since such a concept generally serves as an excuse for those who arrange their lives within a provisional solution full of misdeeds. The lucid application of the formula of the "lesser evil" is, for Weil, the only way to do justice both to the aspiration of the spirit for the perfect good and to the strictures of the social order.[26] Yet she was careful to disassociate herself from the "social-democratic misuse" of the formula of the "lesser evil" that excuses a listless acceptance of the status quo.

This brings us back to the liberal concept of rule as a necessary evil. "The social order, though necessary, is essentially evil, whatever it may be."[27]

In contrast to the individual, a nation cannot attain the status of saintly madness, since it has no soul—or, to put it another way, it is not a subject. "It can only be given to the individual soul, in its most secret manifestations, to follow the path leading to such perfection."[28] For the same reason no nation is in a position to bring the redemptive sacrifice of the just man, which is able to break through the circle of evil by absorbing the blow of the evildoer without passing it on.

"Whoever is uprooted himself uproots others. Whoever is rooted in himself doesn't uproot others."[29] The sacrifice of the just transforms power into suffering and so, in a "supernatural" way, puts a stop to libidinous expansion. "The false God changes suffering into violence; the true God changes violence into suffering."[30] This is one of the principal themes of Weil's unfinished play, "Venise sauvée," embodied in the character of Jaffier.[31] A nation cannot be holy, it cannot consider itself holy, make itself into an idol.[32] A national unity cemented by idolatry is the sign of an artificial identity.[33]

26. *OL*, 192–93 (*OLE*, 145–46).
27. *OL*, 193 (*OLE*, 146).
28. *Ep*, 204 (*NR*, 160).
29. *E*, 49 (*NR*, 48).
30. *C*, 3:143 (*N*, 2:507).
31. *Poèmes suivits de Venise sauvée*, 41–134. See also ibid., 48: "Automatic transmission of evil *[mal]* down to redemptive suffering." See also Rees, *Brave Men*, chap. 10.
32. *Ep*, 188 (*NR*, 147).
33. See Erikson, *Insight and Responsibility*, chap. 3.

The observation remains valid for our day, even if Weil in her anti-historical and anti-Semitic animus projects back to Israel the archetype of the nation gathered around the idol of itself: "No statues used to be erected of Jehovah; but Israel is the statue of Jehovah. This people was . . . [a]n artificial people. They were a tribe when they entered Egypt; they became a nation whilst in bondage. . . . Held together by a terrible violence *[violence]*. . . . Non-assimilable, non-assimilatory."[34]

The observation is certainly correct up to a point. But even here the low threshold of outrage does not allow for a distinction between the inadequate bond of nationalism and the systematic atomizing of the totalitarian second reality, with its absolute claim to validity that shatters all natural bonds. "It is quite unfair to say, for example, that fascism annihilates free thought; in reality it is the lack of free thought which makes it possible to impose by force official doctrines entirely devoid of meaning."[35]

The borderline is drawn by the courage required for free thought under totalitarian conditions and—not least—by the physical strength to resist, which marks the distinction, for example, between someone like Solzhenitsyn and some carping country bumpkin or other or even a hearty syndicalist train engineer. Alain had already noted, "When the fatherland represents the last and highest goal, the whole power system returns."[36]

For Alain the liberalist goal, in part inspired by Kant, is the individual. This objective must never be viewed as the means to other ends. Weil went further by considering the positing of any immanent absolute to be an outrage. This is even truer of collectivities, which as such lack any possibility of sharing in the supernatural absolute except through the presence of holy individuals in their midst.

It is easy to say, with Lamartine, "Ma patrie est partout où rayonne la France. . . . La vérité, c'est mon pays." Unfortunately, this would only make sense if France and truth were synonymous. France sometimes resorts to lying and committing injustice; this

---

34. *C*, 1:167 (*N*, 1:106).
35. *OL*, 155 (*OLE*, 119). See also Arendt, *Origins of Totalitarianism*, 317.
36. *Eléments*, 239.

has happened, is happening, and will happen again. For France is not God, not by a long chalk.[37]

If a nation were holy, radical pacifism would be an almost obligatory notion. Destruction, as the final consequence of refusing to defend oneself, would stand immeasurably higher as an *imitatio Christi* on a national scale than the most glorious resistance. But holiness is forbidden to collectivities.[38]

Because the nation's sacrifice cannot be redemptive, while the *patrie* for its part is the all-encompassing *milieu vital,* excluding all others, the latter must, if the need arises, be defended. Its annihilation would also destroy all other legitimate objects of loyalty. "[T]he members of a population which is enslaved to a foreign State are deprived of all these nucleuses at once, and not merely of the national one. Thus, when a nation finds itself in peril to this extent, the military obligation becomes the unique way of expressing all one's loyalties in this world."[39]

Weil resolved the internal contradiction of patriotic duty—an obligation that, by the nature of obligation, is an absolute as opposed to a limited good—by writing, "It does not require that we should give everything always; but that we should give everything sometimes."[40]

Defining the fatherland as a *milieu vital* avoids the lies and contradictions that surround patriotism.[41] The *patrie* is not good in itself, worthy of love; it is a bridge, an intercession, the embodiment of the special *modi* of a people's access to truth.

Respect and obligation are due a national community as the keeper of customs and historical traditions; they put its members in touch with things that transcend their individual existence and thus supply them with the consciousness of belonging, of being rooted. Weil gave the name of *cité* to any community that, in contrast to the "social," does not declare itself to be the all-devouring end in itself but works to mediate. "A clear label of the social: Intoxicating mixture, which

---

37. *Ep,* 188 (*NR,* 147). See also *Ep,* 168 (*NR,* 131): "To posit one's country as an absolute value that cannot be defiled by evil is manifestly absurd."

38. *Ep,* 204, 188 (*NR,* 160, 147).

39. *Ep,* 208 (*NR,* 163–65). Weil stipulated special conditions that made it possible to be a conscientious objector. In this context she insisted on differentiating between a distaste for killing and the fear of being killed.

40. *Ep,* 203 (*NR,* 159).

41. *Ep,* 206 (*NR,* 161–62).

includes every exuberance. Disguised devil. And yet the city *[cité]* . . . (Venice) . . . But that is not a form of the social; it is a human ambiance, of which we are no more aware than of the air we breathe. Contact with nature, with the past, with tradition: a *metaxy.*"[42]

Like the air we breathe, we become conscious of the goods of the *cité* when we are deprived of them. This, in any case, was the view of Weil, to whom the desolation of the rationalist tabula rasa was not vouchsafed until the collapse of 1940.

---

42. "Venise sauvée," in *Poèmes,* 46. See also *AD,* 174. In addition, see the admirable essay by Janet Patricia Little, "Society as Mediator in Simone Weil's 'Venise sauvée.'"

NINETEEN

Equilibrium and Control

The *cité* is not the Platonic polis, in which power, guided by reason, becomes the ordering factor. It is an attempt to gain the ethical substance of the polis while excluding power—a polis that has banished power. For Simone Weil the *cité* is desirable precisely because of its ephemeral nature, which her dialectic equates with the all-or-nothing of weakness.[1] The unique position of the Free French in London and the symbolic figure of de Gaulle seemed to Weil to offer an almost providential opportunity to initiate France's "taking root," even if realistically she had little expectation of success.[2] The fact that the London movement wielded the authority normally given to the state but, unlike an established state apparatus, had no way of imposing its authority enabled Weil to an extraordinary extent to practice the Socratic art of midwifery, modified with Rousseauian methods, for an entire nation:

> [T]he French movement in London is in the best possible position imaginable, if only it knows how to make use of it. The movement is neither more nor less official than what is required in order to be able to speak in the name of the country. Not possessing any governmental authority—even a nominal, fictitious authority—

---

1. See *Ep,* 218–19 (*NR,* 171–72). On fragile beauty as the thing that "preserves the city," see Little, "Society as Mediator." On the power of the beautiful to reveal reality as seen by Weil, see Miklos Vetö, "Le piège de Dieu: L'idée du beau dans la pensée de Simone Weil."
2. *EL,* 58 ff.

over the French people, based entirely upon free consent, it has something of a spiritual power *[pouvoir spirituel]* about it.[3]

Weil was fully aware that the English allies had the necessary means—the power—to bring about the liberation of France. Pragmatically and loyally she urged close and self-effacing collaboration in a manner that deviated markedly from the style of her leader.[4] But if her functional theory of power, with its claim to universality, were to be applicable, it would follow that France, liberated from the German occupation, would soon find itself under British rule. But evidently the English belonged to a different species. Let us not exaggerate: Weil certified Great Britain to be the least "uprooted" European nation—a judgment that is surely correct. But it becomes clear what a chore it is to have to interpret experienced reality as an exception to a doctrine that is fixed in the stars.

What obedience de Gaulle, working out of London, could find in France could not be anything but voluntary. For Weil that circumstance was the foundation that made legitimacy possible because those who issued the orders were not exposed to the corruptions of power and no fuel was being added to the antigovernment sentiment that was the norm for France. This special circumstance, however, would last only until the moment liberation was accomplished. Then it would become a matter of governing, and it would become essential to actually follow, as much as possible, the principle of the "lesser evil" within the "necessary evil" of government. In an arena of political action that is so narrowly limited, the negative *modi* of securing legitimacy become important.

According to Alain, the corrective assertion of the *esprit* against the authorities could be realized in great measure in the institutional framework of the Third Republic, provided there was constant vigilance. Weil, for her part, absolutely rejected the Third Republic, and along with the majority of the Résistance fighters, she did not mourn its collapse, no matter how much she tried to combat the successor government. Drafts for a possible optimal social condition drawn up during her period of "clear-sighted pessimism" survive; but there are no plans from her pen for any practical realistic approach to this optimum.

3. *Ep,* 250 (*NR,* 197–98). See also *Ep,* 259 (*NR,* 204–5).
4. *Ep,* 260 (*NR,* 206).

Weil did not share her teacher's "euphoria on the level of ultimate things."[5] For Alain the force of the spirit in its Sisyphean task is on a par with the inertia of the rock of the authorities, even though there are different stages in the ascent and frequent backsliding, and even though the hero cannot reach a plateau where he might rest. Weil's Sisyphus, on the other hand, is crushed by his burden, and the best he can do under the weight is to cry out. Only after the Sisyphean absurdity is overcome when an otherworldly finality of action (or of being crushed? the ambiguity cannot be resolved on the basis of Weil's texts) is revealed does the actual consolidation of achievements become thematic again. Additionally, the urgent task, after the Fall of France in 1940, of planning the reorganization of the country after the liberation focused attention on institutional problems. A particular circumstance was added to the raising of problems of principle. The planning office of the Free French, headed by André Philip, entrusted Weil with drafting memoranda concerning the country's reorganization in the postwar period. *L'enracinement* and the companion texts published in *Ecrits de Londres* are the result of this work. According to Weil, there can be justice in society only when gravitational force *(pesanteur)*—that is, the libidinous force of natural law—resolves itself into equilibrium. She quoted from Thucydides' Melian dialogue as if the classical highly stylized moral disintegration at the height of the "greatest cataclysm that ever struck the Greeks" more or less adequately characterized the conditions of human existence under all circumstances, if they are not transfigured by folly, the *folie d'amour.*[6] "The investigation of what is just is undertaken only when the same necessity obtains on every side. Wherever there is a strong man and a weak man, what is possible is carried out by the strong and accepted by the weak."[7]

Only the impact of the "supernatural" provides justice among those who are not equals, and Weil compared even the substantial presence of the "infinitely small" with a point—that is, the fulcrum of equilibrium. But even before she fixed the axis of equilibrium in the ground of transcendence, she wrote an essay that provides an illuminating picture

5. See Davy, *Introduction,* 49.
6. *EL,* 48 (quoting Thucydides, I.1).
7. *EL,* 45 (Thucydides V.89).

of the social balance as she understood it.[8] The social order is both necessary and, when it comes to *pensée,* unbearable. Given this reality, the rebellion of the oppressed can be understood only too easily. Resignation, on the contrary, is a sign of the deep wound of humiliation. In her search for the "manly virtues *[les vertus viriles]*" Weil encountered a topos advanced by the theoretician of *virtù:* Machiavelli was without a doubt the first to see party diversions as possibly advantageous for the republic. This advantage was the practice of virtuous love of liberty; and this was his belief even if long before him the dissolution of the polis had been seen to lie in excessive unification and homogenization.[9] "The struggles between fellow citizens do not spring from a lack of understanding or goodwill; they belong to the nature of things, and cannot be appeased, but can only be smothered by coercion. For anyone who loves liberty, it is not desirable that they should disappear, but only that they should remain short of a certain limit of violence."[10]

To replace Comte's permanent and therefore mitigated revolution of radicals, Weil posits permanent and therefore mitigated civil war. The success of the major strikes of 1936, with the occupation of factories, which culminated in the so-called Matignon accords—which really were the significant turning point of French social policy, in contrast with parliamentary stagnation—encouraged Weil to visualize the creation of a free arena if conflicts were to be settled, not in the form of public debate channeled through the parliamentary parties, but on the model of the *seccessio plebis.*[11] For the rest, in her hunt for abstractions, entered into entirely in the *esprit des années trente* (spirit of the thirties), she would forget the principal weapon of syndicalism, *action directe,* but not because she no longer expected that the coercions

8. "Méditation sur l'obéissance et la liberté," *OL,* 186–93 ("Meditation on Obedience and Liberty," *OLE,* 140–46). Pétrement dates it from 1937–1938; see P, 2:161 (PE, 313).

9. See Machiavelli, *Istorie fiorentine, opere,* book 7, chapter 1; Erwin Faul, "Verfemung, Duldung, und Anerkennung des Parteiwesens."

10. *OL,* 193 (*OLE,* 146).

11. See *EHP,* 265. Thinking about the threat of war, Weil wrote even before the outbreak of the Second World War: "To discriminate between imaginary antagonisms and genuine antagonisms, to cast discredit on empty abstractions and analyse concrete problems—that, if our contemporaries were to consent to such an intellectual effort, would be to diminish the risks of war without forgoing struggle which, according to Heraclitus, is the condition of life." *OL,* 173 (*OLE,* 131).

of the *condition ouvrière* could be overthrown once and for all by applying it. "The hunting down of imaginary entities in all spheres of political and social life thus appears as a task necessary in the interests of public health."[12]

We have referred in passing to the fact that alongside the ritual methods of securing legitimacy, Weil provided for control mechanisms. The control mechanism of monarchy, concern with historical reputation and with dynastic continuity, proves to be unreliable and highly inflexible. Once it has fallen apart, it cannot be put back together.[13] But, understandably, the institutional roots of monarchic legitimacy could not hold Weil's interest for long once she pointed out the significance of symbolic representation. For Alain, monarchic legitimacy was a contradiction in terms, pure and simple, while the modalities of republican legitimacy occupied a prominent position in his political philosophy. For the radical, who derived his doctrines from the historical experiences of Bonapartism and Boulangism, universal suffrage was not a sufficient guarantee of institutional resistance to the "authorities."

> Even universal suffrage does not result in a definition of democracy. Even if the infallible Pope, who is responsible to no one, were legitimated by universal suffrage, the Church would not thereby become democratic; a tyrant chosen by universal suffrage will be no less a tyrant. What makes the difference is not the source of authority but the constant and effective control the subjects exert over the rulers.[14]

The insight that plebiscitary legitimation cannot guarantee a government that proceeds democratically had to force itself on every republican living in a republic erected on the ruins of the Empire, no matter how much that understanding conflicted with the individual's doctrinaire populism and his desire to trust in origins and principles.

The radical republic disposes of an institution of central significance: the member of parliament. There can be no doubt whatever that these representatives are the leading figures in the Third Republic, the embodiment of its political style. As the only officeholder directly

12. *OL,* 173 (*OLE,* 130).
13. *EL,* 66–67.
14. *Politique,* 9.

elected on the national level, the member of parliament enjoys the prestige of being the most immediate representative of the people's sovereignty. The member of parliament acts as a tribune. His principal task is not legislating, and especially not initiating programs. The debate is directed to proclaiming principles and—depending on the speaker's oratorical skills—to raising his renown among his colleagues in the chamber. He is first of all the embodiment of the "constant and efficient control the subjects exert over the rulers," which for Alain constitutes the place of democracy in the republic,

> that third authority, which political science has not defined and which I have called right of supervision [right of control]. It is nothing but the permanent active power to depose kings and specialists in a trice if they do not carry out public affairs in the interest of the majority. For a long time this power was wielded by means of revolutions and barricades. Today it uses question time. Democracy would therefore be a constant striving by the governed against the encroachment of power.[15]

Every civil servant, every stationmaster, is a "king" in the view of the radicals, and the republic is not interested in having the trains run on time but in making sure that the heads of tyrants roll. Unconditional preference in favor of decisions made along party lines over those dictated by purposive reason in public affairs defines the radical *de gauche,* and it is his dominance that gives the republic its leftward list. "The political economist of the right is an economist. The political economist of the left is a politician."[16]

Accordingly, interpolation and intercession are the true tasks of the member of parliament, who is himself an object of suspicion. He is perennially suspected of becoming corrupted by power, with which he is necessarily in contact. Alain imagined the good member of parliament as a good man *(honnête homme)* who has come from his village to teach the Parisians a lesson.[17]

Success, life in the capital, these can loosen his ties to his provincial constituency. His voters and the appropriate election committee will

15. Ibid., 10.
16. Thibaudet, *République des professeurs,* 171.
17. On this and the following see Siegfried, *Tableau,* 214 ff.; J. Fontanet, "Alain ou le citoyen grognard."

be on the lookout for this contingency. Thus a chain of suspicious supervisors comes into being. "I can imagine the most popular man in a town saying, 'It's my job not to be a member of parliament but to supervise the member of parliament.' And then there is the member of parliament saying, 'I was not elected to become a minister but to supervise the ministers.' Such men, on every level, would form the bulwark of [public] opinion."[18]

André Siegfried has given us a description of the tribunitial power in the *régime d'assemblée* of the Third Republic that is less idealized than Alain's: "If in general the wealthy classes might have dropped the idea of a service government, which they put in the dock at the very moment they demand preferential treatment from it, the people, to the contrary, have become fully accustomed to it. If the people no longer clamor for direct democracy, that is only because they believe that it resides in the directly willed and incessant intervention of their representative in parliament."[19]

And, Siegfried added, the name of parliamentarian, which is reminiscent of members of the British House of Commons, can be given to the French delegate only with difficulty. The latter functions primarily as an instrument of his voters' private demands and claims upon the central institution. It is also his business to represent the suspicious dislike of those who elected him vis-à-vis the institution to which he is elected. The single-vote constituency, the *scrutin d'arrondissement,* strengthens both the immediate dependence of the representative, as the tribune of the little man, on his voters and his independence from the "authorities" of the central institution. It strengthens him against the threats, the temptations, the pressure to which his provincial probity and especially his humility are exposed.

Alain unequivocally opposed the abolition of the single-candidate constituency, "the best weapon of the provinces against the Parisian elite." In his view, the introduction of proportional representation was intended to work against the voter, with the aim not of advancing delegates devoted to local interests, the *intérêts de clocher,* but of filling the parliament with ambitious "authorities," who dream of "great politics." The introduction of proportional representation was a perfidious plan

18. *EL,* 132.
19. *Tableau,* 203.

of the Parisian elite, who wished "that great politics, which they call national, be completely withdrawn from the control of the little people, for whom the great thing is to work for a living and to safeguard themselves against risks."[20]

Alain feared most of all that proportional elections based on party lists would solidify the party structures. That prospect repelled Alain not only as a trend toward oligarchy, encouraged by this tightening, but also because it would fundamentally sap the individualistic basis of the radical republic. Labels would replace people, the vote would no longer be given to men but to posters.

> If I demand an accounting of a vote, or of a poorly executed reform, I will be referred to the party leaders, to party discipline, to slogans, and to party resolutions. Instead of having a delegate to serve me, I will have a party congress to rule me. Thank you very much! It is bad enough that the administration's offices are closed. I want the delegate's door to be wide open.[21]

Parliamentary representation would lose its appropriate role as the servant of individual claims against the administration and as the embodiment of the opposition in principle to power. It would itself be changed into part of the mechanism it was meant to combat. Unlike the thinking individual, according to Alain, an organized party is "the social," a collective that as such must obey the blind drives of the lust for power, inordinate ambition, and greed.

And then again, as far as appropriate government affairs are concerned, for Alain the model minister was the editor of the first proclamation of the radical party, Camille Palletan, who, as minister of naval affairs, promoted syndicalism in the shipyards, forced suppliers to make restitution for excessive charges, knew how to humiliate the "clerical" admiralty—and let the fleet become totally dilapidated.[22]

Weil had no wish to reform party democracy; she wanted to abolish it. The controlling agencies of the Third Republic seemed to her not only worn out but fundamentally inadequate. A recent essay by Friedrich Hayek reveals the degree to which the topoi of Weil's criticism

20. *Politique,* 42.
21. Ibid., 15.
22. Ibid., 75.

of party democracy have not fallen out of fashion since her death; or, to put it differently, how Rousseau's ghost haunts discussions of democracy.[23]

If Alain was unwilling to tolerate anything except loosely organized parties, Weil saw no problem in simply abolishing all parties. "A political party is a machine to produce collective passions. A political party is an organization designed in such a way that it exerts collective pressure on every human being belonging to it. The first, and in the last resort the only, objective of all political parties is their own growth, and growth without limits."[24]

Alain was unwilling to vote for a label, and Weil rejected parties because they institutionalized decision making, *parti pris* in the most literal sense. She referred explicitly to the Continental ideological parties and could therefore point with some justification to the deplorable custom of appealing to partisanship in such locutions as "As a liberal, I believe" or, "As a monarchist, it's my opinion" to justify such partisanship.[25] Aside from the observation that parties of the Anglo-Saxon type were based on an alien tradition and therefore not easily imported into France, however, we never learn why institutional reforms, such as adequate ways to exercise the franchise, could not effect changes in the right direction.

The contradiction inherent in parties consists, for Weil, in the circumstance that a predetermined attitude and representation of interests lay claim to universality; they must, in fact, raise such a claim to the degree that each party considers its aims worth pursuing—that is, sees them as identical with the common weal. That is why for Weil every party begins by being totalitarian, and the logical realization of party objectives must result in Trotsky's formula, "One party in power and all others in jail."[26] Such rigorous conclusions depend on Weil's dualistic conviction that everything that is not truth itself is simply untrue, and she therefore lacked that broad-mindedness that her admirer Camus misses in Gabriel Marcel: "M. Marcel wants to defend absolute values, such as shame and the divine truth of mankind. But it is much more

23. Friedrich August von Hayek, "Wohin steuert die Demokratie?"
24. *EL*, 132.
25. Ibid., 126 ff.
26. Ibid., 124.

important to defend the few provisional values that will one day permit M. Marcel to peacefully champion his absolute values."[27]

After all that, Weil believed the control of the radical committee of notables to be completely inadequate. To avoid the "prostitution" of campaigning, the members of the legislative assembly would have to be chosen within the framework of revitalized local life. She proposed that members of parliament be selected by corporations akin to local cooperatives.[28] Hayek for his part preferred an assembly of mature people, of whom only a fifth at any one time are indirectly elected by local age cohorts. In both cases the intention is the same: to constitute an independent assembly, not put together by parties, one that represents "public opinion" instead of special interests, one that should "be made up of persons . . . that take a long-range view of problems and do not depend on the fickle fashions and passions of the inconstant masses."[29]

We can only imagine the devastating consequences in political recruiting of this deliberate elimination of *ira et studium,* which Max Weber called the politician's element.[30] Alain engaged in a controversy against strengthening party discipline in parliament. Almost paradoxically, Weil turned the commandment for freedom of conscience into an absolute, so that the outcome of an election deals with people less than with causes. But which causes? Surely not the guidelines of politics, which some systems leave up to the elected majority or the chief executive, so that the personal election outcome can correspond to a program. Hayek, following the German nineteenth-century jurists, called them laws in the material sense. Weil was intent on differentiating rigorously between government decrees and laws, and she described laws as "mental efforts about fundamental concepts."[31] Laws are interpretations of the declaration of principles so that they can be applied in practice. The laws issued by the legislature before, according to Hayek, it usurped the right to determine government policy, for which he is nostalgic, are very similar:

27. Camus, *Essais,* 373.
28. *EL,* 67, 93 ff.
29. Hayek, "Wohin steuert die Demokratie?"
30. *Politik,* 28 (*Politics,* 20).
31. *EL,* 93–94.

> It is a matter of rules that were designed to delimit the secure private sphere of the individual and that were meant to apply to an indeterminate number of future cases. In every community, predominant public opinion will form about these rules, which are meant to prevent conflicts and on which most people may take one side or the other just as easily. In this way the majority of elected representatives will also find themselves in accord.[32]

In Weil's conception the substance of the laws may, in accord with the overriding significance she assigned to work, differ from Hayek's understanding, but the pattern is identical. Weil mentioned the function of money, the press, and securing respect for work among matters to be determined by law and not simply by regulation. She considered it the task of the legislature to discern the tendencies converging in the *volonté générale,* to translate vague feelings into legal form, and to make sure that the executive and administrative institutions observe the law.[33] Further, she assigned to the legislature a leadership role in public information; this educational function is similar to one she believed the movement of the Free French to be destined for, though it had no power whatever. Weil tried to make a distinction between articulating initially inchoate feelings of connection and the ideologic result of the selective stress of affects and propagandistic suggestion. The effort exposed her to all the difficulties that anyone must incur when Alain's "invincible opinion" is substituted for *homonoia,* while realizing with horror that political homogeneity is then attained by way of propaganda.

Weil, like Hayek, made the trenchant observation that the fact of achieving a numerical majority does not prevent the ruling majority from being criminal, or at least corrupt. Both tried to forestall this possibility by proposing a chamber of disinterested diviners of the general will, in a way that places both rulers and ruled under a superior legal authority. In this arrangement, ruling proceeds according to rules issued by a corporate body that does not take part in power. Hayek wrote, "The majority generally relies on mutual obligation not merely to obey certain principles but to satisfy particular demands."[34]

Pork-barrel democracy results when a sovereign people is also a ruler and therefore always open to flattery and bribery. But it is extremely

32. "Wohin steuert die Demokratie?"
33. *EL,* 94.
34. "Wohin steuert die Demokratie?"

doubtful that this problem can be remedied by inserting a disinterested chamber—one that would therefore also be uninterested. Most of all, such a schema completely disregards the truly crucial element, government policy, except as it conforms to the constitution. It is nevertheless quite logical for Weil to write, "The government is concerned with the absolute minimum. . . . The legislature sees to it that it remains restricted to this minimum."[35]

It seems much more likely that flattery and corruption can be muted in a system that allows responsibility and alternatives to be clearly recognized through a ruling majority and an oppositional minority. But such a solution presupposes that the framework marked out by the rules of the game is not controversial.

The legislature must articulate the popular idea of justice, must think about it in the form of laws. Weil apparently counted on the unanimity of this body because—in her view—anyone who is mistaken is not actually thinking. But this method provides only indirect opportunities to control the government. Given the inefficiency and lack of public openness of the Third Republic's political control mechanism, Weil set no great store by the idea of healing it by introducing something like the right of dissolution and electoral reform; she wanted to replace it with another mechanism—the legal process.[36] The head of government should not be subject to deposition by the chamber—for example, by a vote of no confidence—but should be subject to judicial punishment. On every level political responsibility was to be replaced by responsibility before justice. We need not go into details. The severity of possible punishments was to correspond to the significance of the office, and this applied not only to public offices in the narrower sense but also to any position of authority and influence, such as those of factory manager and journalist. Only this correspondence of sanctions and social position, Weil believed, would create social balance and a legitimating justice.[37]

We must be highly suspicious of the purity of the motives of those who opt for a life of poverty and humility in a social order constituted along these lines. The training of judges becomes of overriding importance in a society conceived in this way. We learn that they are to be given an education that is more spiritual than legal and that within the

35. *EL*, 96.
36. Ibid., 67–68.
37. Ibid., 79; see also *EL*, 95–96.

confines of the proclamation of principles they are to render judgments, not according to the letter of the law, but in the spirit of fairness *(en équité)*. As Weil quite correctly observed, "The hardest part should be to imagine the transitional government, before such mores could be established."[38]

38. *EL*, 97.

TWENTY

Experience and Vocation

In all probability Simone Weil would not have been quite so susceptible to Alain's influence if she had not already had strong natural affinities with his doctrine long before she met him. Her reconstruction of Alain's metaphysical and political propositions allows us to sense Weil's earnest intensity, a harshness peculiar to her. She lacks completely the master's sanguine temperament. For her, Alain's anthropological and cosmological dualism is not merely a speculative explanatory schema; it is the expression of a rupture painfully experienced in her own person. In a much quoted autobiographical essay Weil wrote:

> At fourteen I fell into one of those fits of bottomless despair that come with adolescence, and I seriously thought of dying because of the mediocrity of my natural faculties. The exceptional gifts of my brother, who had a childhood and youth comparable to those of Pascal, brought my own inferiority home to me. I did not mind having no visible successes, but what grieved me was the idea of being excluded from that transcendent kingdom to which only the truly great have access and wherein truth abides. I preferred to die rather than live without that truth.[1]

The fourteen-year-old girl felt acutely that the inadequacy of her talent kept her out of touch with a reality that she suspected existed, one that encompassed truth and beauty and real virtue. "Under the

1. *AD*, 38–39 (*WG*, 64).

name of truth I included beauty, virtue, and every kind of goodness."[2] It is in contact with the fullness of being and truth, sensed in this way, that genuine human greatness becomes manifest. The insight into her inability to realize this virtue—that is, to develop her human potential—cast Weil into "bottomless despair," and life, robbed of its meaning, seemed to her no longer worth living.

The brother against whom Weil measured herself is in fact the brilliant mathematician André Weil, who distinguished himself in a discipline that his sister would come particularly to despise: algebra. She never begrudged him his public success; she always spoke of him with loving admiration, just as she always maintained cordial relations with her family.

> After months of inward darkness, I suddenly had the everlasting conviction that any human being, even though practically devoid of natural faculties, can penetrate to the kingdom of truth reserved for genius, if only he longs for truth and perpetually concentrates all his attention upon its attainment. He thus becomes a genius too, even though for lack of talent his genius cannot be visible from outside.[3]

Her hopelessness was born from the tension between the conviction that contact with the suspected ground of reality is an essential part of humanity and the impossibility, felt in her own person, for a particular person to establish this contact through readily comprehensible skills and modes of knowledge—the virtuosity and instrumental reason represented by, for example, algebra. The "inward darkness" of this despair led to the insight, which solidified into certainty, that it is not an increase of "talents" but a qualitatively different mode of perception that provides the efficient instrument of knowledge. This mode is "attention," which allows the insight of "genius." Thus technical and rationalist talent is countered by genius. After Weil's experience of factory work and the so-called conversion of Solesmes, *attention* changed to *attente,* the expectant opening to the ground of reality.[4] In her *autobiographie spirituelle,* as she herself called her sketch in a letter to Perrin, Weil

2. *AD,* 39 (*WG,* 64).
3. Ibid.
4. Weil, "L'attente est la passivité de la pensée en acte," in *CS,* 47.

continued, "so that for me it was a question of a conception of the relation between grace and desire. The conviction that had come to me was that when one hungers for bread one does not receive stones. But at that time I had not read the Gospel."[5]

This is the language of the late Weil, after her "conversion." The interpreted basic attitude, looking back in terms of the categories of her mature thinking, is the constant that underlies the change of forms of expression, the point where political, philosophical, and religious thinking meet. It is characteristic that those who knew Weil well perceived a coherent impulse, determining the course of her entire life, even if they were unable to bring any understanding to the political or conversely the religious side of her life.

In the late phase of her development, when the text we have just cited was written, she used a Christian vocabulary, albeit in a fairly idiosyncratic fashion. She interpreted the intuition that governed the way she lived her life as love of God, first implicit, then explicit. One of the church fathers called Plato *naturaliter christianus*. The kinship of Weil's *génie* with the Socratic *daimonion* cannot be denied. Clearly we must return to Plato to find the classical counsel for that science of virtue that—in contrast to the specialized sciences—has its own practice for its goal.[6] Weil is Platonic as well when she experiences the loss of reality as a problem not only for the individual soul but also for the society encapsulating this soul. Her work is already historically conditioned in the sense that, not surprisingly, she starts from the specifics of her contemporary crisis. However, her tendency to conceive the phenomena of historical decline in ontological categories, not so much of imperfection as of evil, already points to a dualistic hardening to which she was characteristically prone. Alain provided the intellectual instruction for a train of thought that evinces a greater kinship with neo-Platonic and Manichaean ideas than with, say, the thought of Socrates' great disciple.

Weil's work is historically conditioned in another way as well. Her intellectual devices are, as we saw, adopted from traditions that were widespread in France in the period between the wars, most especially

5. Weil, *AD*, 75 (*WG*, 64).
6. "A mes yeux, rien ne surpasse Platon," *PSO*, 66.

Cartesian rationalism and Neo-Kantianism.[7] Her intuitive openness to the ground of reality was not able to break through the closedness of these systems. She therefore saw the drama of the human psyche not as a struggle for the forming of the soul through participation in the form of the good but as a polar opposition between the upright *(rectus) esprit* and the extension made up of passion and matter. "Just as I was certain that desire has in itself an efficacy in the realm of spiritual goodness whatever its form, I thought it was also possible that it might not be effective in any other realm."[8]

This is the essence of Weil's naturalism, whose manifestations we have encountered many times. The openness to transcendence is not, as we have seen, a *faculté naturelle.* To salvage a modern concept of nature, relating to necessary mechanistic causal conditions rather than to growth and entelechy—from which an equally modern "spirit" tries to tactically fight free—the highest element in man, his actual *differentia,* is presented as something that is not part of his nature!

For Weil, experience is essentially *pathos.* This means for her not least physical suffering. Here the difference from Alain, both in biography and in speculation, is most evident. Extremely delicate even as a child, Weil began at the age of twenty to suffer from headaches of such severity as to turn physical labor, as in the factory, into torture and— of even greater importance—to threaten always to frustrate intellectual concentration, attention. She wrote of this apparent hopelessness of all her efforts: "I was upheld by the belief, which I had gained at the age of fourteen, that no real effort of attention is ever wholly lost, even if directly or indirectly it has not even the slightest visible results."[9]

Noninstrumental attentiveness here represents one pole of that contrast whose other pole is the suffering body. Pain is described in one passage in a way characteristic of Weil's anthropological schema: "around the central point of the nervous system, at the juncture of soul and body."[10] Pain seems to make manifest the body and the part of the psyche assigned to it in all its lack of dignity. Dujardin was correct when he

---

7. Curtius, *Die französische Kultur,* 17. See the useful essay by Rolf Kühn, which seeks to situate Weil's work in the philosophical trends of her day in Kahn, ed., *Philosophe, historienne, et mystique.*
   8. *AD,* 39 (*WG,* 64–65).
   9. *PSO,* 80.
   10. Ibid., 79.

detected in Weil's physical suffering more a subjective confirmation of than a cause for her contempt for her "empirical self." But his argument seems to overlook the fact that for Weil the totality of the *moi haissable* is subject to "biological" mechanisms. Pain helps only as "contact with harsh reality," placing objectivity and lack of dignity of the body and the passions in the sight of the *esprit* that has been thus purified. That was why Weil's greatest fear was that her mind would be clouded by illness.

> [A]t a certain point in time exhaustion and increasing pain made me feel that a horrible collapse *[déchéance]* of my entire soul was imminent to the extent that for several weeks I tormented myself with the question whether dying was not my bounden duty, although it seemed to me terrible to end my life in a condition of loathsomeness . . . only the decisions for a contingent and properly timed death restored peace to me.[11]

The desire for self-annihilation appears here for the second time, though this time not as an act of despair but as a duty. In view of the suspected perfection, the existence of imperfection, represented through her own self, is experienced as a scandal. The immediate extinction of this should–not–be is only delayed, mediated into a "calling" to a *mort conditionelle et à terme* (conditional and temporary death). After her emancipatory hopes shattered in the experience of factory work, work was reinterpreted into a redemptive *imitatio mortis.*

Weil's life and work are the obverse of a flight from suffering in more senses than merely escape from physical pain. Countless anecdotes, which do not need to be repeated here, testify to her inclination, from her earliest childhood, to identify with the misery of others. They testify as well to her stubborn insistence on bearing her share of the burden. The little girl who sat down in the snow in sulking protest because the bag she had been given to carry weighed less than that given her brother is the same person as the teacher who donated every penny of her pay in excess of the amount of unemployment insurance for unskilled labor to unemployment relief, and the collaborator of the Free French in London who refused to eat more than the rations in her occupied homeland would have allowed her. The words *dolorism* and *helotism*—that is, a morbid love for pain and for enslavement—have

11. Ibid., 80.

been used to refer to Weil. Her friends, however, mention her cheerful disposition. If she herself warns against the temptation of perversity— "respond, react to an evil (a hurt, an injury) by doing all one can to augment it"—it is because she clearly recognizes perversity to be an error, a sin.

> [N]ot for her own sake did she submit to this asceticism, not in order to perfect her own personality, to save or redeem her own soul. The ideal of personality, the demand for a well-rounded development of the individual seemed to her downright evil, because they claim privilege for some that can be realized only by unremitting injustice to many. So she takes a stand against Goethe, against Nietzsche, against Gide.[12]

Such an interpretation is certainly preferable to a number of psycho-logical reductions, but in its apologetic benevolence it tends to ignore a few problems. In particular it leaves no room for the hardness and rigor with which Weil followed her vocation and especially for the particular pride that, though it can be reminted into the will to self-sacrifice, can never become humility. "Though utterly and entirely detached from her tastes and needs, she was not detached from her detachment. . . . In the great book of the universe spread often before her, her *ego* was, as it were, a word which she may perhaps have succeeded in *effacing,* but which was still *underlined.*"[13]

I am not competent to render a psychopathological analysis of Weil's basic stance, though it would surely be of great interest. Dujardin's criti-cal objection, however, that earlier interpreters rejected a psychological interpretation for reasons of self-interest and with irrational arguments is once again simply a way to denigrate positions after first misrepresenting them. It is not because Weil transcends "the measure of man"—as Dujardin quotes Davy—that she is beyond the scope of psychological analysis; rather, psychological analysis can never furnish a *sufficient* ex-planation if it means the reduction of higher levels of consciousness to lower ones. What is certain is that Weil's humanity manifested itself as, literally, com-passion—that is, suffering with others—and that she had a thoroughly radical understanding of her duty to mankind, including

12. Friedhelm Kemp, "Das Werk von Simone Weil," 1194.
13. Perrin and Thibon, *Telle que nous l'avons connue,* 139 (*As We Knew Her,* 119).

her own humanity: "in view of the general and permanent condition of humanity it may well be that to eat one's fill is always a kind of theft."[14]

Seeking to share in man's misfortune is also to attempt to touch reality, and this in two ways: On the one hand, as we have seen, experience is on principle *pathos*. On the other, compassion results in the search for a remedy, which in turn requires a view of reality free of illusion. Such a view reveals the *condicio* of the suffering person. Maurice Schumann described this circle trenchantly: "Truth leads to wretchedness [*malheur*], and wretchedness opens the soul to the truth. The being who feels compassion for others becomes aware of their unhappiness; and this compassion, which first emerges as attentiveness, forces the search for a remedy—that is, to get to the bottom of reality."[15]

Compassion and the search for knowledge, joined like ebb and flow, are two phases of the same movement. Weil herself wrote: "Once the little that is given me to do for the good of others is laid aside, life has no other meaning for me and at heart has never had any other meaning except waiting [*attente*] for the truth."[16] The unity of the search for truth and compassion also means the intentional unity of reflection and action. This means first of all that action must conform strictly to thought: "I think that we must always stand up for what we believe, even if we support an error over a truth. But at the same time we must always pray to gain more truth, and always be ready to abandon any of our opinions at the moment when our understanding receives more light. But not before."[17] From her late, heightened perspective, after having been "possessed by Christ," the behavioral pattern reflected here would appear as obedience. In Weil's earlier phases, this premonition of the vocation that appears as the cardinal virtue is simply called courage. "If you recognize something as a good, you must seize it. To hold back would be cowardice."[18]

Here we see Weil's clear preference for what is certain and willed over what is vague and hesitant, even at the risk of choosing something that is false or even criminal. The context of the above quotation, for example, is that Hitler—unlike the halfhearted imperialists who, in

14. *CS*, 177 (*FLN*, 219).
15. *La mort*, 86.
16. Quoted in ibid., 83.
17. *AD*, 248.
18. *E*, 192–93.

Weil's view, make up the majority of French public opinion—does not just think of colonial expansion as a good but is also prepared to act on what he believes to be true. For one thing, what is operating here is Alain's doctrine that in the last resort true volition can only be goodwill because by definition it acts by free will and the decision is therefore pure. On the other hand, what is manifest here is that natural kinship of which Helmut Kuhn speaks, "with the spiritual climate of a time that is more tolerant of a lack of balance than of a lack of resoluteness."[19] At the same time there is a hint of the teleological direction of Weil's vision of courage, which is an erotic pull toward the good, which in its dynamic itself includes the aspired good, even if in error she takes her bearings from an imaginary good. This perversion cannot be compensated for by loosening the attraction but only by a correction concerning objectives. Julien Sorel, the hero of Stendhal's *Le rouge et le noir,* can serve as the model of courage. In an essay written for Alain, Weil remarked, "Julien does not trouble himself about God at all. . . . He does not despair because he has killed; there is only one failing that he could never forgive himself for, and that is losing courage. For all of his short life Julien cared about only one thing: to keep himself in check, never to be a coward. . . . *Le rouge et le noir* could well be called the bible of humanity, a bible that in every respect is the opposite of the real Bible."[20]

The stress Weil placed on the erotic orientation as well as the disorientation of courage should by no means be seen as an attempt at justification. She never viewed Hitler's conquests and the murder committed by Julien Sorel as anything but criminal. For Weil external problems of execution do not justify any discrepancy between thought and action. "There is no difficulty whatever, once one has decided to act, in maintaining intact, on the level of action, those very hopes which a critical examination has shown to be wellnigh unfounded; in that lies the very essence of courage."[21]

What is remarkable is the juxtaposition of courage and hope, with hope being subordinated to courage. Maintaining hope even in the face of apparently insurmountable difficulties is possible if for no other

19. "Die Philosophie des 'laisser faire Dieu,'" 595.
20. P, 1:96.
21. *OL,* 36 (*OLE,* 22).

reason than because the external results of the action, while not in-different, are by no means the only motive. Because it is a matter of practicing a virtue, the repercussions on the actor are what counts. More precisely, what counts is that the actor, for his own sake, act virtuously regardless of the outcome. In her late phase, however, when courage had fallen victim to vocation, cowardice became the corrupt alternative: "Owing to the physical deficiency of my nature, there is no possible half-way house for me between total sacrifice and cowardice." The ethical polarity, for which once again the body and its frailty are held partially responsible, corresponds closely to an intellectual polarity: "And my intellectual situation is the same. I have no alternative between creative attention and mental nullity,—because my capacity for every other kind of attention is paralysed."[22]

The split within herself, the compassion, the scandal of imperfection in view of the experience of perfection, the passion for truth—all of these are encompassed in one sentence found in a letter to Maurice Schumann: "I feel an ever increasing sense of devastation, both in my intellect and in the centre of my heart, at my inability to think truthfully at the same time about the affliction of men, the perfection of God, and the link between the two."[23]

Commenting on this admission, Schumann rightly calls attention to the significance of the order in which the elements are listed. The link becomes a problem for Weil not in the descent from God's perfection but in the ascent from man's wretchedness. The classical solutions of the freedom of will of the beloved creature therefore remain closed to her. The fundamental experience is not that of the divine presence but that of human wretchedness—that is, precisely, the absence of God. Weil's god is experienced only in and through his absence. If he is to be pure essence, he cannot be existent. Her *engagement* is dedicated to alleviating human wretchedness. Wretchedness that cannot be alleviated—and after her year of working in the factory, this imperative would appear infinitely more important—must be shared by her. "Hardship and danger are essential because of my particular mentality. . . . The suffering all over the world obsesses and overwhelms me to the point of annihilating my faculties and the only way I can revive

22. *EL,* 208, 209 (*SL,* 174, 175).
23. *EL,* 213 (*SL,* 178).

them and release myself from the obsession is by getting for myself a large share of danger and hardship."[24]

In the same breath Weil begged to be sent back to France on a daring and dangerous mission for the Free French. To deprive her of such a task would be to condemn her to becoming "fruitlessly eaten up by grief." It is typical that the sacrifice was to be made for a lost country. Like her God, the reality of her country became manifest to her only in its absence.[25]

The woman who for many years was an antinationalist and pacifist may have fulfilled her vocation by surrendering her own existence to an entity that has been purified by its absence into an essence. For practical reasons—her physical awkwardness, her easy identifiability—she was not assigned a mission. She continued to work in the London office of France Libre, until, *consumée par le chagrin* soon after, she had to be taken to the sanatorium in Ashford in Kent. She died on August 24, 1943. On her death certificate the English doctor noted: "cardial failure due to myocardial degeneration of the heart muscles due to starvation and pulmonary tuberculosis. The deceased did kill and slay herself by refusing to eat whilst the balance of her mind was disturbed."[26] The concluding sentence is the formula used for suicide in British bureaucratic jargon. Schumann remarked on this, not without a certain unintentional irony, "England is too convinced of the stability of the values on which its long history is based to be able to admit that it is possible to become the clear-sighted killer of oneself."[27]

24. *EL,* 199 (*SL,* 156).
25. *E,* 139 (*NR,* 159).
26. P, 2:517 (PE, 537).
27. Schumann, *La mort,* 63.

AFTERWORD

The evolution of Simone Weil's thought reveals the interpretation of a basic intuition in light of a series of influences, encounters, and experiences. The analytic schema by which Weil sought to grasp reality and—of special interest to us—political reality sprang from an existential stance that began to manifest itself in her earliest childhood. This psychological direction had two aspects: a passion for truth and a will to self-control. But they must be understood as two aspects of a single drive that would not tolerate any discrepancy between knowledge and morality, thought and deed. For Weil, such a discrepancy would have amounted to something like both an ethical lapse and a loss of truth. All her aspirations, however, especially her political commitment and her reflections on the political sphere, were nothing but an attempt to erase error and injustice wherever possible, or at least to curtail them. The special characteristic of this effort is the search for the place where truth and justice meet—a juncture that alone allows them to be realized. This search is tempered with a refusal to yield to the temptation of locating the connection—because she desired it so ardently—at too low a level and thus ideologically misrepresenting both elements of the intended harmony.

Childish and youthful premonitions crystallized under the influence of Alain—professor of philosophy, polemicist, and theoretician of radicalism—into an analytic framework. In this, she came under the influence of a *philosophie de l'esprit* that was practiced, not at the university, but at the major Paris lycées. In accordance with this intellectual trend, Weil disavowed a sociological way of thinking that, following Durkheim, tends rashly to equate the spirit with society, but she also rejected the neo-Kantianism of Leon Brunschwicg at the Sorbonne, which threatened to reduce the development of critical rationality to

233

the progress made in the various distinct academic disciplines. Her philosophical critique goes hand in hand with a political critique. What develops on one level as philosophical reflection manifests itself on the other as cultural defense of a humanity that Weil sees as threatened in two ways: for one, by idolizing the collective; for another, by the alienating specialization in a social order that relies increasingly on division of labor; such a society is no longer merely technical but has already evolved into technocracy. Weil followed her mentor Alain into a particular variant of Kantianism, which attempts to overcome the discontinuity between pure and practical reason by the creative circumvention called work. Work, according to Weil, was to mediate between the experience of the world of everyday life and the mathematical conception of a world equated with natural law.

By this means work becomes the privileged mode of participation—of principle accessible to everyone—of particular subjectivities in a universal that was to be both the transcendental a priori and the concrete condition for existence. Work, in that it is a roundabout path of desire in which reason serves as a control consciousness, is perceived as asceticism: it requires the deferment of instant gratification and subdues physical impulsiveness by instrumentalizing it with a view to a finality that points beyond itself.

The circumstance that self-control and the search for truth can be united in the most elemental of human activities also complies with Weil's egalitarianism. The concept of work, with its social connotations, offered her the opportunity to regard her politics as an extension of her critical philosophy. If she stressed the concrete grasp of reality in Alain's epistemology, she also sharpened the sociocritical aspects of his doctrine. But if her political activity went far beyond the radical teachings of Alain, to end up in syndicalist-revolutionary *engagement,* the specifics of this eventuality are hard to reconcile with her philosophy. Weil herself explained that the prestige of the great classical thinkers of socialism had led her to a kind of intellectual self-effacement that subsequently she felt to be wrong.

Particularly when she was analyzing political phenomena, she pushed her own analytical construct into the background, though she never abandoned it entirely. This was a period in which there was a discrepancy between "philosophy" and "politics." The actual experience of the French labor movement, which she saw "from the inside," as well as—and especially—her analysis of the German crisis take the borrowed categories ad absurdum and reveal that, in the face of the triumphal progress of Stalinism and nationalism, revolutionary hopes are simply an expectation of harmony that comes from self-deception; their plausibility is based on the forcible reduction of the poles of the existential antinomy of human existence. The revolution stands revealed as a phantom, precisely the opposite of work as seen by Weil. Thus she would search for the direct contact provided by work.

As we saw, what followed was a period of persisting in binary tension. The experience of factory work gave Weil the certainty that this tension cannot be resolved on the "natural" plane. But if the human, social, cosmic *restitutio ad integrum* cannot be postulated as the consequence of revolutionary action, and certainly not as the quasi-automatic result of the course of history, and if work in itself cannot bring about liberation, what remains is the courageous certainty that a polarized reality nevertheless tends to form an entity. This entity, however, is for Weil quite emphatically not to be found in a near or distant future. Her criticism of Marxism is inscribed into a fundamental critique of progressivism, which starts from the premise that significant value cannot be found in a dimension commensurable with time.

The persistence seems to be answered by the discovery of a God who manifests himself precisely by his radical absence; this discovery was made by a "contact experience" of an ecstatic nature. The "sudden possession" by Christ permits the spiritual excess of the analytic schema whose main features derive from Alain, and it points to a resolution of the existential tension beyond this world.

Weil's breakthrough into transcendence, however, remained incomplete. What was transcended was not really the world but only historicity. If this breakthrough enabled her to develop transhistorical standards of political order, it also promoted a feeling for tradition and vital milieus. These convey ways of self-interpretation and, given the proper circumstances, can lead to the crucial opening.

In a close analogy to the experience of God, Weil perceived the *patria abscondita*. The fall of France allowed her, out of the emotion of the vacuum that remained, a *reevaluation* of the political order. This order could no longer be understood in the category of the pure totalitarian state but must be seen as the *milieu vital par excellence*. And its revitalization must be fought for. From this moment on, differences between nature and the distortion of the political order could be made.

"For every tree is known by his own fruit" (Luke 6:44). Weil never tired of recalling this gospel phrase, and she saw in it a methodical principle. With its help, she believed, we could find a way through the thicket of ideological controversy to penetrate to reality. The adventure of the modern subject, who thinks of himself as autonomous, is measured by its results, manifest in what has been called the crisis of the liberal system, and found wanting. The apparently pointless project needs to be thought through radically. But the rationalist stringency— itself obligated to modernity—with which Weil applied the biblical principle to the contingent social *metaxy*—the contingent region of society—leads to significant weaknesses in her treatment of political institutions.

Weil searched for the root of the contemporary crisis and discovered it to be the autonomous individual; she therefore tried to fight against autonomy as "something that should not be." But she was marked by the modernist reduction of the perception of reality to such a degree that she turned a historical lapse in consciousness into a constant human trait.

Weil's spiritual peripeteia, experienced in existential authenticity, can be interpreted less as the striving of a particular consciousness to return to its ground than as an attempt to regain the whole of the ground itself by abolishing individual existence. This effort signifies a reversal of the imperial expansion of the self, which aims to control the whole of reality. Not action but passion brings about the *restitutio ad integrum* for which she longed. But what is restored is not humanity's integrity but that of the deified world. The element that restores the world to an ordered cosmos is revealed to be the abolition of the creature between heaven and earth. This process results from a speculative assimilation of the vegetative and animalistic realms to the *res extensa* and from elimination of the disorderly passionality that should not be. Weil counters the current modernist dream of the human being at one with himself, brought about by man's creative action, with the conception of restoring God's integrity brought about by man's decreation.

Under these auspices work is assigned an almost sacramental function, as imitation or prefiguration of decreation *(la mort se fit fatigue)*, as passion, as experience, and as an exercise: as asceticism.

BIBLIOGRAPHY

The Association pour l' étude de la pensée de Simone Weil, 5, rue Monticelli, 75014 Paris publishes *Cahiers Simone Weil* directed by Michel Narcy, 14, Residence du Bois du Roi, 91940 Les Ulis. Besides valuable articles the *Cahiers* contain reviews, updates on the literature, reports on conferences, and so forth.

A landmark in Weil studies was Janet Patricia Little, *Simone Weil, a Bibliography* (London: Grant and Cutler, 1973); and the *Supplement* (1979).

Rolf Kühn, *Deuten als Entwerden: Eine Synthese des Werkes Simone Weils in hermeneutisch-religionsphilosophischer Sicht,* Freiburger Theologische Schriften 136 (Freiburg: Herder, 1989), contains a very full bibliography, including the key to classification of the Weil papers in the Bibliothèque Nationale, as well as listings of many separate editions and secondary works in all languages.

Joan Nordquist, *Simone Weil: A Bibliography,* Social Theory: Bibliographical Series no. 38 (Santa Cruz, Calif.: Reference and Research Services, 1995), includes works by Simone Weil in French but is otherwise limited to publications in English. It has the advantages and disadvantages of a bibliography prepared by computer. Texts are usefully keyed to reviews, there are key-word indexes, but also strange omissions—for example, the second edition of Weil's *Cahiers.*

See also the bibliographical essays in: Michel Thiout, "Jalons sur la route de Simone Weil. I: La recherche de la vérité de Simone Weil; II: Essai de bibliographie des écrits de Simone Weil," *Archives des Lettres Modernes* 3 (1959): nos. 25–26; Ana Luisa Janeira, *Conhocer Simone Weil* (Braga, 1973); Adriano Marchetti, "Simone Weil: Coscienza delle contradizioni presenti nella letteratura francese degli anni trenta, con una bibliografia sistematica," in *Atti dell'Accademia delle Scienze dell'Istituto di Bologna,* Classe di Scienze Morali 73 (Bologna 1977), 7–82; George Abbot White, ed, *Simone Weil: Interpretations of a Life* (Amherst, 1981); and Heinz Robert Schlette, "Simone Weil: Ein Porträt," *Information Philosophie* (December 1986): 38–48.

Thomas R. Nevin, *Simone Weil: Portrait of a Self-Exiled Jew* (Chapel Hill, 1991), seeks to lay the foundation of a "Rezeptionsgeschichte."

Works by Simone Weil

The monumental *Oeuvres complètes* under the general editorship of André A. Devaux, founding president of the French Weil association, and Florence de Lucy, custodian of the Weil manuscripts at the Bibliothèque Nationale, is being published by Gallimard, beginning in 1988. The following volumes are available by the end of 1997.

Vol. I. *Premiers écrits philosophiques,* edited by Gilbert Kahn and Rolf Kühn. 1988. 2d ed. 1991.

Vol. II, pt. 1. *Ecrits historiques et politiques: L'engagement syndical (1927–1934),* edited by G. Leroy. 1988.

Vol. II, pt. 2. *Ecrits historiques et politiques: L'expérience ouvrière et l'adieu à la révolution* (1934–1937), edited by Gerald Leroy and Anne Roche. 1991.

Vol. II, pt. 3. *Ecrits historiques et politiques: Vers la guerre* (1937–1940), edited by S. Fraisse. 1989. 2d ed. 1991.

Vol. VI, pt. 1. *Cahiers* (1933–Sept. 1941), edited by Alyette Degraces, Pierre Kaplan, Florence de Lucy, and Michel Narcy. 2d ed. 1994.

This authoritative edition should eliminate many sources of misunderstanding and biased reception.

Because English translations of Weil's works are keyed to the earlier editions, note references are to those editions.

La pesanteur et la grâce. Edited by Gustave Thibon. Paris: Plon, 1947. In English: *Gravity and Grace.* Translated by Emma Craufurd. London: Routledge and Kegan Paul, 1952.

L'enracinement. Edited by Albert Camus. Paris: Gallimard, 1949. The final pages missing in this edition are included in the 1970 paperback edition. In English: *The Need for Roots: Prelude to a Declaration of Duties toward Mankind.* Translated by Arthur F. Wills. Preface by T. S. Eliot. New York: Putnam's Sons, 1952.

Attente de Dieu. Paris, Fayard, 1950. In English: *Waiting for God.* Translated by Emma Craufurd. Preface by Leslie Fiedler. New York: Putnam's Sons, 1951.

La connaissance surnaturelle. Paris: Gallimard, 1950.

Lettre à un religieux. Paris: Gallimard, 1951. In English: *Letter to a Priest.* Translated by Arthur F. Wills. New York: Putnam's Sons, 1971.

Les intuitions pré-chrétiennes. Paris: La Colombe, 1951.

La condition ouvrière. Paris: Gallimard, 1951; paperback ed., 1972.

Cahiers I. Paris: Plon, 1951.

Cahiers II. Paris: Plon, 1953.

Cahiers III. Paris: Plon, 1955. All three volumes in English in *The Notebooks of Simone Weil.* 2 vols. Translated by Arthur F. Wills. New York: Putnam's Sons, 1956.

La source grecque. Paris: Gallimard, 1953.

Oppression et liberté. Paris: Gallimard, 1955. In English: *Oppression and Liberty.* Translated by Arthur Wills and John Petrie. Introduction by F. C. Ellert. Amherst: University of Massachusetts Press, 1973. (Translation originally published London: Routlege and Kegan Paul, 1958.)

Venise sauvée. Paris: Gallimard, 1955. Now in: *Poèmes suivit de Venise sauvée.* Paris: Gallimard, 1968.

Ecrits de Londres et dernières lettres. Paris: Gallimard, 1957.

Leçons de philosophie. Presented by Anne Reynaud. Paris: Plon, 1959. In English: *Lectures on Philosophy.* Translated by Hugh Price. New York: Cambridge University Press, 1978.

Ecrits historiques et politiques. Paris: Gallimard, 1960.

Pensées sans ordre concernant l'amour de Dieu. Paris: Gallimard, 1962.

Sur la science. Paris: Gallimard, 1966. In English: *Lectures on Science.* Translated by Hugh Price. Introduction by Peter Winch and Anne Reynauld-Geurithault. Cambridge: Cambridge University Press, 1978.

Cahiers I, II, III. 2d ed., with a slightly different arrangement from the 1st ed. and including a previously unpublished notebook. Paris: Plon, 1970, 1972, 1974.

A great number of essays not included in the anthologies listed above appeared in the periodicals *Libres Propos, Bulletin de la Section de la Haute Loire du Syndicat National des Institutrices et Instituteurs Publics de France et des Colonies* (Le Puy), *L'Effort* (Lyon), *La Tribune* (Saint-Etienne), *La*

Révolution Prolétarienne, La Critique Sociale, Feuilles Libres de la Quinzaine, Le Libertaire, Syndicats, Cahiers du Sud, and others.

Additional Anthologies in English

First and Last Notebooks. Translated by Richard Rees. London: Oxford University Press, 1970.

Formative Writings, 1929–1941. Edited and translated by Dorothy Tuck McFarland and Wilhelmina van Ness. Amherst: University of Massachusetts Press, 1987.

Gateway to God. Edited by David Raper, with the collaboration of Malcolm Muggeridge and Vernon Sproxton. New York: Crossroad, 1974.

Intimations of Christianity. Collected and translated by Elisabeth Chase Geissbuhler. London: Routledge and Kegan Paul, 1957.

On Science, Necessity, and the Love of God. Collected, translated, and edited by Richard Rees. London: Oxford University Press, 1968.

Seventy Letters. Translated and arranged by Richard Rees. London: Oxford University Press, 1965.

Simone Weil: An Anthology. Edited and introduction by Siân Miles. London and New York: Weidenfeld and Nicholson, 1986.

The Simone Weil Reader. Edited by George A. Panichas. New York: McKay, 1977.

For a detailed listing, see Janet Patricia Little, *Simone Weil, a Bibliography* (London: Grant and Cutler, 1973), and the *Supplement* (1979); and Miklos Vetö, *La métaphysique religieuse de Simone Weil* (Paris: Vrin, 1971); in English: *The Religious Metaphysics of Simone Weil* (Albany: State University of New York Press, 1994).

Books and Dissertations on Simone Weil

An indispensable guide is: Simone Pétrement, *La vie de Simone Weil,* 2 vols. (Paris: Fayard, 1973); in English: *Simone Weil: A Life,* translated by Raymond Rosenthal (New York: Pantheon, 1976).

The most careful doxographic work on Simone Weil's thought, though it explicitly excludes the political dimension, is: Miklos Vetö,

La métaphysique religieuse de Simone Weil (Paris: Vrin, 1971); in English: *The Religious Metaphysics of Simone Weil* (Albany: State University of New York Press, 1994).

Abosch, Heinz. *Simone Weil: An Introduction*. New York: Pennbridge Books, 1994.

Allen, Diogenes. *Three Outsiders: Pascal, Kierkegaard, Simone Weil*. Cambridge, Mass.: Cowley, 1983.

Allen, Diogenes, and Eric O. Springsted, eds. *Spirit, Nature and Community: Issues in the Thought of Simone Weil*. Albany: State University of New York Press, 1994.

Anderson, David. *Simone Weil*. London: SCM Press, 1971.

Bell, Richard, ed. *Simone Weil's Philosophy of Culture: Readings toward a Divine Humanity*. New York: Cambridge University Press, 1993.

Blech-Lidolf, Luce. *La pensée philosophique et sociale de Simone Weil*. Bern and Frankfurt: Lang, 1976.

Blum, Lawrence A., and Victor J. Seidler. *A Truer Liberty: Simone Weil and Marxism*. New York: Routledge, 1989.

Bourgeois, Michel. "La spiritualité du travail selon Simone Weil." Ph.D. diss., Free Faculty of Protestant Theology, Paris, 1961.

Bugnion-Secretan, Paule. *Simone Weil: Itinéraire politique et spirituel*. Neuchâtel: Messeiller, 1954.

Cabaud, Jacques. *L'expérience vécue de Simone Weil*. Paris: Plon, 1957. The German version, *Simone Weil: Die Logik der Liebe* (Freiburg: K. Alber, 1968), is expanded relative to the French original. In English: *Simone Weil: A Fellowship in Love*. New York: Channel Press, 1965.

———. *Simone Weil à New York et à Londres*. Paris: Plon, 1967.

Canciani, Domenico. *Simone Weil prima di Simone Weil: Gli anni di formazione di un' intellettuale francese degli anni trenta*. Padua: Cleup, 1983.

Coles, Robert. *Simone Weil: A Modern Pilgrimage*. Reading, Mass.: Addison Wesley, 1987.

Danielou, Jean, et al. *Réponses aux questions de Simone Weil*. Paris: Aubier Montaigne, 1964.

Davy, Marie-Madeleine. *Introduction au message de Simone Weil*. Paris: Plon, 1954.

———. *The Mysticism of Simone Weil*. Boston: Beacon, 1951.

————. *Simone Weil*. Classiques du XXe Siècle. Preface by Gabriel Marcel. Paris: Editions Universitaires, 1961.

————. *Simone Weil: Sa vie son oeuvre avec un exposé da sa philosophie.* Paris: Universitaires de France, 1961.

Debidour, Victor-Henri. *Simone Weil ou la transparence.* Paris: Plon, 1963.

Del Noce, Augusto, ed. *Simone Weil: L'amore di Dio.* Turin, 1968.

Dietz, Mary Golden. *Between the Human and the Divine: The Political Thought of Simone Weil.* Totowa, N.J.: Rowman and Littlefield, 1988.

Dufresne, Jacques. "Simone Weil et la tradition dualiste." Ph.D. diss. Faculty of Letters, Dijon, 1965.

Dujardin, Philippe. *Simone Weil: Idéologie et politique.* Foreword by Colette Andry. Paris: Maspéro, 1975.

Dunaway, John. *Simone Weil.* Boston: Twayne, 1984.

Epting, Karl. *Der geistige Weg der Simone Weil.* Stuttgart: Vorweck, 1955.

Fiori, Gabriella. *Simone Weil: An Intellectual Biography.* Athens: University of Georgia Press, 1989.

Fleuré, Eugène. *Simone Weil ouvrière.* Paris: Fernand Lanore, 1955.

Giniewski, Paul. *Simone Weil ou la haine de soi.* Paris: Berg International, 1978.

Goldschlager, Alain. *Simone Weil et Spinoza.* Sherbrooke: Editions Naaman, 1982.

Hautefeuille, François d'. *Le tourment de Simone Weil.* Paris: Desclée de Brouwer, 1970.

Heidsieck, François. *Simone Weil.* Paris: Seghers, 1965. 2d ed., 1967.

Hellman, John. *Simone Weil: An Introduction to Her Thought.* Waterloo: Wilfrid Laurier University Press, 1982.

Janeira, Ana Luisa. *Conhocer Simone Weil.* Braga: Livrarie Cruz, 1973.

Kahn, Gilbert, ed. *Simone Weil: Philosophe, historienne, et mystique.* Paris: Aubier Montaigne, 1978.

King, Paul. "The Social and Political Thought of Simone Weil." Ph.D. diss., UCLA, 1975.

Krogmann, Angelica. *Simone Weil in Selbstzeugnissen und Bilddokumenten.* Hamburg: Rowohlt, 1970.

Kühn, Rolf. *Deuten als Entwerden: Eine Synthese des Werkes Simone Weils in hermeneutisch-religionsphilosophischer Sicht.* Freiburger Theologische Schriften 136. Freiburg: Herder, 1989.

Little, Janet Patricia. *Simone Weil, a Bibliography.* London: Grant and Cutler, 1973.

————. *Simone Weil, a Bibliography: Supplement.* London: Grant and Cutler, 1979.

Malan, Ivo. *L'enracinement de Simone Weil.* Paris: Didier, 1960.

Marchetti, Adriano. *Politeia e sapienza: In questione con Simone Weil.* Bologna: Pàtron, 1993.

McFarland, Dorothy Tuck. *Simone Weil.* New York: Unger, 1983.

McLane-Iles, Betty. *Uprooting and Integration in the Writings of Simone Weil.* American University Studies, Series VII, Theology and Religion, vol. 20. New York: Peter Lang, 1987.

McLellan, David. *Utopian Pessimist: The Life and Thought of Simone Weil.* New York: Poseidon, 1990.

Narcy, Michel. *Simone Weil: Malheur et beauté du monde.* Paris: Centurion, 1967.

Nevin, Thomas R. *Simone Weil: Portrait of a Self-Exiled Jew.* Chapel Hill: University of North Carolina Press, 1991.

Nordquist, Joan. *Simone Weil: A Bibliography.* Social Theory: Bibliographical Series no. 38. Santa Cruz, Calif.: Reference and Research Services, 1995.

Nye, Andrea. *Philosophia: The Thought of Rosa Luxemburg, Simone Weil, and Hannah Arendt.* New York: Routledge, 1994.

Ottensmeyer, Hilary. *Le thème de l'amour dans l'oeuvre de Simone Weil.* Paris: Lettres Modernes, 1958.

Oxenhandler, Neal. *Looking for Heroes in Postwar France: Albert Camus, Max Jacob, Simone Weil.* Hanover, N.H.: University Press of New England, 1995.

Perrin, Jean Marie, and Gustave Thibon, *Simone Weil telle que nous l'avons connue.* Paris: La Colombe, 1952. 2d ed., 1967. In English: *Simone Weil: As We Knew Her.* Translated by Emma Craufurd. London: Routledge and Kegan Paul, 1953.

Pétrement, Simone. *La vie de Simone Weil.* 2 vols. Paris: Fayard, 1973. In English: *Simone Weil: A Life.* Translated by Raymond Rosenthal. New York: Pantheon, 1976.

Piccard, Eulalie. *Simone Weil: Essai biographique et critique suivi d'une anthologie.* Paris: Presses Universitaires de France, 1960.

Raper, David. "Simone Weil's Critique of the Old Testament." Ph.D. diss., McMaster University, 1968.

Rees, Richard, *Brave Men: A Study of D. H. Lawrence and Simone Weil*. Carbondale: Southern Illinois University Press, 1959.

————. *Simone Weil: A Sketch for a Portrait*. Carbondale: Southern Illinois University Press, 1966.

Schlette, Heinz Robert, and André Devaux, eds. *Simone Weil: Philosophie, Religion, Politik*. Frankfurt am Main: Knecht, 1985.

Schumann, Maurice. *La mort née de leur propre vie: Peguy, Simone Weil, Gandhi*. Paris: Fayard, 1974.

Springsted, Eric O. *Christus Mediator: Platonic Mediation in the Thought of Simone Weil*. Chico, Calif.: Scholars Press, 1983.

————. *Simone Weil and the Suffering of Love*. Cambridge, Mass.: Cowley, 1983.

Strickland, Stephanie. *The Red Virgin: A Poem of Simone Weil*. Madison: University of Wisconsin Press, 1993.

Suzzoni, Alexis. "La pensée politique de Simone Weil de 1931 a 1939." Thèse IIIe Cycle, Lettres Modernes, Paris III, 1977.

Terry, Megan. *Approaching Simone: A Drama in Two Acts*. Introduction by Phyllis Jane Wagner. Old Westbury, N.Y.: Feminist Press, 1973.

Tomlin, Eric Walter Frederic. *Simone Weil*. New Haven: Yale University Press, 1954.

Vetö, Miklos. *La métaphysique religieuse de Simone Weil*. Paris: Vrin, 1971. In English: *The Religious Metaphysics of Simone Weil*. Albany: State University of New York Press, 1994.

White, George Abbot, ed. *Simone Weil: Interpretations of a Life*. Amherst: University of Massachusetts Press, 1981.

Winch, Peter. *Simone Weil: "The Just Balance."* New York: Cambridge University Press, 1989.

Articles on Simone Weil

Abosch, Heinz. "Die Gesellschaftskritik Simone Weils." *Neue Rundschau* 3 (1972): 528–39.

Alain [pseudonym of Émile Chartier]. "Simone Weil." *La Table Ronde* 28 (April 1950): 47–51.

Bataille, George. "La victoire militaire et la banqueroute de la morale qui maudit." *Critique* 5:40 (September 1949): 788–803.

Buber, Martin. "The Silent Question: On Henri Bergson and Simone Weil." In *At the Turning: Three Addresses on Judaism,* 29–43. New York, 1952.

Camus, Albert. "Simone Weil *L'enracinement:* Projet de preface." In *Essais,* 2:1700–1702. Paris: Gallimard, 1965.

Chevanier, Robert. "Simone Weil: 'La haine juive de soi'?" *Cahiers Simone Weil* 14:4 (December 1991): 291–328.

Cranston, Maurice. "Reactionary Mystic." *The Guardian,* October 19, 1962, p. 7.

Davy, Marie-Madeleine. "Die geistige Erfahrung der Simone Weil." *Zeitschrift für philosophische Forschung* 8 (1954): 118–38.

Dreyfuss, Dina. "La transcendance contre l'histoire chez Simone Weil." *Mercure de France* 1053 (May 1, 1951): 65–80.

Eliot, T. S. Preface. In *The Need for Roots: Prelude to a Declaration of Duties toward Mankind,* translated by Arthur Wills, v–xii. New York, 1952.

Elshtain, Jean Bethke. "The Vexation of Simone Weil." In *Power Trips and Other Journeys: Essays in Feminism as Civic Discourse,* 13–37. Madison: University of Wisconsin Press, 1990.

Fiedler, Leslie. "Simone Weil: Prophet out of Israel, Saint of the Absurd." *Commentary* 1 (January 1951): 38–46. Rpt. in *Arguments and Doctrines: A Reader of Jewish Thinking in the Aftermath of the Holocaust,* ed. A. Cohen, 52–69. New York, 1970.

Gollancz, Victor. "Waiting for God." In *More for Timothy,* 83–136. London, 1953.

Grant, George. "In Defense of Simone Weil." *The Idler* (Toronto) 15 (January–February 1988): 36–40.

Greene, Graham. "Simone Weil." In *Collected Essays,* 372–75. London, 1969.

Guitton, Jean. Afterword. In *La mort née de leur propre vie. Péguy, Simone Weil, Gandhi,* by Maurice Schumann, 169–74. Paris, 1974.

Kadt, Jaques de. "Chez Simone Weil: Rupture avec Trotsky." *Le Contrat Social* 11:3 (1967): 139–45.

Kemp, Friedhelm. "Das Werk von Simone Weil." *Merkur* 5 (1951): 1194–97.

Kuhn, Helmut. "Die Philosophie des 'laisser faire Dieu.'" *Merkur* 6 (1957): 592–95.

Levinas, Emmanuel. "Simone Weil contre la Bible." In *Difficile liberté: Essais sur le Judaisme,* 160–70. Paris: Albin Michel, 1963.

Lichtheim, George. "Simone Weil." *Cambridge Journal* (March 1951), under the pseudonym G. L. Arnold. Reprinted in *Collected Essays,* 458–76. New York: Viking, 1973.

Little, Janet Patricia. "Society as Mediator in Simone Weil's 'Venise sauvée.'" *Modern Language Review* 65:2 (1970): 298–305.

Lohman, H.-M. Book reviews. *Archiv für Rechts- und Sozialpolitik* 52:2 (1976): 299–300.

Lynd, Staughton. "Marxism-Leninism and the Language of *Politics* Magazine: The First New Left and the Third." In *Simone Weil: Interpretations of a Life,* ed. George Abbot White, 111–36. Amherst: University of Massachusetts Press, 1981.

Macdonald, Dwight. "A Formula to Give a War-Torn Society New Roots." *New York Times Book Review,* July 6, 1952, p. 6.

Marcel, Gabriel. Preface. In Davy, *Simone Weil,* 5–8. Classiques du XXe Siècle. Paris, 1961.

———. "Simone Weil." *The Month* (July 1949): 9–18.

Marchetti, Adriano. "Simone Weil: Coscienza delle contradizioni presenti nella letteratura francese degli anni trenta, con una bibliografia sistematica." In *Atti dell' Accademia delle Scienze dell' Istituto di Bologna,* 7–82. Classe di Scienze Morali 73. Bologna, 1977.

Merton, Thomas. "Pacifism and Resistance in Simone Weil." In *Faith and Violence: Christian Teaching and Christian Practice,* 76–84. West Bend, Ind.: University of Notre Dame Press, 1968.

Moeller, Charles. "Simone Weil et l'incroyance des croyants." In *Litterature du XXe siècle et christianism,* 1:246–81. 2d ed. Paris: Casterman, 1967.

Monseau, Marcelle. "L'humanisme de Simone Weil dans la condition ouvrière." *Revue de l'Université Laval* (Quebec) 12:5 (January 1958): 454–62.

Muggeridge, Malcolm. Interview with André Weil. *The Listener* 83 (May 24, 1973): 673–79.

Pétrement, Simone, "La critique du marxisme chez Simone Weil." *Le Contrat Social* 4 (September 1957): 230–36.

———. "Sur la religion d'Alain avec quelque remarques concernant celle de Simone Weil." *Revue de Metaphysique et de Morale* 3 (July–October 1955): 306–30.

Pierce, Roy. "Simone Weil: Sociology, Utopia and Faith." In *Contemporary French Political Thought*, 89–121. London and New York: Oxford University Press, 1966.

Rabi, Wladimir. "La conception weilienne de la Création: Rencontre avec la kabbale juive." In *Simone Weil, philosophe, historienne, et mystique*, ed. Gilbert Kahn. Paris, 1978.

Rosen, Fred, "Labour and Liberty: Simone Weil and the Human Condition." *Theoria to Theory* 7 (1979): 33–47.

————. "Marxism, Mysticism, and Liberty: The Influence of Simone Weil on Albert Camus." *Political Theory* 7:3 (August 1979): 301–19.

Savinel, P. "Simone Weil et l'hellénisme." *Bulletin de l'Association Guillaume Budé* (March 1960): 122–44.

Schlette, Heinz Robert. "Simone Weil. Ein Porträt." *Information Philosophie* (December 1986): 38–48.

Sontag, Susan. *Against Interpretation and Other Essays.* New York: Farrar, Straus and Giroux, 1966.

Taubes, Susan Anima. "The Absent God." *Journal of Religion* 35:1 (January 1955): 6–16.

Thiout, Michel. "Jalons sur la route de Simone Weil. I: La recherche de la vérité de Simone Weil; II: Essai de bibliographie des écrits de Simone Weil." *Archives des Lettres Modernes* 3 (1959): nos. 25–26.

Vetö, Miklos. "Le piège de Dieu: L'idée du beau dans la pensée de Simone Weil." *La Table Ronde* 197 (June 1964): 70–88.

————. "Thèmes kantiens dans la pensée de Simone Weil." *Cahiers Simone Weil* 8:1 (March 1985): 42–49.

————. "Uprootedness and Alienation." *Blackfriars* (1962): 383–95.

Wall, E. "Simone Weil and Metapolitics." *Religion and Life* 24 (1955): 417–29.

Welton, Anthony. "Simone Weil." In *Martyrs: Contemporary Writers on Modern Lives of Faith*, ed. Susan Bergman, 182–96. San Francisco: Harper, 1996.

Winch, Peter. Introduction to *Lectures on Philosophy* by Simone Weil, translated by Hugh Price, 1–23. New York: Cambridge University Press, 1978.

Woulker-Kamarinea, Maria, trans. "Simone Weil: The Iliad or the Poem of Force" (in Greek). Athens: Bibliophilia, 1984.

General Bibliography

It is in the nature of a work such as this that it is directly or indirectly in the debt of a broad range of reading matter. It is impossible and not to much purpose to document every allusion with bibliographic data. I have acknowledged my direct references in the notes. The following selected list of titles provides the complete publication information for the works cited in the notes.

Alain [pseudonym of Emile Chartier]. *Le citoyen contre les pouvoirs.* Paris: Ed. du Sagittaire, 1926.

―――. *Définitions.* Paris: Gallimard, 1953.

―――. *Les dieux.* Paris: Gallimard, 1947.

―――. *Eléments d'une doctrine radicale.* Paris: Gallimard, 1925. 2d ed., 1933.

―――. *Politique.* Edited by Michel Alexandre. 2d ed. Paris: Presses Universitaires de France, 1951.

―――. *Propos sur la religion.* Paris: Presses Universitaires de France, 1951.

Albertini, Rudolf von. "Die Dritte Republik." In *Geschichte in Wissenschaft und Unterricht* 6 (1955): 492–504.

―――. *Freiheit und Demokratie in Frankreich.* Freiburg and Munich: K. Alber, 1957.

Andreu, Pierre. "Les idées politiques de la jeunesse intellectuelle de 1927 à la guerre." *Revue des Travaux de l'Académie des Sciences Morales et Politiques Comptes pendues* 11, 4th ser. (1967; second semester, meeting of July 8, 1957): 17–35.

Arendt, Hannah. *The Human Condition.* Chicago: University of Chicago Press, 1958.

―――. *The Origins of Totalitarianism.* 2d ed. New York: Meridian, 1958.

Aron, Raymond. *Les grandes doctrines de sociologie historique.* Centre de Documents, n.p., n.d. In English: *Main Currents in Social Thought.* Translated by Richard Howard and Helen Weaver. 2 vols. New York: Basic Books, 1965–1967.

―――. *L'homme contre les tyrans.* New York: Editions de la Maison Française, 1944.

―――. *L'opium des intellectuels.* Paris: Calmann Levy, 1955. In English:

The Opium of the Intellectuals. Translated by Terence Kilmartin. New York: Norton, 1957.

Arvon, Henri. *La philosophie du travail.* Paris: Presses Universitaires de France, 1960.

Augustine, Saint. *Confessiones. Sancti Aurelii Augustini Opera,* vol. 1/1. Vienna: Tempsky, 1887– .

————. *De utilitate credendi. Sancti Aurelii Augustini Opera,* vol. 6/1. Vienna: Tempsky, 1887– .

Azéma, Jean Pierre, and Michel Winook. *La Troisième République.* Paris: Calmann Levy, 1976.

Beauvoir, Simone de, *Mémoires d'un jeune fille rangée.* Paris, Gallimard, 1958. In English: *Memoirs of a Dutiful Daughter.* Translated by James Kirkup. New York: Harper Colophon, 1974.

Benjamin, Walter. *Ursprung des deutschen Trauerspiels.* Frankfurt am Main: Suhrkamp, 1972.

Bergsträsser, Arnold. *Staat und Wirtschaft in Frankreich.* Vol. 2 of *Frankreich,* by Ernst Robert Curtius and Bergsträsser. Berlin and Leipzig, 1930.

Bonnefous, Georges. *Histoire politique de la Troisième République.* 7 vols. Paris: Presses Universitaires de France, 1956–1967.

Bridoux, André. *Alain, sa vie, son oeuvre.* Paris: Presses Universitaires de France, 1964. Contains extracts from the works.

Brogan, Dennis W. *The Development of Modern France, 1870–1939.* Rev. ed., Gloucester, Mass.: Peter Smith, 1970.

Camus, Albert. *Essais.* Pléiade. Introduction by R. Quillot. Paris: Gallimard, 1965.

Caute, David. *Communism and the French Intellectuals.* Oxford: Oxford University Press, 1964.

Centenaire de la Troisième République. Actes du Colloque de Rennes, May 15–17, 1975. Paris, 1975.

Christian, Lynda G. "Metamorphoses of Erasmus' Folly." *Journal of the History of Ideas* 32 (April–June 1971): 289–94.

Cobban, Alfred. *A History of Modern France.* Vol. 3. Harmondsworth: Pelican, 1965.

Crossman, Richard H. S., ed. *The God That Failed.* New York: Bantam, 1965.

Curtius, Ernst Robert. *Die französische Kultur.* Vol. 1 of *Frankreich,* by

Curtius and Arnold Bergsträsser. Berlin and Leipzig, 1930. 2d ed. Bern and Munich, 1975.

Dewitt, S. *Alain: Essai bibliographique.* Brussels, 1961.

Dolléans, Edouard, *Histoire du mouvement ouvrier,* vol. 3, *1921 à nos jours.* Paris: A. Colin, 1953.

Duverger, Maurice. *La démocratie sans le peuple.* Paris: Seuil, 1967.

————. *Institutions politiques et droit constitutionnel.* Paris: Presses Universitaires de France, 1955.

Erikson, Erik. *Insight and Responsibility.* New York: Norton, 1964.

Faul, Erwin. "Verfemung, Duldung, und Anerkennung des Parteiwesens." *Politische Vierteljahresschrift* 5 (1968).

Fetscher, Iring. "Rousseaus Freiheitsvorstellungen." *Politische Vierteljahresschrift* 1 (1960).

Fohlen, Claude. *La France de l'entre deux guerres.* Paris, 1966.

Fontanet, J. "Alain ou le citoyen grognard." *Terre humaine* 2 (1952): 48–59.

Goguel, François. *La Politique des partis sous la Troisième République.* 2d ed. Paris: Seuil, 1958.

Gooch, Robert K. "The Antiparliamentary Movement in France." *American Political Science Review* 21:3 (August 1927): 552–72.

Gruner, Shirley M. *Economic Materialism and Social Moralism.* The Hague: Mouton, 1973.

Gurvitch, Georges. "Social Structure in Pre-War France." *American Journal of Sociology* 18:5 (1943): 535–55.

Habermas, Jürgen. *Theorie und Praxis.* Neuwied–Berlin: Luchterhand, 1963. In English: *Theory and Practice.* Translated by John Viertel. Boston: Beacon, 1973.

Hayek, Friedrich August von. "Wohin steuert die Demokratie?" *Frankfurter Allgemeine Zeitung* 6 (January 8, 1977): 11.

Hegel, Georg W. F. *Phänomenologie des Geistes.* Edited by Johannes Hoffmeister. Hamburg: Meiner, 1952.

Hermens, Ferdinand A. *Verfassungslehre.* Cologne, 1968.

Hobbes, Thomas. *Leviathan.* Edited by A. D. Lindsay. London: J. M. Dent, 1914.

Hoffmann, Stanley, et al. *In Search of France.* Cambridge: Harvard University Press, 1963.

Hughes, H. Stuart. *Consciousness and Society: The Reorientation of European Social Thought, 1890–1930.* New York: Knopf, 1958.

————. *The Obstructed Path: French Social Thought in the Years of Desperation 1930–1960*. New York: Harper and Row, 1966.

Husserl, Edmund. *Die Krise der europäischen Wissenschaften und die transzendentale Phänomenologie*. Husserliana, vol. 6. The Hague: M. Nihjoff, 1962.

Huszar, George Bertrand de, ed. *The Intellectuals: A Controversial Portrait*. Glencoe: Free Press, 1960.

Joll, James, ed. *The Anarchists*. Boston: Little Brown, 1964.

————. *Decline of the Third Republic*. London: Chatto and Windus, 1959.

Jouvenel, Bertrand de. *Über Souveränität*. Neuwied-Berlin: Luchterhand, 1963.

Jouvenel, Robert de. *La république des camarades*. Paris: B. Grasset, 1934.

Kayser, J. *Les grandes batailles du radicalisme*. Paris, n.d.

————. "Le radicalisme des radicaux." In *Tendances politiques dans la vie française depuis 1789*. Colloques, Cahiers de civilisation, edited by Guy Michaud (1960): 65–88.

Lagneau, G. "Radicalism, Radicalisme: Essai d'identification des idéologies radicales." *L'Année Sociologique* 22 (1971): 129–52.

Lefebvre, Henri. *La somme et le reste*. Paris, n.d.

Lefranc, Georges. *Histoire du front populaire*. Paris: Payot, 1965.

Lessing, Theodor. *Der jüdische Selbsthass*. Berlin: Zionistischer Bücher-Bund, 1930.

Lichtheim, George. *Europa im zwanzigsten Jahrhundert*. N.p.: Kindler, 1973. Originally: *Europe in the Twentieth Century*. London: Weidenfeld and Nicholson, 1971.

————. *Kurze Geschichte des Sozialismus*. Munich: dtv, 1975. Originally: *A Short History of Socialism*. New York: Praeger, 1970.

————. *Marxism in Modern France*. New York: Columbia University Press, 1966.

Lorwin, Val Rogin. *The French Labor Movement*. Cambridge: Harvard University Press, 1954.

Loubet del Bayle, J. L. *Les non-conformistes des années 30*. Paris: Seuil, 1969.

Lubac, Henri de. *Proudhon et le christianisme*. Paris: Seuil, 1945.

Luther, Martin. *Von weltlicher Obrigkeit: Wie weit man ihr Gehorsam schuldig sei*. Kritische Gesammtausgabe, Bohlan, Weimar, 1883–1919. Reprint, 1964.

Machiavelli, Nicolò. *Istorie fiorentine, opere.* Edited by Ezio Raimondi. Milan and Paris, 1976.

Marcus Aurelius. *Pensées.* Edited and translated by A. I. Trannoy. Preface by Aimé Puech. 1925. Rpt. Paris: Belles Lettres, 1969.

Marcuse, Herbert. "Über die philosophischen Grundlagen des wirtschafswissenschaflichen Arbeitsbegriffes." *Archiv für Sozialwissenschaft and Sozialpolitik* 69 (1933): 257 ff. Reprinted in *Kultur und Gesellschaft,* Frankfurt am Main: Suhrkamp, 1965.

Maurois, André. *Alain.* Paris: Gallimard, 1959.

Mayer, Jacob Peter. *Political Thought in France from the Revolution to the Fifth Republic.* 3d ed. London: Faber and Faber, 1961.

Michel, Henri, and Boris Mirkine-Guetzévitch. *Les idées politiques et sociales de la résistance.* Paris: Presses Universitaires de France, 1954.

Molnar, Thomas. *Kampf und Untergang der Intellektuellen.* Munich, 1966. In English: *The Decline of the Intellectual.* New Rochelle, N.Y.: Arlington House, 1973.

Mondor, H. *Alain.* Paris: Gallimard, 1953.

Mounier, Emmanuel. *La révolution personnaliste et communautaire.* In *Oeuvres,* 1:129–416. Paris: Seuil, 1961.

Nicolet, Claude. *Le radicalisme.* Paris: Presses Universitaires de France, 1957.

Nizan, Paul. *La conspiration.* 1938; rpt. Paris: Edition Folio, 1973. In English: *The Conspiracy.* Translated by Quintin Hoare. London and New York: Verso, 1988.

Oakeshott, Michael. *Rationalism in Politics.* Expanded ed. Indianapolis and London: Liberty Press, 1991.

Popper, Karl R. *The Open Society and Its Enemies.* 4th ed. Vol. 2. New York: Harper and Row, 1966.

Proudhon, Pierre-Joseph. *De la capacité politique des classes ouvrières.* Paris: Dentu, 1865.

———. *La guerre et la paix.* Paris: Lacroix, 1861.

———. *Qu'est ce que c'est la propriété?* Edited by E. James. Paris: Garnier-Flammarion. 1966. In English: *What Is Property?* New York: H. Fertig, 1966.

———. *Théorie de la propriété.* Paris: Lacroix, 1866.

Rauch, R. William. *Politics and Belief in Contemporary France.* The Hague: M. Nijhoff, 1972.

Rémond, René. *Les catholiques, le communisme et les crises.* Paris: A. Colin, 1960.

Ridley, Frederick F. *Revolutionary Syndicalism in France.* Cambridge: Cambridge University Press, 1970.

Sauvy, Alfred. *Histoire économique de la France entre les deux guerres.* 4 vols. Paris: Fayard, 1965–1975.

Schabert, Tilo. *Natur und Revolution.* Munich: List, 1969.

Scott, John Anthony. *Republican Ideas and the Liberal Tradition in France.* New York: Columbia University Press, 1951.

Serret, Gilbert. *Le syndicalisme dans l'enseignement.* Paris, 1957.

Shirer, William L. *The Collapse of the Third Republic.* New York: Pocket Books, 1971.

Siegfried, André. *Tableau des partis en France.* Paris: B. Grasset, 1930.

Steiner, George. *Language and Silence.* New York: Atheneum, 1967.

Sur, Marie-Thérèse. "Alain et la théorie démocratique." Ph.D. diss., University of Caen, 1976.

Tarr, Francis de. *The French Radical Party.* London: Oxford University Press, 1961.

Thibaudet, Albert. *La république des professeurs.* Paris: B. Grasset, 1927.

Thomson, David. *Democracy in France since 1870.* 5th ed. London: Oxford University Press, 1969.

Touchard, Jean. "L'esprit des années 30: Une tentative de renouvellement de la pensée politique française." In *Tendances politiques dans la vie française depuis 1789.* Colloques, Cahiers de civilisation, edited by Guy Michaud (1960): 89 ff.

———. *La gauche en France depuis 1900.* Paris: Seuil, 1977.

Voegelin, Eric. *Anamnesis.* Munich, 1966. In English: *Anamnesis.* Translated by Gerhart Niemeyer. Columbia: University of Missouri Press, 1990.

———. *Order and History.* Vol. 4, *The Ecumenic Age.* Baton Rouge: Louisiana State University Press, 1974.

Wallace-Hadrill, John Michael, and John McManners, eds. *France: Government and Society.* London: Methuen, 1957.

Weber, Max, *Politik als Beruf.* 3d ed. Berlin: Dunker and Humblot, 1958. In English: *Politics as a Vocation.* Philadelphia: Fortress Press, 1965.

Yale French Studies. Vol. 15: *Social and Political France, 1955.* Contributions by Edouard Daladier, Pierre Mendes-France, André Philip,

André Malraux, Raymond Aron, Maurice Duverger, François Goguel, R. Herr, Alfred Sauvy, André Siegfried, Eric Weil, and others.

Zeldin, Theodore. *France, 1848–1945.* 2 vols. Oxford: Clarendon Press, 1973–1977.

Ziebura, Gilbert, ed. *Wirtschaft und Gesellschaft in Frankreich seit 1789.* Cologne: Kiepenheuer and Witsch, 1975.

INDEX

255